For the Love of the World

BOOKS BY EDWIN ZACKRISON

Melvin Campbell and Edwin Zackrison. *Interactive Readings for Christian Worship*. (Lincoln, NE: iUniverse, 2003).
———. *Readers Theatre for Christian Worship; Biblical Stories of Courage and Faith*. (Lincoln, NE: iUniverse, 2003).

Edwin Zackrison. *In the Loins of Adam; A Historical Study of Original Sin in Adventist Theology*. (Lincoln, NE: iUniverse, 2004).
———. *The First Temptation; Seventh-day Adventists and Original Sin*. (Bloomington, IN: iUniverse, 2015).
———. *About Tomorrow, Let God Worry; The Place of Time*. (Bloomington, IN: iUniverse, 2019).
———. *God's Camelot; The Security of the Kingdom*. (Bloomington, IN: iUniverse, 2019).
———. *Christians Are Recovering Human Beings; Returning to God's Reality*. (Bloomington, IN: iUniverse, 2019).
———. *People Under Construction; Life is a Journey*. (Pittsburgh, PA: Dorrance Publishing, 2020).
———. *Profile of a Religious Man; Confessions of a Religion Addict*. (Eugene, OR: Resource Publications, 2020).

For the Love of the World

For God So Loved

EDWIN ZACKRISON

Foreword by Lorena Jeske

RESOURCE *Publications* · Eugene, Oregon

FOR THE LOVE OF THE WORLD
For God So Loved

Copyright © 2021 Edwin Zackrison. All rights reserved. Except for brief quotations in critical publications or reviews, no part of this book may be reproduced in any manner without prior written permission from the publisher. Write: Permissions, Wipf and Stock Publishers, 199 W. 8th Ave., Suite 3, Eugene, OR 97401.

Resource Publications
An Imprint of Wipf and Stock Publishers
199 W. 8th Ave., Suite 3
Eugene, OR 97401

www.wipfandstock.com

PAPERBACK ISBN: 978-1-6667-0709-0
HARDCOVER ISBN: 978-1-6667-0710-6
EBOOK ISBN: 978-1-6667-0711-3

JULY 21, 2021

All Biblical quotations, unless otherwise indicated, are from the Revised Standard Version of the Bible. Copyright 1946, 1952, 1971, 1973 by the Division of Christian Education of the National Council of the Churches of Christ in the United States of America.

Quotations appearing at the beginning of each chapter are taken from Ted Goodman (ed), The Forbes Book of Business Quotations (New York: Black Dog and Leventhal Publishers, 1997); and Laurence J. Peter, Peter's Quotations: Ideas for our Time (New York: Bantam Books, 1980).

To FLORENCE YOUNG, Ed.D.

Educator, Administrator, Author and Colleague

As an exemplary Dean of Women, she has demonstrated her care for hundreds of college students through the years.

Contents

Foreword by Lorna Jeske | ix

Preface | xi

CHAPTER 1	FOR THE LOVE OF THE WORLD	1
CHAPTER 2	HOW TO BE A NEW CREATION	9
CHAPTER 3	CATCHING THE FORCE	18
CHAPTER 4	PRAISING IN THE NEW YEAR	24
CHAPTER 5	HOW TO BE RIGHTEOUS	30
CHAPTER 6	APPEAL OF MOSES AND ELIJAH	37
CHAPTER 7	LAY DOWN YOUR BURDEN	44
CHAPTER 8	GET UP AND BEGIN AGAIN	52
CHAPTER 9	ACTING LIKE CHILDREN	59
CHAPTER 10	FINDING A NEED TO SUFFER	66
CHAPTER 11	NO GOD, NO HOPE	72
CHAPTER 12	EAT, DRINK, BREAD, BLOOD	79
CHAPTER 13	TASTE OF NEW WINE	86
CHAPTER 14	THE RESURRECTION OF JESUS CHRIST	93
CHAPTER 15	THE PRIVILEGE OF MATURING	99
CHAPTER 16	HOW TO ESCAPE TEMPTATION	107
CHAPTER 17	THE RESURRECTION BODY	113
CHAPTER 18	IS "FATHER" THE BEST TERM?	118

CHAPTER 19	OUR FATHER IN HEAVEN	124
CHAPTER 20	HALLOWED BE THY NAME	132
CHAPTER 21	THY KINGDOM COME, THY WILL BE DONE	138
CHAPTER 22	GIVE US THIS DAY, OUR DAILY BREAD	146
CHAPTER 23	TRUTH IS IN THE TASTING	152
CHAPTER 24	HAPPY ARE THE THANKFUL	157
CHAPTER 25	REMOVING THE CUP	164
CHAPTER 26	WATCHING UNTO LIFE	170
CHAPTER 27	THE RAPTURE	177
CHAPTER 28	AT PEACE WITH GOD	185
CHAPTER 29	YOU ARE THE LIGHT OF GOD	192
CHAPTER 30	TUESDAYS WITH MORRIE	199
CHAPTER 31	THE CLASS OF '57 HAD ITS DREAMS	205
CHAPTER 32	PRAYING IN THE ENEMY'S LAND	211

Bibliography | 222

Foreword

RECENTLY I READ A post on Facebook: "Religion: 'I messed up. My Dad is gonna kill me.' Gospel: 'I messed up. I need to call my Dad.'" In Dr. Zackrison's *For the Love of the World: For God so Loved* he writes about the "gospel God," not the "religion God." The gospel God loves us unconditionally and wants us to know that.

This inspirational book is thirty-two chapters of Dr. Zackrison's writing over the past fifty-five plus years in several states: California, Georgia, Michigan, Tennessee, and Washington State. During those years on both the west coast and east coast, he pastored three churches, was a professor at three universities, two colleges, and adjunct professor at three others. He has spoken for spiritual emphasis weeks, convocations, religion retreats, pastoral seminars, and workshops, written seven books, and co-authored two. This in addition of many published articles. He has served as book editor for university publications.

Dr. Zackrison is forthright in his writing as he presents familiar verses, people and events from the Bible, new perspectives, the hills and valleys of personal experiences, both his and others, all woven with vignettes throughout the chapters. Within these pages, you will discover stories of hope, joy, happiness, and peace, as well as accounts of disappointment, disillusionment, betrayal, and discouragement. Stories of emotional, mental, spiritual, and physical pain, stress, death, dying. Stories of mistakes made; lessons learned. Stories of God's impact on and in people's lives, and his hard-for-many-to-understand great love for this world.

The chapters in this book are short. Although each chapter stands alone, they are intertwined with a focus on God, Jesus, and reconciliation. Dr. Zackrison writes, "The message of the gospel involves a message of two enemies who have been reconciled: God and human beings." (Chapter 6). He notes, "The Lord has authority in our lives because he has earned it. He made us, he saved us, he died and lives for us." (Chapter 11). He comments that Paul "presents the gospel as the only hope, as the only future, as the only stabilizing factor in a life of separation, alienation and estrangement from God." (Chapter 15). And he explains, "As it is Jesus' right-doing that saves us, so it is God's faithfulness to us that we have assurance of salvation." (Chapter 20). He states, "Peace comes through reconciliation with God. . . . I find no evidence that this is anything but personal in its final application." (Chapter 28).

A tall, crewcut, blond-haired, handsome teenager with a ready smile, arrived from California during the fall of 1957 to join our junior class at Auburn Academy, a co-educational Christian boarding high school located in the western foothills of Mount Rainier in northwestern Washington State. I soon learned his name was Ed, the name by which I have since always called him. After we graduated in 1959 our paths would cross during on-campus high school alumni weekends, of which our honor-year high school class reunions were a part, and during honor-year class reunions in California. Ed provided worship service discourses at five of these reunions. Now that we have both entered our years of retirement, we have available time for lengthy long-distance phone discussions that cover a great diversity of subjects and topics.

I was surprised when Ed invited me to write the Foreword to his new book, *For the Love of the World: For God So Loved*. I am honored and delighted to accept his invitation. He has been my friend for more than sixty years.

Learning about God is a continuous journey with new discoveries. I believe that readers of this book will discover the chapters add to such a journey. Additionally, it can assist those just beginning their journey of searching. This book dispels the stereotype of God traditionally taught to many of us as young children and teenagers. For some, this book may provide new perspectives, and for others words to ponder or words of encouragement. And for those on their journey, whether continuous or beginning, a reinforcement of the God who loves.

Thank you, Ed, for writing this book about our "gospel God."

Lorena Jeske, MN
Public Health Nurse (Retired)
Washington State Department of Health

Preface

I GREW UP IN a denomination that was very "world" aware. Being worldly was presented as a serious offense against God. New members needed an outline of what the congregation understood "worldly" to mean. Loving God meant hating the world. But that needed to be explained. The world was quickly understood as being the enemy of the Almighty.

As a young person in the church, I memorized the scriptural texts given to me by my elders. They were strong and seemed clear from scripture.

> [15] I do not pray that thou shouldst take them out of the world, but that thou shouldst keep them from the evil one. (John 17:15)

Here the connection between the evil one and the world appeared to be quite well-defined. And some texts were even stronger than this one.

> [2] Do not be conformed to this world but be transformed by the renewal of your mind, that you may prove what is the will of God, what is good and acceptable and perfect. (Romans 12:2)

> [19] If you were of the world, the world would love its own; but because you are not of the world, but I chose you out of the world, therefore the world hates you. (John 15:19)

The world is our enemy. The ways of the world would lead us to eternal separation from God, which meant eternal death. And this was the specific purpose of the evil one.

> [4] In their case the god of this world has blinded the minds of the unbelievers, to keep them from seeing the light of the gospel of the glory of Christ, who is the likeness of God. (2 Corinthians 4:4)

The New Testament sharply pleaded with believers to reject the world.

> [20] If with Christ you died to the elemental spirits of the universe, why do you live as if you still belonged to the world? (Colossians 2:20)

The world is at times presented as a desertion of the mission of Christ.

> [10] For Demas, in love with this present world, has deserted me. (2 Timothy 4:10)

And the world puts a "stain" on the believer.

> [27] Religion that is pure and undefiled before God and the Father is this: to visit orphans and widows in their affliction, and to keep oneself *unstained* from the world. (James 1:27. Emphasis supplied)

Friendship with the world is even deemed as being an enemy of God.

> [4] Unfaithful creatures! Do you not know that friendship with the world is enmity with God? Therefore whoever wishes to be a friend of the world makes himself an enemy of God. (James 4:4)

This is a frequent theme throughout the Bible.

> [18] If the world hates you, know that it has hated me before it hated you. (John 15:18)

And movement for believers is encouraged and expected.

> [15] Do not love the world or the things of the world. If any one loves the world, love for the Father is not in him. [16] For all that is in the world, the lust of the flesh and the lust of the eyes and the pride of life, is not of the Father but is of the world. (1 John 2:15-16)

> [19] It is these who set up divisions, worldly people, devoid of the Spirit. (Jude 1:19)

Texts of this nature are spread through the New Testament. Often "the world" is used as a geographical location created by God and where the Son was sent to do his salvific work. Not all of the references carry this negative connotation. But because of the evil in the world many of the notions display these implications.

> [12] For we are not contending against flesh and blood, but against the principalities, against the powers, against the world rulers of this present darkness, against the spiritual hosts of wickedness in the heavenly places. (Ephesians 6:12)

> [19] We know that we are of God, and the whole world is in the power of the evil one. (1 John 5:19)

In spite of these suggestions of the world's hatred and the *worldliness* of sinful humanity, the most popular text in the Bible still speaks of God's *love* of the world!

> [16] For *God so loved the world* that he gave his only Son, that whoever believes in him should not perish but have eternal life. [17] For God sent the Son into the world, not to condemn the world, but that the world might be saved through him. (John 3:16-17. Emphasis supplied)

So, the greatest of all paradoxes is set up by the inspired authors of the scriptures: Love the world but hate the world if you want to be a follower of God. In this book, we will look realistically at this idea. A paradox can cause confusion if taken as a logical contradiction. But it can cause exciting truth to those who allow it to function according to its literary purpose.

The world can be subject to interpretations that cause believers to disagree and fight. Unfortunately, these interpretations often end up in startling dispute. For my sectarian generation, *the world* included the inheritance of other denominational interpretations. That usually presented a historically conditioned conclusion that was taken within its context. Some of those for my sect included bearing military arms, dancing, smoking, marijuana and heroin, competitive sports, theatre, and movies. There were others, but these were emphasized. The booklets produced by the denomination for young people were largely on these subjects. This was *the world* for us.

We will not spend a lot of time on the specifics in this book. We will instead seek to discuss *the world* from the viewpoint of God's salvation. This is a book about the gospel. The specifics can be sorted out by the many believers who will deal with the philosophical data. Our concern is about *the world* that God loves and how that involves us as believers.

Edwin Zackrison, PhD, MBA
Former Professor of Theology and Ministry
La Sierra University, Riverside, California
July, 2021

CHAPTER ONE

FOR THE LOVE OF THE WORLD

> "The real trouble with this world of ours is not that it is an unreasonable one. The trouble is that it is nearly reasonable, but not quite."
>
> —G. K. CHESTERTON

JOHN 3:1-17

¹ Now there was a man of the Pharisees, named Nicodemus, a ruler of the Jews. ² This man came to Jesus by night and said to him, "Rabbi, we know that you are a teacher come from God; for no one can do these signs that you do, unless God is with him." ³ Jesus answered him, "Truly, truly, I say to you, unless one is born anew, he cannot see the kingdom of God."

⁴ Nicodemus said to him, "How can a man be born when he is old? Can he enter a second time into his mother's womb and be born?" ⁵ Jesus answered, "Truly, truly, I say to you, unless one is born of water and the Spirit, he cannot enter the kingdom of God. ⁶ That which is born of the flesh is flesh, and that which is born of the Spirit is spirit. ⁷ Do not marvel that I said to you, 'You must be born anew.'

⁸ "The wind blows where it wills, and you hear the sound of it, but you do not know whence it comes or whither it goes; so it is with every one who is born of the Spirit." ⁹ Nicodemus

said to him, "How can this be?" [10] Jesus answered him, "Are you a teacher of Israel, and yet you do not understand this? [11] Truly, truly, I say to you, we speak of what we know, and bear witness to what we have seen; but you do not receive our testimony. [12] If I have told you earthly things and you do not believe, how can you believe if I tell you heavenly things? [13] No one has ascended into heaven but he who descended from heaven, the Son of man. [14] And as Moses lifted up the serpent in the wilderness, so must the Son of man be lifted up, [15] that whoever believes in him may have eternal life."

[16] For God so loved the world that he gave his only Son, that whoever believes in him should not perish but have eternal life. [17] For God sent the Son into the world, not to condemn the world, but that the world might be saved through him.

LET THE PASTOR GO LAST

On my first Thanksgiving away from home I was invited to a church member's home for dinner. These people went all out. There was a full spread of typical holiday foods—cranberry sauce, fresh breads of all kinds, delicious juices, sweet potatoes, mashed potatoes, gravy, dressing, a plate of vegetarian meats for those who didn't indulge in the beast, and a huge turkey. They acted like they considered it an honor to have the pastor there and they really played it up.

As we sat down to this magnificent feast, the hostess, at the head of the table, asked us to join hands in unity and then, rather than saying grace, she said, "Let's go around the table and have each person recite a favorite memorized verse from scripture."

When you are given such an assignment on the spot you hope they will let the pastor go first because you know you are on the spot. What if, by the time they get to you, all the others at the table have taken all the verses you can remember? You could not just repeat a verse someone had already taken. I was a divinity student, and I was their student pastor, and I would be expected to have memorized something in scripture. Then she dropped the bombshell, "Let's have the pastor go last and then finish with a Thanksgiving grace after he gives his favorite text."

There were fifteen people at that table, and I watched one text after another go by until I was sure the whole Bible had been taken. The guy next to me gave as his favorite text: "Jesus wept." That is the shortest verse in the Bible. I had not even thought of using that one. But when my turn came I was able to paraphrase something from Romans. All the texts I knew were gone.

As you can probably guess, the first text used that happy afternoon was everyone's favorite:

> ¹⁶ For God so loved the world that he gave his only Son, that whoever believes in him should not perish but have eternal life. (John 3:16)

I had hoped to get that one—that was a text every Christian had learned from birth in a Christian home—but no such luck. It was gone immediately.

THE CENTER OF THE BIBLICAL MESSAGE

In this chapter I have no competition. So, I will look at that most-loved, most-quoted, most-memorized, most-remembered text. As Christians we cling to that passage and Christians have done so through the ages since it was written in the Gospel of John.

The sentence comes as a commentary on an evening conversation that Jesus had with a "ruler of the Jews," Nicodemus. This man wanted to cut to the chase. He got together with Jesus at night, perhaps so no one would see him. He started his conversation with Jesus by making a pointed observation.

> ² This man came to Jesus by night and said to him, "Rabbi, we know that you are a teacher come from God; for no one can do these signs that you do, unless God is with him." (John 3:2)

In other words, God must be with you since you do what you do. Nicodemus had noticed. But unlike so many of the other Pharisees, Nicodemus had looked through eyes of faith. And now he was in audience with the miracle-worker to see what he had to say to him alone.

Don't we do things like that? A late-night TV host interviewed an American Olympic gold medal winner by way of satellite. He asked the young girl, now that she was famous and could probably have anything she wanted, what would she like now more than anything else? This young athlete answered: "I would like to get the autograph of Britany Spears!"

Winning the gold was great but getting an autograph was right up there too! And she had no sooner said that than Britany Spears appeared on the stage screen in the TV studio and began talking to her by way of satellite. What were the first words out of Britany Spears' mouth? She looked at the gold medal winner by way of satellite and asked her, "Do you suppose I could get your autograph?"

This response of admiration is paradoxical. Here was a leader in Israel, yet he wanted to see Jesus in private. He wanted to know what made him function—what contributed to his ministry. And Jesus responded with a few questions. Here was a great rabbi in the presence of who he considered the great rabbi, and the whole conversation followed suit. Jesus saw that here was a teachable heart—at last!

THE QUESTIONS

Jesus immediately began his instruction.

> [3] Jesus answered him, "Truly, truly, I say to you, unless one is born anew, he cannot see the kingdom of God." (John 3:3)

Many of us are probably so familiar with this story that it seems like pretty plain teaching. But Nicodemus is going through it for the first time, so he probes Jesus to make sure he understands. And at first, Nicodemus acts like he is taking Jesus literally, so he asks questions.

> [4] Nicodemus said to him, "How can a man be born when he is old? Can he enter a second time into his mother's womb and be born?" (John 3:4)

A pharisee of his standing should have known better but it may be that the truth was getting close and so he used a defense mechanism—like when you came in late and there was Dad waiting up for you, and he said, "You're late—your curfew is 11:00 pm, and you are home at 11:15 pm." And you said, "Those are nice pajamas, Dad, did you get those at Belk?"

Nicodemus does the same sort of thing. He evades the real meaning of the situation with a rather inane remark about being literally re-born. But Jesus is not deterred. He stays right on topic and adds to it.

> [6] "That which is born of the flesh is flesh, and that which is born of the Spirit is spirit. [7] Do not marvel that I said to you, 'You must be born anew.' [8] The wind blows where it wills, and you hear the sound of it, but you do not know whence it comes or whither it goes; so it is with every one who is born of the Spirit." (John 3:6-8)

You were not meant to be simply a fleshy human being on a level with the rest of the mammals—Darwin will jog your mind—but he will be wrong about that notion. You are a spiritual being. You can relate to each other on a higher level than the physical. You can do more than make babies— you can make love. You have available to you a level of relationship that no animal could ever have. As great as all the animals are on this earth, none was created to be in the same special relationship with God.

Some time ago several big dogs were destroyed because they attacked and killed a lady as she was opening the door to her apartment in the city. They were Rottweilers and apparently had been trained to kill. So, they attacked the lady's neck and crushed her trachea. There followed an intense trial in the municipality.

But the dogs were not tried—they were simply destroyed without a trial. The owners of the dogs were tried for manslaughter because they kept dangerous dogs. We don't try animals because we innately know that animals don't have that spiritual ability to live ethical, moral, spiritual, and responsible lives. Consequently, we don't hold them responsible. If they are dangerous we simply snuff them out; we do it humanely because we are spiritual beings, but we don't put them through the ten to thirty years of court proceedings that human killers often get.

There are human beings who act lower than other mammals. And in some cases, they are tried and retried, and tried and retried again, and they appeal, and they are tried again. Why? Because we call that "holding people responsible for their actions." Because we still have that innate understanding that human beings should know better. Christians believe that human beings were created in the "image of God."

> [26] Then God said, "*Let us make man in our image, after our likeness;* and let them have dominion over the fish of the sea, and over the birds of the air, and over the cattle, and over all the earth, and over every creeping thing that creeps upon the earth." [27] So *God created man in his own image, in the image of God he created him;* male and female he created them. [28] And God blessed them, and God said to them, "Be fruitful and multiply, and fill the earth and subdue it; and have dominion over the fish of the sea and over the birds of the air and over every living thing that moves upon the earth." (Genesis 1:26-28. Emphases supplied)

Therefore, they are responsible beings. Human beings were to be superintendents of the other animals, not vice versa. Interestingly, even atheists insist on a fair trial. Christians insist that human beings were created with a capacity to relate to God. Christians believe that through that original sin of Adam his descendants lost the fullness of that spiritual capacity. But most Christians believe that their spiritual nature has never been destroyed; it is wounded, but some trace of it still exists.

THE PRIVILEGE OF REBIRTH

When I see the handiwork of men and women I marvel. I go to the library and look at the books and I say, How could people write so many books? Some of them are four inches thick. Some of them are series of ten books, each four inches thick. I look at the automobiles on the freeway; I look at the homes around that represent everything from simple to excessive. And I see the creative abilities that God included in making them in "the image of God."

I have had animals as pets. They have done everything from destroying my radios to chewing up my blankets or wetting on my camcorder. But of all the animals I have had, I have never had an animal that fixed the blankets they chewed up, or the radios they destroyed or either repairing the camcorder or replacing it. These things about "the image of God in humankind" are easy to understand.

Nicodemus was operating on one of these lower levels when he asked the questions.

> [4] Nicodemus said to him, "How can a man be born when he is old? Can he enter a second time into his mother's womb and be born?" (John 3:4)

What blind questions! What an inane observation! At best it was an evasive one. But Jesus stays with Nicodemus. He is a precious soul in leadership—one who knows better—that knowledge just needs a little awakening. But not without chiding him.

Nicodemus earned that.

> [10] Jesus answered him, "Are you a teacher of Israel, and yet you do not understand this?" (John 3:10)

He was playing a game with God. Because we are created with superior intellects we play many games with God. Adam and Eve played games; Cain and Abel played games; Moses and Aaron played games. We all play games. We know better. Who do we think we are fooling?

An irritated Grandpa told my son to get out of his hair. My clever little boy said, "Grandpa, you don't have any hair—you're bald." Sometimes it comes down to playing games with our soul. The Bible makes it clear that when we play games too long we create what adds up to a callous on our soul—we can't hear anymore. We put off our commitment, we put off our total response, we resist the Spirit, and we find other things in which to invest our magnificent creativity. That spiritual nature gradually faints and starves and almost ceases to exist.

Nicodemus was playing a game with God. He knew what God was asking but he didn't want to know. He was not ready.

FOR THE LOVE OF THE WORLD

Jesus played along but he never let Nicodemus stray from where he wanted to direct his thinking. Can you see the wind? No, but you know it is there because it rustles the leaves. The Spirit can't be seen but you know of his work in your soul. The work of the Spirit is to rekindle that belief in God's work to save you to an everlasting life.

It was an important audience that Nicodemus had that night. He never forgot it. He went back to the Jewish ruling council and became a staunch supporter of the early church. He was one who anointed the body of Christ for a proper burial.

> [38] After this Joseph of Arimathea, who was a disciple of Jesus, but secretly, for fear of the Jews, asked Pilate that he might take away the body of Jesus, and Pilate gave him leave. So, he came and took away his body. [39] Nicodemus also, who had at first come to him by night, came bringing a mixture of myrrh and aloes, about a hundred pounds' weight.
> [40] They took the body of Jesus, and bound it in linen cloths with the spices, as is the burial custom of the Jews. [41] Now in the place where he was crucified there was a garden, and in the garden a new tomb where no one had ever been laid. [42] So because of the Jewish day of Preparation, as the tomb was close at hand, they laid Jesus there. (John 19:38-42)

He was one who finally expended all his earthly resources to make sure the message he received that night in the dark went to the entire world. As Jesus went through that whole message, he gave illustrations to bring Nicodemus into the spiritual arena of understanding. He appealed to that spiritual capacity that he knew Nicodemus had. The leaves, the wind, the birth, the snake in the wilderness. All of these illustrations were meaningful especially in the context of Pharisaic Judaism.

The most important point in the dialogue is the end of the passage of Jesus' words where he says,

> [14] "And as Moses lifted up the serpent in the wilderness, so must the Son of man be lifted up, [15] that whoever believes in him may have eternal life." (John 3:14-15)

For the love of the world he had created, God sent someone to rescue us. Not all rescue missions succeed. President Carter learned this the hard way. We learned that when the Wall Street journalist was beheaded at the hands of his kidnappers. But the rescue mission of God to a world trapped by that original sin must not fail.

The rescuer was killed but in his death was the victory of the rescue. It is the greatest paradox in the content or context of any religion on this earth. God created a world in his image. It became tarnished, dirtied, injured, and wounded by God's enemies. And now, for the love of that world and what he intended for it to be, that rescuer appeared.

> [16] For God so loved the world that he gave his only Son, that whoever believes in him should not perish but have eternal life. [17] For God sent the Son into the world, not to condemn the world, but that the world might be saved through him. (John 3:16-17)

CHAPTER TWO

How to Be A New Creation

> "Religion is life and lifts you out of yourself.
> We must believe God is too big to fail."
>
> —Samuel H. Sweeney

2 CORINTHIANS 5:16-21

[16] From now on, therefore, we regard no one from a human point of view; even though we once regarded Christ from a human point of view, we regard him thus no longer. [17] Therefore, if any one is in Christ, he is a new creation; the old has passed away, behold, the new has come. [18] All this is from God, who through Christ reconciled us to himself and gave us the ministry of reconciliation; [19] that is, in Christ God was reconciling the world to himself, not counting their trespasses against them, and entrusting to us the message of reconciliation.

[20] So we are ambassadors for Christ, God making his appeal through us. We beseech you on behalf of Christ, be reconciled to God. [21] For our sake he made him to be sin who knew no sin, so that in him we might become the righteousness of God.

A RIGHTEOUS MAN

Every temptation that Christ faced had to do with believing or doubting the word of his heavenly Father. Likewise, every temptation we face will center in faith. To what extent do we believe God will keep his word to us? That is the essential question in temptation. Jesus came to this earth as "the second Adam," to prove that a human being, as God made him, can remain obedient to God. Had Adam believed, he would have been victorious, and sin would never have occurred.

> [45] Thus it is written, "The first man Adam became a living being;" the last Adam became a life-giving spirit. (1 Corinthians 15:45)

There was another time where the life of Abraham was called "righteous." How could a man be called "righteous?" The scriptures say that when he believed God, he was credited as righteous. The New Testament draws the comparison: those who believe Christ are righteous, or accounted righteous, or declared right with God, acquitted of all the charges of sin. The old death decree, that old arrest warrant, held in the hand of the great accuser of the brethren, Satan himself, and strengthened by God's own law, was nailed to the cross.

> [13] And you, who were dead in trespasses and the uncircumcision of your flesh, God made alive together with him, having forgiven us all our trespasses, [14] having *canceled the bond which stood against us* with its legal demands; *this he set aside, nailing it to the cross.* [15] He disarmed the principalities and powers and made a public example of them, triumphing over them in him. As Abraham was *declared* righteous when he believed, so we are declared righteous when we believe in the work of Christ on our behalf. (Colossians 2:13-15. Emphases supplied)

Just as Jesus was given the power to stand up to temptation, so we are given that power. That is where our own belief becomes important. And the temptation not to believe is never stronger than the will to believe. God's wish for us to be strong, to stand firm for what is right, and good, moral, ethical, and healthful is carried out in our lives through faith. No temptation is ever so strong that we must capitulate.

THE SNAGS OF LIFE

We have the promise that there is no temptation that can overcome us. There is no temptation that can leave us in despair. As we face the hardships of life—children who cause us pain, parents who are suffering in their old age, bosses who we see as incarnated devils, diseases that create suffering, health problems that won't improve, people around us who are not as perfect as we are, addictions this age brings us and leaves us in confusion and discomfort—none of these will overwhelm us because we are in Christ—as a "new creation."

The more you study the gospel, the more you will be intrigued. Jesus' parables may seem to make no sense because when Christ spoke in parables he intended to make us think. So many of us resist the whole notion of really thinking. We bounce along through life from Safeway to Shell to Taco Bell to American Idol. We bounce along from work to work, to play, to meal, to fight with the family, to misunderstanding with kids, to board meeting, to bed. Where does thinking enter this picture?—how does thinking find its way into our routine? Not that we don't think in a way for all those peculiarities—but thinking and pondering in silent moments that seem so rare? Life is hectic—who has time to really consider? And yet when confronted by the newness of the angel's message, Mary *pondered* all these things in her heart—that's the thinking to consider.

When we hit a snag in life, Jesus is standing there. He asks, "Have you really thought about this?" The snags of life are clues to the meaning points of life. A kid offers you a joint at school. "Come on, take it, it's in." Jesus is there, and he says to us, "Have you really thought about this?" A snag of life—a little pressure point, a directional situation. A conflict of interest arises at work, a little insider information, the chance to slander someone you don't like, the snags of life, and Jesus is there at these turning points that could change our lives and he asks, "Have you really thought about where this will lead?"

I listen to my students—mostly adults now—people who often wish they hadn't stopped thinking when they graduated from high school—wish they had worked on their college education before this where they have a family and a job and all the complications that includes. They are thrilled to be doing the job now—and yet the snags are there. "I was so busy this week I just couldn't get that assignment done." Don't tell me—I had no choice in the matter. I can't say—"Hey, I was so busy this week I couldn't get ready to teach you for four hours tonight."

Someone asks us, "What do you believe?" What? "What do you believe?" About what? "You know, about life, about Jesus, about God, death, sin, the universe, the world, conflict in marriage." And we stand there, and Jesus is there, and he asks, "Have you really thought about this?" Why is thinking so far down on the totem pole of our existence? Is life just in slow motion? Is life in Powerglide? What does it take to wake us up? The snags of life help!

I'm not suggesting that those profoundly serious snags that many of us have run into this past year were either welcomed or directed at us from God, or even something we thought we deserved. Death, separation, divorce, and joblessness are right up there at the top of the list of horrible stressors. In fact, if you get too many of these things in short duration they can do you in. Every college psychology textbook has a list of them, and they are numbered for effect. You can add up the numbers and figure out how close you are to breaking down.

NEW CREATION HAS ROOTS IN RECONCILIATION

The message of the gospel involves a message of two enemies who have been reconciled: God and human beings. Throughout the scriptures we find the same theme: Cain and Abel, Jacob and Esau, Pharaoh and Moses, David, and Jonathan; the stories don't cease. And as we listen to these stories we begin to get the point that the highest form of fellowship on this earth occurs after reconciliation. These are stories that illustrate the rift between God and humanity.

In Christ we are reconciled.

> [18] All this is from God, who through Christ reconciled us to himself and gave us the ministry of reconciliation; [19] that is, in Christ God was reconciling the world to himself, not counting their trespasses against them, and entrusting to us the message of reconciliation. (2 Corinthians 5:18-19)

Here is another paradox. As we die to sin we live to God. We cannot be an old creation and a new one at the same time. The church is the *fellowship of the reconciled.* It is not just a social club where you come to see your friends. That is not its purpose. That is not its mission. That is a by-product of the genuine article.

Scripture does not teach us to neglect or reject our friends. When you go to the fellowship dinner don't ignore anyone who is there and think you are fulfilling the true meaning of reconciliation. If the church is a place at all it is a place where you bring the unreconciled to God. In the process they meet reconciled people. And that is crucial and important. It's a matter of perspective. In Christianity we are concerned with order. Friendship is seen through the eyes of God—as a result of our friendship with God. It is all very delicate. We are reconciled to God in Christ, and now there is fellowship with others who have the same experience. How this is accomplished in a church is through the courage God gives us to make things right among ourselves.

In Matthew 18 Jesus gave an answer of reconciliation between brothers and sisters. If a brother has sinned against you, go to him alone and talk to him. If he listens you have gained a brother. If not, and you think it is still important—take a couple people with you and talk to him. If he still will not listen, and it's still important to you, take it before the congregation and if he won't accept the judgment of the church, treat him like a Gentile. If this kind of communication is not happening in the church then there can be no ministry of reconciliation.

> [15] If your brother sins against you, go and tell him his fault, between you and him alone. If he listens to you, you have gained your brother. [16] But if he does not listen, take one or two others along with you, that every word may be confirmed by the evidence of two or three witnesses. [17] If he refuses to listen to them, tell it to the church; and if he refuses to listen even to the church, let him be to you as a Gentile and a tax collector. [18] Truly, I say to you, whatever you bind on earth shall be bound in heaven, and whatever you loose on earth shall be loosed in heaven. [19] Again I say to you, if two of you agree on earth about anything they ask, it will be done for them by my Father in heaven. [20] For where two or three are gathered in my name, there am I in the midst of them. (Matthew 18:15-20)

How delicately this operation must be carried on. I have listened to church members sharing this whole notion of the ministry of reconciliation week after week. In their conversations they hit some points that are tough because they are real, truthful, practical and they rise above the abstract ideas that many of us have.

How do we treat people like a Gentile or a tax collector? In theory, in abstraction, this may mean we are to reject, ignore or shun them—they are sinners, they have not responded, they are doomed, damned, and relegated to the lower regions. But watch how Christians respond to people who don't believe like them—at concerts or guest presentations—we often give them standing ovations, we praise their abilities to communicate with us. They appear in the cultural lyceums of the school, they speak for assemblies, sharing their ideas in life. They even come on as political rivals.

During my freshman year in college, the administration invited Senator Albert Gore, Sr., to speak for assembly. A sitting U. S. senator from Tennessee! And I came to the assembly expecting something exciting. No one protested, there was an electricity in the air as the students came in. And then I saw how the hall had been decorated—Kennedy banners (John F. Kennedy—a Democrat Roman Catholic, running for president).

I didn't know any Democrats—like Daddy Warbucks in *Annie* said when he invited President Roosevelt to a Christmas dinner—"What do Democrats eat?" These banners were all around the assembly hall. I never thought about the trappings that would come along with the presence of a political celebrity. I was shocked because I hadn't thought about it. But Albert Gore, Sr., was the recipient of the most courteous treatment. I don't remember what he said—it was long ago, and I was still processing all those Kennedy banners—wondering why our predominantly Republican campus would be supporting a Catholic Democrat—Oh! The baggage!

Treat him like a *Gentile*. Time to think about that a little more. To become a clinical psychologist, you must go through therapy, and so it is to be a reconciling church you must go through personal reconciliation with those people in the church who are giving you a "problem." This is the essence of being a new creation: to have a ministry of reconciliation—and it is something we need to think about in those quiet moments—when we think.

Our response should never be like that line from *Inherit the Wind* where Colonel Brady is confronted with Colonel Drummond's question about his thinking processes, and he says glibly, "I don't think about things I don't think about!"

THE MENTALITY OF THE NEW CREATION

When we become a new creation through faith we see God's side of the picture, not just the human side. We live in an age where God's side of the picture is hardly considered at all. Even many Christians are often functional atheists in that God's side of the story hardly goes noticed. How would you solve the problem of estrangement if you were God? Many of the answers we suggest are irrational, poorly thought out, and yet Paul is not really talking about argumentation here. What is our behavior? Our demonstration? How do we act in the face of hardship, not just what do we say?

In the past fifty years many evangelical denominations have joined together to discuss such things as "mission" and "vision." When I was growing up we thought we had all that nailed down, but then we never believed we would even have time to go to college or get married or have a family because Christ was returning any day! Talk about living on borrowed time! I'm retired now. That isn't even something I want to think about.

I get together with my high school graduating class every ten years. Can you imagine that the next time we get together we will be in our late 80s? We've always had 50-60 people at our ten-year gatherings—how about next time? Most of those people who told us Christ would come before we graduated from college are dead now. And so, the church has had to rethink why it's here and where it is going. Enter—vision and mission explained.

I've watched congregations struggle with this over the past several decades. If a church grows too rapidly it must be letting down the standards and it is time to shake out the dead wood and the sinners. And then if the congregation gets too small it is not carrying out its vision and mission. It must have the wrong definition of the gospel and the cycle starts up again and again. Such is the mentality that often dominates a congregation.

Many congregations today have a mission statement printed in their bulletins each week. If your congregation has this you should take it home and think about it in those moments of quietness. Your time will not be wasted. Ask yourself in those quiet moments, what do I think God wants done with our church? Believe it or not your church does not belong to you. The money in the bank is not yours, that is just something God has entrusted you with as you get organized.

The old creation sees things selfishly. The new creation attempts to see things through God's eyes. What does God want the mission to be? The vision to be? The vision tells you where you expect to be in ten years. The mission is what you will be doing during all that time.

New creation thinking sees the end from the beginning. I saw a bumper sticker that said, "I know the future . . . God wins!" There is an advantage that a Christian has—we know who will win because we know who has won. It's just a matter of sorting out the details. We may not know what the future holds, but we know who holds the future. And we've got news for Satan: God is going to win (because he has already won). The new creation affirms that God is going to win, and we are going to act as winners not losers.

What I appreciated most about the last year was a reconciliation with my older daughter. When I was in hills and valleys on an hourly basis I shared a lot of my grief with her. She is a physician, teacher, and author—a person of very impressive judgment. I told her I had never thought that my life would be in such a dumper that I couldn't even make my car payment. She wrote back—"Your life is not over, Dad. And as far as worrying about finances—the cattle on a thousand hills belong to God. We need not ask when things look dark: are we out of money? We need to ask, are we out of faith? Dad, you need to learn surrender. He will take care of you."

I could have heard myself in that counsel, but I was too oppressed to think right then. When I gradually recovered and ascended one of those hilltops I asked the question seriously, are we unable to move because we have no resources? Or are all our resources simply human ones? The new creation thinks from God's point of view and sees the end from the beginning—God is the winner. And there is a bonus in that thinking, that God has already won—we just have details left to sort out.

The cross was the great victory. We can believe God—we can take God at his word when he promises to bless us and to go with us through the valleys that present scary, new ideas. God accounts that belief to us as *righteousness*. As righteous people through faith in Christ's work we are called "a new creation." This is a position of authority. God is indeed with us.

A PARABLE OF MANAGEMENT

Toward the end of the Gospel of Matthew, Jesus illustrates what we could call "new creation thinking." We will update some of the attachments in this story.

Jesus tells the story of a Chief Executive Officer, who had three managers under him. He wanted to test these managers for a high position that he knew was coming open. So, he called them into his office one day and instructed, "Gentlemen, I am going away for a while and I'm not sure when I will be back. But I need you, as my trusted managers, to manage things while I'm gone." So, he said to the first manager, "I'm leaving ten million in the account of your division of the business. I want you to protect it, care for it, and make sure it is effectively used." He said to the second manager, "I'm leaving five million in the account of your division of the business. I want you to protect it, care for it, and make sure it is effectively used." And he said to the third manager, "I'm leaving five hundred thousand in the account of your division of the business. I want you to protect it, care for it, and make sure it is effectively used."

The first manager went to the financial advisors and got the best advice he could get, invested it wisely, built up his end of the business and worked hard to see that the money was rightly used. The second manager also went to financial advisors and got the best advice he could, invested it wisely, built up his end of the business and worked hard to see that the money was rightly used. But the third manager was offended that he was given so little in comparison with the other managers. He was not motivated to build it, but he did want to protect it, so he put it in the bank and used it for maintenance on his end of the business.

The CEO returned in due time and looked at the books. The first manager had doubled the ten million by creatively investing and building up his end of the business. The second manager had doubled the five million by creatively investing and building up his end of the business. And the third manager handed back the original five hundred thousand—he hadn't lost anything, and he thought that was impressive. He had simply maintained his end of the business.

Two managers were promoted because they had a new creation mentality. The third was fired because his kind would never help the business thrive. It is time to practice new creation mentality. It is called in the business world, "vision." But in the biblical world it is called thinking as a member of the kingdom.

CHAPTER THREE

Catching the Force

> "In the general course of human nature, a power over a man's subsistence amounts to a power over his will."
>
> —Alexander Hamilton

MATTHEW 8:14-20

[14] And when Jesus entered Peter's house, he saw his mother-in-law lying sick with a fever; [15] he touched her hand, and the fever left her, and she rose and served him. [16] That evening they brought to him many who were possessed with demons; and he cast out the spirits with a word, and healed all who were sick. [17] This was to fulfil what was spoken by the prophet Isaiah, "He took our infirmities and bore our diseases."

[18] Now when Jesus saw great crowds around him, he gave orders to go over to the other side. [19] And a scribe came up and said to him, "Teacher, I will follow you wherever you go." [20] And Jesus said to him, "Foxes have holes, and birds of the air have nests; but the Son of man has nowhere to lay his head."

THE PROPOSITION OF YOUR LIFE

One of the great philosophical questions of life has to do with why we are here. The Bible suggests that most of us get threescore and ten years to decide the answer to that question. Some in your congregation may have passed that mark. They are not living on borrowed time; they are just those who are greatly blessed and for whom we are thankful to God.

My father lived to be seventy-four, my mother to be eighty-nine. They were both greatly blessed as were their children. In today's world there are forces that keep us alive longer but also there are forces that threaten to shorten our lives every time we go on the freeway or down the stairs. So, if we get roughly seventy years to decide why we are here, how are we doing in answering that question?

In college we used to write down the objectives for classes we would someday teach or sermons we would someday preach. In Homiletics we called it "a proposition." What do you propose to say in the number of minutes allotted to you? If we couldn't say it in twenty minutes then maybe we didn't know what we really intended to say at all. So, what is the proposition of your life? What is the objective of your existence? Propositions change. Objectives change. People change. We set out on a track and evidence piles up on one side or the other. We become more certain of some things and less sure about others. As a kid I read the Bible stories and believed them. I read the fairy tales and knew they were fairy tales. As an adult I have other frames of reference and wonder what to do with the similarities in the two genre of stories? How does the Bible help me frame my purpose?

OUR PERCEPTIONS CHANGE WITH TIME

I marvel when I hear of someone who grew up in Nebraska and lived on her farm all her life and the farthest she ever traveled was to town five miles away. You may have known people like that. No TV, perhaps a radio, perhaps a paper occasionally, but otherwise truly little contact with the world off the farm. Where we grew up and what our family taught us, or where we lived, or who we went to school with affects how we answer the question of why we are here.

Several years ago, two young people enrolled in one of my classes at the university where I taught. One was my nephew who had just returned from Honduras where his Dad was a missionary. The other was a co-ed from Knoxville. I asked the students to pick any seat they wished to sit in for the semester and these two ended up with seats next to each other. Neither had met the other until they chose those seats. By the end of the term, they were dating. Today they live in Knoxville. She is a nurse; he is a businessman. They have two daughters: one is a nurse; the other is a clinical psychologist. Who we marry sometimes has a lot to do with how we answer the question, Why are we here? The decisions we make early in life are sometimes good, sometimes bad, but those are judgments we make in trying to answer that bigger question, "Why are we here?"

Who our parents are can also have something to do to answer that question. An impressive example of this is the story of a teacher I once had. As a young man he grew up in a relatively well-to-do home. His father gave him a graduation present from high school: a fully paid vacation to South America. As he sat on the balcony of the hotel restaurant overlooking the bay, he overheard an older couple at another table talking.

The husband said, "Well, dear, here we are! Our whole life has been devoted to this day. We saved for forty years so we could take this vacation and sit and look over this bay. Finally, we are retired, and we have accomplished our dream!" As the young man heard that conversation he thought, "Their whole life! . . . Planning for this trip! I'm nineteen and I am here. So, what will be the plan for my life? Where will I be when I'm sixty-five? What is my dream?"

JESUS' LIFE IS A CLUE TO ANSWERING THIS QUESTION

There are many interpretations of Jesus' life. Jesus was a controversial figure. We claim to be disciples of Jesus Christ. I can safely assume that that claim has impacted our personal thinking about why we are here. To be a disciple of Christ means to learn from Christ. To learn from Christ incorporates thinking, pondering, considering, if it incorporates anything at all. In Matthew 8 we see Jesus at the height of his ministry dealing with people where they were. A woman with a fever. People who were demon-possessed, mentally ill, bodies that were sick. Old, young, middle-aged, all coming to Jesus because they carried diseases and had infirmities. And he healed them.

You have a hard time answering the question when you are sick or in pain or feel weak? When I am sick I wonder if I will ever feel well again.

At that time, I appreciate like at no other time what it means to be well. I may ask, "Why am I here?" But I can't think too deeply about it. Some people answer that question most effectively, when they are sick, in the form of resolutions. Sometimes that answer comes in the form of bargaining: "Lord, if you will make me well I will do your will." Sometimes it comes in the form of anger: "God, where are you? And why are you doing this to me?" It is sometimes in the form of denial. And sometimes it is in the form of acceptance.

Jesus cared about his community.

> [15] He touched her hand, and the fever left her, and she rose and served him. (Matthew 8:15)

This example gives a clue to why we are here. When the young man heard the old couple testify that they had finally carried out a lifelong aspiration, he knew there had to be more to life than that for him. He returned home and announced to his father that he had decided to plant a church in his hometown area.

SO WHY ARE WE HERE?

If Jesus' ministry is our clue to why we are here, then the answer is straightforward. We are here to minister to others. That ministry comes in many different forms. For some it is professional. When I was sixteen years of age, I made my decision to become a professional minister. I have never escaped that decision. I have wavered in my human frailty. I have attempted other things, but ministry has always been central.

As a college professor, I realized that ministry was more important to me than the knowledge I imparted. I must admit I would never have predicted where that commitment to ministry would eventually take me. The road has not been easy. Like one of my friends said about his own ministry, "I must be awfully valuable to God because the devil has tried everything in the book to get me out of ministry!"

In my experience I have learned that the religious leader types of Jesus' day are still around today. But they can't stop you from doing ministry. I have learned that those closest to you can use everything to discourage you, but they can't stop you from doing ministry. Ministry is not just professional from the standpoint of salary. Ministry includes every interest you take in another person as a result of your recognizing your value to God. Put another way: when you see evidence that you are valuable to God your natural response is to "minister."

> [15] He touched her hand, and the fever left her, and she rose and served him. (Matthew 8:15)

Using today's jargon, she *caught the force*. "Catching the force" means she was spontaneously grateful. And that spontaneity, that natural response, that gratitude, would take shape as time went on. I'm not sure what God did to me at sixteen, but it was the right place and time for the most important decision I ever made: to get up and wait on him. That waiting involved caring and seeking to understand. In getting up and waiting on him, that lady caught the force that day and finally understood why she was here. It's not the last thought she ever thought. But it was a directional thought that would lead her on a journey.

CHURCH CATCHES THE FORCE

Each of us has caught the force. That's why we join a congregation and enjoy the physical presence of other disciples. And that force is melding its way in your congregation in a special way. That force is gradually putting together a new start, a fresh view of ministry to your city. Jesus has touched us, and the fever has left. Then we get up and begin to wait on him in new and fresh ways. When the young high school graduate caught the force in South America, "the fever left him" and he got up and began to wait on Jesus. He came home, talked to friends, and they united and started a new congregation, which over the years has grown.

They took the business principles that they had learned at his father's feet and applied them to congregational life. When I attended their congregation, they were targeting baby boomers. They studied them and sought to bring new life to them through service to Jesus. They held a meeting, and a few young people came. It was a beginning.

Out of that little group of peers to whom they chose to minister, came one of the most significant churches in America today.

> [14] And when Jesus entered Peter's house, he saw his mother-in-law lying sick with a fever; [15] he touched her hand, and the fever left her, and she rose and served him. [16] That evening they brought to him many who were possessed with demons; and he cast out the spirits with a word, and healed all who were

sick. [17] This was to fulfil what was spoken by the prophet Isaiah, "He took our infirmities and bore our diseases." (Matthew 8:14-17)

CHAPTER FOUR

Praising in the New Year

"We all are imbued with the love of praise."
—Cicero

PSALM 148

¹ Praise the Lord!
   Praise the Lord from the heavens,
   praise him in the heights!
² Praise him, all his angels,
   praise him, all his host!
³ Praise him, sun and moon,
   praise him, all you shining stars!
⁴ Praise him, you highest heavens,
   and you waters above the heavens!
⁵ Let them praise the name of the Lord!
   For he commanded and they were created.
⁶ And he established them for ever and ever;
   he fixed their bounds which cannot be passed.
⁷ Praise the Lord from the earth,
   you sea monsters and all deeps,
⁸ fire and hail, snow and frost,
   stormy wind fulfilling his command!
⁹ Mountains and all hills,
   fruit trees and all cedars!

¹⁰ Beasts and all cattle,
    creeping things and flying birds!
¹¹ Kings of the earth and all peoples,
    princes and all rulers of the earth!
¹² Young men and maidens together,
    old men and children!
¹³ Let them praise the name of the Lord,
    for his name alone is exalted;
    his glory is above earth and heaven.
¹⁴ He has raised up a horn for his people,
    praise for all his saints,
    for the people of Israel who are near to him.
Praise the Lord!

MY FATHER'S WORLD

Coming to the close of the second decade in a new millennium it seems fitting that we think on the element that resides at the center of our existence as Christians. That element is praise.

> This is my father's world, and to my listening ears,
> All nature sings and round me rings the music of the spheres.
> This is my father's world; I rest me in the thought
> Of rocks and trees, of skies and seas;
> God's hands the wonders wrought.
>
> This is my father's world; the birds their carols raise.
> The morning light, the flowers bright, declare their maker's praise.
> Our God has made this world and shines in all that's fair;
> In rustling grass I hear God pass, who speaks to me everywhere.
>
> Our God has made this world; oh, let us ne'er forget
> That though the wrong seems oft so strong, God is the ruler yet.
> God trust us with this world to keep it clean and fair.
> All earth and trees, the skies and seas, God's creatures everywhere.[1]

In Psalm 148, the writer dwells on the fact that all creation gyrates at the thought of God's creative power. He sees all of creation coming alive in praise to the creator, the beginning and finisher, the designer of all that works together to make nature the most fascinating subject of our thoughts.

1. Babcock, *The United Methodist Hymnal*, 144.

NATURE IS A MYSTERY TO MOST OF US

Throughout history men and women have looked at the heavens with ambivalent response. Before the scientific age there was a certain kind of superstition connected with nature. Men in their finite wisdom saw forces at work. And these forces were subjected to various kinds of interpretation. Some saw these as objects for worship. The scorching sun became a symbol of anger. The warming sun became a symbol of peace and tranquility. The storms and plagues of nature were interpreted as attacks on evil, whatever forms that evil took. Unfaithfulness to the human spirit brought punishment and required offerings and sacrifices, many times in the form of a virgin or a child. These were unfortunate interpretations, for they depreciated the nature of the true God and they deadened the human spirit.

For the Hebrews, God was one—he was not the creation but rather the maker of all creation, while the "pagan" personified all nature as god or gods. If the crops failed, it was because of an angry outburst by the gods. If the crops succeeded, it meant that all was well. But regardless, divinity was at the center of human existence. Dances represented either ways to placate gods or ways to praise gods, depending on what was happening on earth. We call much of this "superstition" for we have come of age. We are mature now, we say. In Christianity, the Hebrew view of God has flourished and continues to hold its own despite this "enlightened" modern view of life through science.

Some of you have cable or satellite television and are aware of the many channels on animals and nature, which captivate the attention of the viewing public. *The Crocodile Hunter*, now in reruns due to his untimely death, has become a favorite of children and adults alike as he excitedly discovers some of the secrets of nature. The Discovery Channel concentrates on the dinosaur period, and the nature of scary animals like sharks and threatening animals like snakes and fierce beasts.

FOR THE PSALMIST THERE WAS ANOTHER KIND OF MYSTERY

I watched a TV show called, "When Dinosaurs Ruled." It was fascinating even though I questioned much of the timeline and much of the theory, which was presented as scientific fact. Seeking to explain the size and nature of these giants of the past the scientists injected much of their theory on history. Tens of millions of years were needed to explain the evolution of these beasts that would have terrified any human being. And yet I couldn't help but notice that "one day" a flower appeared which changed everything.

How and why or where and what brought that flower was not made clear. Why it took several million years to produce a dinosaur and only one day to produce a flower remained a mystery, which the scientists glossed over. But the change in the world that one flower brought also eventually ended in the extinction of the dinosaurs. The show went on for several hours and I slumbered through some of it, but when I was awake I would sometimes say, no, this does not have to be the way he is speculating it. There is no way that nature would need that much time. Just as one eruption of Mount St. Helens created natural havoc in a matter of minutes, so all of this could have taken place in a noticeably short time.

Even these evolutionist theories indicate a kind of worship. As we look at the mysteries of nature we wonder. We find ourselves fascinated by the way in which nature evolves and works. In our little time capsule we stand amazed at the stars and the universes that our telescopes and modern technologies seem to indicate. Carl Sagan, a lifelong student of the universe, inspired a movie called *Contact*.

In this film plot a young female scientist seeks to observe any kind of messages that might be coming in from the depths of the universe. She finally receives a message that results in her making a trip to another planet or level of existence. She was not a religious type person even though a close friend was a Christian minister. But when she returns from her trip where she experiences another dimension of existence and has a chance to talk to her deceased father whom she loved dearly; she cannot adequately explain to the satisfaction of her fellow scientists what happened.

PRAISE COMES IN MANY FORMS

These fascinations with nature also carry with them forms of praise. Whether we agree with the timelines or the interpretations of evolutionism, has been bases for battle between creationism and evolutionism. Yet the movie *Contact* suggests that the closer we come to the center of truth, the closer we can come to some agreement.

One night when my son was about two years old, we were sitting outside enjoying the cool air. He is half Scandinavian and I have referred to him as craving arctic air. He never liked to sleep in pajamas, he never relished coats. And we sat there looking up at the black sky with only two objects in it: a sliver of a moon and a planet directly opposite its center. He was fascinated. He pointed and jumped up and down as he screamed, "Moon, moon, moon!" The fascination had already begun in his two-year-old mind.

As an heir of a scientific age, I cannot help but question some of the notions I grew up with as a believer in scripture. I find a lot of what I learned to be quite surface and uncritical. I find many unanswered questions that I can only hold in suspended judgment. I do not find my faith nailing down many facts regarding the universe, but I can't find evolutionism doing much better. And I must believe that there is a common denominator between science and faith.

I believe that common denominator to have something to do with this fascination that we all share. I'm sorry when science and religion battle it out with their preconceived ideas and sometimes cynical conclusions. I just don't think it is simplistic. But somewhere there is reason to praise, regardless of the side you observe from.

The psalmist chose to see the universe as something that came from the hand of God. And every element in that universe bears witness to praise. "Praise the Lord from the heavens"—from the highest forms of creation—angels and all of God's hosts praise him. All the shining stars praise him. They praise him because he commanded, and they appeared. He created them in order and fixed them in their limits; and in those boundaries, they praise him. The sun and the moon praise him.

> [1] "Praise the LORD! Praise the LORD from the heavens, praise him in the heights!" (Psalm 148:1)

From the monsters that live in the sea to the fire and hail, the snow and the frost, the storm and the quiet. The mountains and the hills. The birds and the beasts, the fruit trees and the cedars, the creeping things, and the cattle. And finally, the human beings of all levels—kings and princes, rulers and young people, seniors, and children. All praise him!

GOD CREATED ALL NATURE

We may look at this as a series of commands, but we don't need to. We can see this as simple descriptions of what goes on. Regardless of how you interpret what you see—creationism, evolutionism, science, religion, you have a demonstration of fascination. And that is a form of praise. Were you not fascinated you would not stay. And in your fascination you look, you ponder, you interpret, and you wonder. And that is praise.

Why? Because God has earned that praise. For the psalmist he has created all nature and all nature is the subject of our fascination. In scripture there is behind all nature a designer, a maker, a director, a producer, and a guiding hand. In time we will meet this person, but until then we are invited to be fascinated. We are invited to study and be amazed and to watch and enjoy.

According to the psalmist this is the God who has "raised up a horn for his people." (Psalm 148:14) The horn on some animals gave them an advantage and so "the horn" became a symbol for superiority and strength, of integrity and power. And here, says the psalmist, is the God who has given Israel its strength. When you are in the presence of such power, such intelligence, such creative ability, what do you do? You praise. You stand transfixed with fascination. You stand in awe, lacking understanding.

It is not important that every interpretation you make be accurate. It is enough to be fascinated, to recognize that here is something beyond you. Here is something approaching the center of your being. "Praise the Lord."

CHAPTER FIVE

How to Be Righteous

> "The superior man seeks what is right; the inferior one, what is profitable."
>
> —Confucius

GENESIS 15:1-12, 17-18

¹ After these things the word of the Lord came to Abram in a vision, "Fear not, Abram, I am your shield; your reward shall be very great." ² But Abram said, "O Lord God, what wilt thou give me, for I continue childless, and the heir of my house is Eliezer of Damascus?" ³ And Abram said, "Behold, thou hast given me no offspring; and a slave born in my house will be my heir." ⁴ And behold, the word of the Lord came to him, "This man shall not be your heir; your own son shall be your heir."

⁵ And he brought him outside and said, "Look toward heaven, and number the stars, if you are able to number them." Then he said to him, "So shall your descendants be." ⁶ And he believed the Lord; and he reckoned it to him as righteousness.

⁷ And he said to him, "I am the Lord who brought you from Ur of the Chaldeans, to give you this land to possess." ⁸ But he said, "O Lord God, how am I to know that I shall possess it?" ⁹ He said to him, "Bring me a heifer three years old, a she-goat three years old, a ram three years old, a turtledove, and a young pigeon." ¹⁰ And he brought him all these, cut them in two, and laid each half over against the other; but he did not cut the

birds in two. ⁱⁱ And when birds of prey came down upon the carcasses, Abram drove them away.

¹² As the sun was going down, a deep sleep fell on Abram; and lo, a dread and great darkness fell upon him.

¹⁷ When the sun had gone down and it was dark, behold, a smoking fire pot and a flaming torch passed between these pieces. ¹⁸ On that day the LORD made a covenant with Abram, saying, "To your descendants I give this land, from the river of Egypt to the great river, the river Euphrates."

HEAVEN WILL BE FILLED WITH RIGHTEOUS PEOPLE

Of all the important single passages in scripture, this one ranks high. The apostle Paul loved to quote this text as evidence that we do not work our way to heaven. Rather we believe God and we are reckoned or considered *righteous*. And since righteousness is our passport to eternal life it is important that we understand how we get it.

As a youngster I was told in my Bible classes in church school that heaven will only be filled with righteous people. And to me that always meant I had to be a good boy. I listened to all the stories of good people and how faithful they had been to God. If you sinned you asked forgiveness. But the ideal was never to sin to begin with.

Then I learned that we are born sinful, so even if we never sinned again we would still have that sinful nature to contend with. I would try to do my best. I would try to keep all sinful thoughts out of my mind. I would try not to get angry and not to be mean. And most of my friends were Christians so I would use that as a benchmark for my righteousness. Perhaps if I only associated with good people I would become good. At night, before going to bed, I would try to recall all the sins I had committed that day, and all the sinful thoughts I had had that day so I could repent of all of that and ask forgiveness. So, I would get them all back for just a moment.

As I grew up I realized that no matter how hard I tried I made mistakes and some of those mistakes I didn't even realize I had made. I was sure I wasn't recalling everything at my bedtime prayer. How could I ever be righteous? It was a serious business with me because it was kept before me all the time. Then I learned that even if I thought about doing something sinful I was guilty of the act—if I didn't commit the act of sin but just thought about committing it!

THE HOPELESSNESS OF THE SINFUL STATE

As I grew older I was confronted with new sins all the time. I read those long lists of sins in the New Testament. I read of all the mistakes even the great men of God made in the Old Testament and it all seemed hopeless. I wondered why people like David seemed so special to God when he committed sins I had never seriously even thought of committing.

As I studied my Bible more earnestly I came to understand that sin was not just an act but a state. That didn't help me either. When I got my first job picking gladiolas I thought I understood things a little more clearly. I worked for a whole day and the man paid me ten cents. It wasn't much but I knew one thing: when I picked up my dime at 5:00 pm, I had clearly earned that dime. I only worked at that job for one day. Down in the middle of my brain I connected working all day for a dime with working to be righteous. If I did so many good things in a day perhaps God would reward me with eternal life. It seemed clear enough. When Christ returns he will reward those who have been faithful by taking them to heaven and giving them the new earth. That made sense to a kid's mind.

Then as I got older, I opened my first bank account. I was about sixteen years old. And I learned another lesson about life. I would pick up my check and take it to the bank and I could write a check. But I learned that I could only write a check if there was money in the bank to cover the check. That was an important fact of life. I heard Dad talk about some kid who had written "bad" checks and was going to prison for a while. So, writing "bad" checks was sinful and punishable. That meant that he had written a check to pay a bill but did not have the money in the bank to cover the check. So that check was an empty piece of paper.

One day it hit me—what if I wrote a "bad" check for heaven? What if, when Jesus returned to pick me up he looked in my heavenly bank account of good works and there weren't enough good works there to cover the price for my eternal life? That would be serious. And this opened a new door of understanding for me that made everything I had understood about eternal life confusing.

There I stood before the heavenly tribunal. My record would be studied, and my resume of righteousness might prove faulty. Naturally, God would look at me and say, "Sorry, Ed; I know you want to live forever, but you have just not done enough good things to get in here. Bye." When the religious speaker would exclaim, "Young people, this is the greatest day to be living—Jesus could come before this school year ends! Isn't that great!!" It wasn't great—because I had a lot to do yet. And I knew, increasingly, that it would not be done by the end of that school year.

NO ONE REALLY EXPLAINED ABRAHAM TO ME

At least I don't remember that anyone did. Abraham was a rich man. Abraham was a good man. Abraham was a lot like me, only I wasn't rich or that good. But Abraham wanted to do God's will and so did I. I wanted to live forever. I didn't want to go to hell. I wanted to go to heaven. But you can't go to the show without a ticket and I knew I didn't have enough money to buy the ticket. How do you get enough money to buy a ticket to heaven?

Have you ever faced the fact that the car you want to buy is the car you can't afford? Have you ever had the problem that your money ran out before the month ran out? When I give students a group project to do I require that they dress up for their presentation. The last day of class is glorious. Here are students you are used to seeing in blue jeans and black tee shirts and beat-up sneakers, appearing before you in suits and dress shirts and ties.

I tell my class the week before—"Next week when you walk into this classroom I don't want to be able to recognize you—you must look so good that I am already biased to give you an 'A!'" But invariably, a student comes to me and says, "I don't even own a tie. All my money has gone to pay for school, I can't afford a suit. I don't have any dress shoes." One student's wife came to me and said, "Al is embarrassed to tell you this, but he is so big that all he owns are sweatpants and sweatshirts. Can you make an exception for him?" And I say, "No, if he is not in a suit he will lose points."

That was my view of heaven. If I didn't have on the wedding garment, I couldn't attend the wedding and there were no exceptions. I might try to sneak in, but I would be spotted. The people who were there were going to see a Cinemascope production of the lives of everyone who ever lived—and when my movie was played I would be embarrassingly yanked out and sent to the other place. It was a terrifying thought.

To help me out of my dilemma a church schoolteacher pointed out to me one day texts in 1 John.

> [4] Every one who commits sin is guilty of lawlessness; sin is lawlessness. (1 John 3:4)

> ²⁹ If you know that he is righteous, you may be sure that *every one who does right* is born of him. (1 John 2:2. Emphasis supplied)

> ⁷ Little children, let no one deceive you. He who *does right* is righteous, as he is righteous. (1 John 3:7. Emphasis supplied)

> ¹⁰ By this it may be seen who are the children of God, and who are the children of the devil: whoever does not do right is not of God, nor he who does not love his brother. (1 John 3:10)

Righteousness is right doing. For years that was my definition of righteousness. It only helped to curtail the idea that righteousness might include "right-thinking," or "right-desiring," or "right-intending." All those thoughts could now be dropped. But if your life is not continually "right doing," you would not inherit the kingdom of God. So, I entered the legalism phase of my life. There was clearly a connection between "doing good" and "receiving eternal life."

As I associated with people who defined righteousness this way, however, I noticed that some of them pushed "right doing" to the extreme. This notion was not to be understood as mostly right doing or occasionally right doing or making as few mistakes as possible, but rather: totally right doing. And they seemed genuinely concerned about my right doing—or wrongdoing—even more than their own. They inspected my cupboards for pepper and coffee. They noticed what I wore. They checked up on my respect for the corners of the Sabbath. And I followed suit.

IN THEIR FUNDAMENTAL DEFINITION THEY WERE RIGHT—ALMOST

Heaven will be the gift to those who are righteous. That means those who are totally, wholly, through and through right doing people. I once put on a brand-new shirt. By the time I got to work I had spilled coffee on it. So now it had a stain on it. I couldn't go forty miles back home and get another shirt. I scrubbed it in the bathroom at school but no matter how hard I worked I couldn't get it completely clean. I tried covering it with my tie, but it wasn't placed exactly right. I kept my coat on, but it still showed. But the wedding garment has no stain. The "white raiment" of the saved is totally white—there is no rip, no spot, no dirt, no flaw.

When the Hebrew brought the lamb to be slain it was to have no blemishes of any kind. If it had a cut and a scar or a genetic imperfection it was discarded. Isn't that a clear picture? Even a child could not miss that. You can't get into heaven with any moral or spiritual scars. You must be totally, wholly, through and through righteous. Of that we must be clear.

So, is righteousness right doing? Yes. But I looked at my life and I saw a lack. For me righteousness was largely defined by what I didn't do: not smoking, not drinking, not eating pork, not going to movies, not stealing, not killing, not committing adultery, not coveting, not breaking the Sabbath, not wearing jewelry, and more. I got out my check list.

Then someone gave me a brochure, published in Southern California, entitled, "One hundred sins God's people must eliminate to get to heaven." That added a lot of things I hadn't thought of. I couldn't be translated if I ate meat. Not a snack or a morsel of food could pass between my lips between meals. And I worked on those for a while. Until one day I got to thinking, why one hundred sins? What if I got to that tribunal and discovered that there were one hundred one sins, and I had relied on this brochure? Would I be in trouble! So, the dilemma built. There seemed to be no answer because I never understood the word "reckoned." I'm sure I had read it, and someone probably tried to explain it, but I was so caught up with "right doing" that I wasn't ready to hear it.

One day I was shopping with my son. He was about ten years old. He saw something he wanted me to buy and I said, "It would be nice if I could buy that for you, but I don't have enough money." And he said, "You don't have to have the money, just write a check!" Sure, why not? Who needs money?—just write a check. I explained to him, in order to write a check, you have to have money in the bank to cover the check. I didn't have the money in the bank so if I had written a check it would have been a "bad" check. Bingo! There is the answer.

THE BANK OF SALVATION

None of us has enough money in the bank of salvation to write a check for heaven. But the answer is in this text, certainly one of the most important texts in all the scriptures.

> ⁵ And he brought him outside and said, "Look toward heaven, and number the stars, if you are able to number them." Then he

said to him, "So shall your descendants be." ⁶ And he believed the Lord; *and he reckoned it to him as righteousness.* (Genesis 15:5-6. Emphasis supplied)

The answer to the question, "How does one become righteous?" is in that text. The whole answer, the entire solution to our dilemma of salvation; and it all centers in the word "reckoned."

It is impossible to be good enough to be saved. It is impossible to look at our right doing and see that there is enough money in our bank to cover the cost of heaven. The cost of eternal life is perfect righteousness. It is perfect death for any wrongdoing. One sin equals the death penalty. As the Israelite brought his perfect lamb, with no blemish, that lamb represented a perfect sacrifice—and it became a substitute for the flaw-filled life of the Israelite. He then believed that this stood for him and he was reckoned, considered, judged, righteous.

Is righteousness right doing? Yes. *But it is not my right doing* that saves me. I come to God and ask for forgiveness based on a bank account in heaven filled with perfect sinlessness. And every time I ask forgiveness and believe that God forgives me, I draw from that bank account. It is not money I have put in, but rather *money that Christ put in*: his perfect life, his paying the death penalty on the cross. Does that make sense?

I don't know when it dawned on me that saving righteousness was *Christ's right doing,* not mine. But I remember the sense of liberty and freedom it brought me. And as you and I believe in the substitutionary life and death of Jesus Christ we are reckoned righteous. How do you become righteous? By believing that the work of Christ as a human being on this earth was for you. Not by believing that you have any right doing that can save you. Do you still attempt to do right? Of course, but that is in joyful response, not a "righteousness" that saves you. We can rejoice by believing in the right doing of Christ for us—for Christ is our righteousness. That is the gospel!

CHAPTER SIX

Appeal of Moses and Elijah

"There is no medicine like hope, no incentive so great, no tonic so powerful as expectation of something tomorrow."

—Orison S. Marden

MATTHEW 17:1-10

¹ And after six days Jesus took with him Peter and James and John his brother, and led them up a high mountain apart. ² And he was transfigured before them, and his face shone like the sun, and his garments became white as light. ³ And behold, there appeared to them Moses and Elijah, talking with him.

⁴ And Peter said to Jesus, "Lord, it is well that we are here; if you wish, I will make three booths here, one for you and one for Moses and one for Elijah." ⁵ He was still speaking, when lo, a bright cloud overshadowed them, and a voice from the cloud said, "This is my beloved Son, with whom I am well pleased; listen to him." ⁶ When the disciples heard this, they fell on their faces, and were filled with awe. ⁷ But Jesus came and touched them, saying, "Rise, and have no fear." ⁸ And when they lifted up their eyes, they saw no one but Jesus only.

⁹ And as they were coming down the mountain, Jesus commanded them, "Tell no one the vision, until the Son of man is

raised from the dead." [10] And the disciples asked him, "Then why do the scribes say that first Elijah must come?"

CLYDE BEATTY AND HIS CIRCUS

Have you ever wanted something so bad that others tried to comfort you? When I was about ten years old I used to listen to the radio in the evenings. One of my favorite programs was the Clyde Beatty Show. I thought Clyde Beatty could do anything. He hunted animals for his circus. He was a world-traveler—from the jungles of India to the plains of Africa he travelled on his great hunts. And I could see him in my mind's eye—carrying out his responsibility to humanity and touring throughout the country with his circus.

Clyde Beatty was a real person. He did tour the world and hunt animals for his circus. And he really did have a circus. It wasn't as big as the Ringling Bros. and Barnum & Bailey Circus, but it was the "Clyde Beatty Circus," and he was my hero.

One day I heard an announcement that the Clyde Beatty Circus would be performing in Riverside. I pled with Dad who was dubious because in our religious tradition circuses were suspect—a circus was one of those borderline amusements that Christians probably didn't want to be caught attending. After all, what if Jesus should come that day and you were at the circus? But Dad knew how much Clyde Beatty meant to me. He had watched me get into my white clothes and get out my whip and line up the chairs and imagine there were lions and tigers on them. He knew the radio program was healthy and educational. So, he announced to the family that we would go to the Clyde Beatty Circus on Wednesday night. I was ecstatic. I was wild. And I couldn't wait to tell my best friends.

On Tuesday morning I saw my friend Barry[1] and told him about the plans Dad had announced. Barry was also a big fan of Clyde Beatty. He said he was going home and ask his parents to take him. But I had a better idea, "Why don't you go home and ask your parents if you can go with us to the Clyde Beatty Circus?"

It was a thoughtless act on my part—one of those times when you are caught up in the ecstasy of the moment—where you are so excited you don't stop to think of implications. You don't stop to think of what you are asking. You don't stop to examine what you are suggesting. You

---

1. Name supplied.

can't imagine that such an innocent request could have any kind of repercussions that could ruin everything. You are ten years old.

On Monday evening the phone rang. Dad looked up from his newspaper and reached for the phone. "Hello," . . . "yes," . . . "oh, really?" . . . "No, I don't think so." "Thank you." "Good-bye." He hung up the phone in silence. But he didn't go back to reading his paper. And I knew something was up. Finally, he spoke, "Eddie, . . . that was Barry's mother. . . . She says you invited Barry to go with us to the circus and wanted to know whether that was okay with me."

I waited for time to end. There was something about the look on his face that told me this was not cool. The silence was heavy. And he spoke again. "I told her that we were not going to the circus." It wasn't a lie. He had planned to take us but because of this little indiscretion he had changed his mind and now I would never see Clyde Beatty!

I cannot remember a time in my childhood that my disappointment was surpassed. I ran to my room and threw myself on the bed and cried and cried and cried. I remember through my tears hearing my brother trying to reason with Dad. I heard Mom intervene. I remember them both trying to dissuade him from this knee-jerk reaction.

"He knew I had reservations about going to the circus at all, and now probably the whole community will think that we go to circuses." I was devastated. Nothing could comfort me. Sometime that night I went to sleep. The next morning, I looked like a lawn mower had run over me.

THE DISAPPOINTMENT OF EXPECTATIONS

Someone told me once that your discouragements or disappointments are directly proportional to your expectations. When we get low we need to ask, what did we expect? The higher our expectations, the greater our discouragements. Jesus was pressing toward Jerusalem and he was talking suffering, hardship, death. It was weighing on the disciples because they were expecting something different. They were expecting kingship, royalty, kingdom, power, authority. And Jesus was talking rejection, suffering and death. He wouldn't give up the subject.

Finally, Peter took him aside to give him some fatherly advice. And he rebuked Jesus:

> [22] And Peter took him and began to rebuke him, saying, "God forbid, Lord! This shall never happen to you." [23] But he turned

> and said to Peter, "Get behind me, Satan! You are a hindrance to me; for you are not on the side of God, but of men." (Matthew 16:22-23)

The irony of the situation is that Peter had just given his famous confession that Jesus is the Son of God. So quickly things can turn around in our weak human condition. Jesus was ever in touch with the human weakness, and so he talked quietly with the disciples.

> ²⁴ Then Jesus told his disciples, "If any man would come after me, let him deny himself and take up his cross and follow me. ²⁵ For whoever would save his life will lose it, and whoever loses his life for my sake will find it. ²⁶ For what will it profit a man, if he gains the whole world and forfeits his life? Or what shall a man give in return for his life? ²⁷ For the Son of man is to come with his angels in the glory of his Father, and then he will repay every man for what he has done. ²⁸ Truly, I say to you, there are some standing here who will not taste death before they see the Son of man coming in his kingdom." (Matthew 16:24-28)

With that his counsel ended and they were in silence. He changed nothing. He still talked of death and suffering, but he brought solace. He said these were necessary things for their understanding of the mystery of life.

THE ENCOURAGEMENT OF ACTION

The obsession of Jesus to tell the disciples things they didn't want to hear is curious. He was compelled to straighten out their thinking about the kingdom. His prediction that some of them would see him in his glory caused them wonder. What did he mean? To this day people wonder what he meant. But the context should give us a hint.

Wednesday night Clyde Beatty performed in Riverside and I sat on my bed listening to his radio program. I wasn't sure I had forgiven Dad. The thought of never seeing my hero when he meant so much to me was overwhelming. I couldn't imagine why anyone would not take a little boy to a circus. I didn't care about religious convictions on circuses—they were invasive. What was the connection anyway?

On Friday we got out of school at noon. Dad and my brother picked me up at school. Dad began, "I know how disappointed you are about not going to see Clyde Beatty," he said, "so we are going to Riverside to get you something."

Well, that was nice, I thought, but it surely wouldn't take the place of my hero. We went to Sears in downtown Riverside, right near the Mission Inn. We went to the sports department. We went to the baseball bats and mitts and baseballs. And there Dad laid out a ton of money for my first baseball bat, baseball mitt, and baseball. That was nice. It wasn't Clyde Beatty, but they were trying.

When your heart is aching, it is nice to have people around you who try to comfort you. And I saw that Dad and Jim were doing that. So, we climbed in the car to go home and presumably play some ball. We went the long way home—across the Rubidoux bridge and to the east. And when we got to Fontana I saw the tent with the flags. My heart pounded again. At least I would get to see the tents of the circus.

Barry's parents had taken him to the circus when Dad had changed our plans. But suddenly I became aware that we had turned into the dirt parking lot under the big sign that read, *The Clyde Beatty Circus*. I was slow. I still refused to believe that there was a connection between the circus and me. But there was. Jim had prevailed. Dad had repented. And we spent the afternoon at the Clyde Beatty Circus!

MT. HERMON

The disciples walked with Jesus in their disappointment. They were resigned to Jesus' words even if those words did not make them happy. And then Jesus did what Jesus often did.

> [1] And after six days Jesus took with him Peter and James and John his brother, and led them up a high mountain apart. (Matthew 17:1)

Mt. Hermon is over nine thousand feet tall. It is the highest point in Syria. They didn't climb to the top, but they climbed up a ways. It got dark. Jesus prayed and the disciples slept again. And then Jesus took his three closest disciples on up the trail. And suddenly a cloud enshrouded him. The three disciples fell to the ground and shaded their eyes for the light was too bright.

There before them stood Jesus talking to two men who were identified as Elijah and Moses. These were two figures from Hebrew history who were larger than life. Both had been mysteriously taken to heaven, one without seeing death, had ridden a glorious chariot.[2] The other had seen death but was resurrected and carried by the angels.[3] One represented those who will die and be resurrected. The other represented those who will be alive when Christ returns.

These two men were in heaven on condition. And the condition was clear. Jesus was going to the cross. The disciples had rebuked him and chided him for his suicidal thoughts. They did not understand. But if there were two human beings in the universe who did understand the issues it was Moses and Elijah. If Jesus were to fail in his mission, their lives would end. And so, they come to encourage Jesus amid the disciples who should have been doing the job. There is no record that they said anything. Why would they need to say anything? Just seeing them would be encouragement for Jesus as he heads into the final storm of his life.

When I despaired at ever seeing Clyde Beatty, Dad surprised me with a vision of my hero. When his disciples despaired of ever seeing the kingdom, Jesus stood before them in glory with Moses and Elijah—all the earthly hosts to be saved and gave them the encouragement they would need to face the next few days. Being surrounded by those who love us means being surrounded by those who understand our needs.

> [2] And he was transfigured before them, and his face shone like the sun, and his garments became white as light. [3] And behold, there appeared to them Moses and Elijah, talking with him. [4] And Peter said to Jesus, "Lord, it is well that we are here; if you wish, I will make three booths here, one for you and one for Moses and one for Elijah."
>
> [5] He was still speaking, when lo, a bright cloud overshadowed them, and a voice from the cloud said, "This is my beloved Son, with whom I am well pleased; listen to him." [6] When the disciples heard this, they fell on their faces, and were filled with awe. [7] But Jesus came and touched them, saying, "Rise, and have no fear." (Matthew 17:2-7)

Peter stepped forth and offered to build a shrine. But Peter missed the point. The shrine was in their hearts. Knowing that in those worst moments of our lives we have people who will share what those moments mean is the most important shrine.

Several years ago, when a cable TV religious scandal broke, the host's goods went up for auction, and the host went to jail. A man flew

---

2. 2 Kings 2:11.
3. Jude 9.

down from Northern California to buy his desk. The auction went on and the price kept getting higher and higher, but the man was determined to get this desk and finally at an extremely high price the desk was sold to him. When asked why he would pay so much more for a desk, he said, several years ago when he and his wife were about to split up they went to this man for counseling and sat at that desk as he helped them put their marriage back together. He could imagine someone getting that desk who saw no more meaning in it than wood and glue.

When I played with that bat and mitt and ball, I thought of the Clyde Beatty Circus. When that man sat at the desk he thought of the marriage that was almost lost. In a sense these all became shrines. But for the disciples there was to be no shrine.

> [5] He was still speaking, when lo, a bright cloud overshadowed them, and a voice from the cloud said, "This is my beloved Son, with whom I am well pleased; listen to him." [6] When the disciples heard this, they fell on their faces, and were filled with awe. (Matthew 17:5-6)

This experience was to carry them through the days ahead. And ever since, Christians have thought of that moment on Mt. Hermon when God showed the disciples that they were going to receive God's reward. And they realized that the appeal of Moses and Elijah broadened the scope to include anyone whose heart was set on seeing the best things in life become theirs.

CHAPTER SEVEN

Lay Down Your Burden

"Life is neither to be wept over nor to be laughed at but to be understood."
—Arthur Schopenhauer

MARK 2:23-28

> [23] One sabbath he was going through the grainfields; and as they made their way his disciples began to pluck heads of grain. [24] And the Pharisees said to him, "Look, why are they doing what is not lawful on the sabbath?" [25] And he said to them, "Have you never read what David did, when he was in need and was hungry, he and those who were with him: [26] how he entered the house of God, when Abiathar was high priest, and ate the bread of the Presence, which it is not lawful for any but the priests to eat, and also gave it to those who were with him?" [27] And he said to them, "The sabbath was made for man, not man for the sabbath; [28] so the Son of man is lord even of the sabbath."

THE SABBATH COMMANDMENT

For the Jews there was no day like the Sabbath—the "seventh day" of the week. All the days of the week pointed to or were counted from the

Sabbath. The Sabbath was the "queen" of the week. And the children learned from their earliest days that this queen arrived every seven days.

The days were not named like they are in our society—Sunday, Monday, Tuesday, and so on. They were numbered or counted—from the Sabbath or to the Sabbath. Sunday was "the first day" from the Sabbath, Monday, the "second day" from the Sabbath, and so on until you got to Wednesday which was the third day until the Sabbath and the countdown began. Friday brought the excitement to its peak. Friday was the "preparation day" for the Hebrews.[1] And when Friday came everything began to switch into high gear—the queen would arrive at sundown!

Even the word for "week" in Greek became *sabbaton*, the same word for Sabbath, and the whole week took on the cast of the Sabbath. Some of us understand that whole dynamic for we grew up in Sabbath-keeping homes, essentially "Jewish" homes with respect to the Sabbath. The Sabbath commandment was at the heart of the Ten Commandment law given at Mt. Sinai. And as time passed the rules for keeping the Sabbath multiplied. The queen needed protection and so the Jews hedged the Sabbath with many requirements that they claimed were implied in the Sabbath commandment. They formulated thirty-nine categories of activities that were forbidden on the Sabbath and each of these categories had literally hundreds of clarifications and sub-rules.

In this passage we see Jesus and his disciples walking through a crop field on the Sabbath. And as they walk along, the disciples are lost in thought as they listen to Jesus teaching them. Apparently without thinking, they pull off pieces of grain, rub them together and nibble on them as they listen. In doing that, they broke four of the Jewish regulations on how to keep the Sabbath: (1) reaping, (2) winnowing (blowing away the chaff), (3) threshing, and (4) preparing a meal. All four were condemned by official Jewish law.

Christians have traditionally deplored the Sabbath laws of the Jews. And yet throughout their history Christians have done the equivalent with their creeds and their artificial insistence on trivia. As a graduate student I did a project on the history of Christian Sabbath-keeping and I found Sabbath manuals prepared in early America by the Puritans. These were lists of rules for keeping the Sabbath. My first thought was, I didn't realize that Puritans kept the Sabbath. But I soon came to realize that these were laws for keeping the Puritan Sabbath, which was Sunday!

---

1. Mark 15:42; Luke 23:54; John 19:31.

According to these Sabbath laws of the Puritans a Christian could not take a bath on Sunday. A Christian could not polish shoes on Sunday. A Christian must avoid traveling on Sunday. No work, no business, no personally gratifying amusement, no games. These were the Christian equivalents to the Talmudic Sabbath laws of the Jews. You might say, they were ways to help God out by going beyond anything God had commanded.[2]

If you followed that, on Sunday morning you didn't take a bath before church. You wouldn't go shopping after church. In modern times that would mean no videos, no football in the afternoon. You wouldn't be doing any business, or going swimming, or today, riding in your power boats, or participating in amusements. Sound familiar? You don't find many Sunday-keeping Christians following this kind of regime do you? That was the Puritans.

In many states this mentality created what are still called the Sunday "blue laws." Attempts to help God to enforce a life-style—to protect Sunday as the Christian Sabbath. Nothing new really. The Jews did it all before. And on the surface things sound good—God tells us to "remember" something important but then we make rules for ourselves and everybody else that can make us lose the spirit of what he intended.

THE PHARISEES OBJECTED TO WHAT THE DISCIPLES WERE DOING

There isn't a scrap of evidence that Jesus ever observed any other weekly day than the Jewish Sabbath. He was a good Jew—he honored the "queen" just like any other strict Jewish boy or man. But that is not the issue here. In his reply to the legalistic criticism of the Pharisees, Jesus focuses on why the Sabbath was given. Because in all their attempts to help God out these people had lost sight of what God was trying to do when he introduced the Sabbath in the first place.

The issue was not obeying God. The issue was their attempts to help God out. Think about it—when we try to help God out we may really be saying, God can't do it, but we can. Isn't God up to the task of solving his own problems?

God promised Abraham and Sarah that they would have a child. They apparently didn't think he could pull it off. So, they tried to help

---

2. Earles, *The Sabbath in Puritan New England.*

him out by doing it themselves. Granted, they did it legally. The laws of the day allowed Abraham to sleep with Hagar, Sarah's servant girl. But the underlying tragedy from the beginning was the belief that God couldn't pull it off—so we need to help him. Instead of following God they decided to lead him.

Cain was told to bring a lamb without blemish for a sacrifice, but he was a gardener, so he decided to help God out by bringing his best fruits and field crops. God had a lesson for Cain to learn in this little ritual but because Cain didn't do what God was asking him to do he never learned the lesson. He had a better idea. And the rest is history. We say, it was lost on Cain.

Organized religion tries to help God out all the time. Early American denominations were sometimes viciously anti-creedal. They said that if you write a creed you will eventually use that creed to test fellowship, then you will try members by that creed, and denounce them as heretics if they do not subscribe to all points of the creed. The result will be persecution of these people by shunning or torturing or even by death decree. History substantiates all of this.

Gradually most of these churches began writing creeds once they were established as organizations. As you analyze it, in the theological sense of societal control, creeds may be another of those human attempts to help God out, because he just is not up to the job.

So, the people had tried to help God out by making hundreds of Sabbath laws because the simple commandment was not enough. The thought that people are intelligent enough to stand before God without help was too intimidating. But these rules had destroyed the meaning of the Sabbath for many Jews of Jesus' day. People were not enjoying the day of rest because they were working so hard to keep it!

WHAT WAS THE PURPOSE OF THE SABBATH?

If you read the Ten Commandments carefully you will find that the Sabbath was given to God's people to show them that they could lay their burdens down. Jesus quietly reminds these human judges, these very human people, steeped in self-righteousness, that "the Sabbath was made for man, not man for the Sabbath."[3] Imbedded in that simple statement are several

---

3. Mark 2:27-28.

truths for us today that will help us lay our burdens down and get over that anxiety that we need to help God out.

First truth: We can rest in God with total confidence. The Hebrew word *shabbath* means "to rest." It is immortalized in the Bible through the creation story. As you read this story you find God finishing his work of creation. It is perfect. It is complete. It is done. And herein is the truth that can transform us. He finished the work. He did the work. He rested to prove that it was finished. Not we . . . *he*!

Things are little different today. If we are going to eternity with God it will be through God's effort. If we are going to have power to resist evil, it will be because of God's faithfulness. If we are going to maintain an equilibrium through those hard times of sorrow, disappointment, betrayal, or pain, it will be God's doing. And so, the writer of the letter to the Hebrews uses the Sabbath as a symbol of this rest.

> [1] Therefore, while the promise of entering his rest remains, let us fear lest any of you be judged to have failed to reach it. [2] For good news came to us just as to them; but the message which they heard did not benefit them, because it did not meet with faith in the hearers. [3] For we who have believed enter that rest, as he has said,
>
> "As I swore in my wrath, they shall never enter my rest," although his works were finished from the foundation of the world. [4] For he has somewhere spoken of the seventh day in this way, "And God rested on the seventh day from all his works." [5] And again in this place he said,
>
> "They shall never enter my rest." [6] Since therefore it remains for some to enter it, and those who formerly received the good news failed to enter because of disobedience, [7] again he sets a certain day, "Today," saying through David so long afterward, in the words already quoted,
>
> "Today, when you hear his voice, do not harden your hearts." (Hebrews 4:1-7)

Enter God's rest, he says in Hebrews 4. And he chastises those who try to help God out. Don't waste your time on the unnecessary. Don't try to do it your way. Seek God and his ways and rest in him.

Dad was a very particular Christian. As I was growing into my own independence I would rebel against rules that I thought were too restrictive and he would appeal to God's will for my life. But there were times when he came across legalistic—at least I evaluated it that way. And I remember as his health began to deteriorate I asked him, "Dad, what do you think? Have you attained the righteous life you think is acceptable to God? You've had several decades to attain this perfection—do you think you have made it?" And his words are burned in my heart to this day: "I guess I will just have to leave that up to God!"

Why couldn't I have heard those words when I was growing up? Such meaningful words—words that give birth to great gospel thoughts. *Leaving it up to God.* It seems natural for us to help God out. But God is able. God can do it. We don't have to improve on anything he has given. We are only asked to trust him—to enter his rest. And that's the first great truth here: the Sabbath, the rest was made for us. We are told to enter that rest and trust him.

Second truth: the letter of the law will kill you; the spirit of the law invigorates. In answer to the charges of the Pharisees, Jesus tells a story. He does not argue. He just tells a story. Rabbis always told stories—that's how they taught, that was their methodology. And then you were supposed to draw the conclusion. So, Jesus uses that method and tells of David, the greatest king of the Hebrew nation. When David was hungry he went into the holy place of the temple and ate the sacred bread and fed it to his soldiers.

Could you do that? No. Could David do it? He was the king. Who was going to stop him? And the people approved. But was it legal? No. The people gave him a pass on that, but he was still breaking the law. Did being king give him the right to break the law? No. But, Jesus says, you will overlook that because he is the king. Jesus knew they would not condemn David for doing that—his soldiers were hungry, so he stole from the temple.

Jesus was saying why can't you see that God gives his instructions for certain reasons. In the case of the Sabbath, you should see the necessity of relationship and easing human suffering not how many steps you can take on the Sabbath without violating the day. God's instructions were given for living a life in the spirit of the law. They were given to carry out human justice and mercy. They are not instructions that are designed to grind everyone up in a meat grinder of legalism.

Jesus is essentially saying to these people, resting in God makes you naturally compassionate people, not slandering, gossiping, or judgmental. And because David was king you entered God's rest and you didn't judge him for breaking one of your rituals! That is what entering the spirit of the law means! The law was given for us—we were not given for the law! Enter that spirit. King David was not arguing to help God out. He was demonstrating what the bread was for to begin with—and he broke the law to save his men. Well—be careful with that . . . but chew on it.

Third truth: Jesus is Lord of the Sabbath. A few years ago, a group of Sabbath-keeping Christians in New England began a crisis collection of foods and medicines for the victims of one of the worst hurricanes ever to hit Florida. They started their journey from Massachusetts after collecting a truck full of relief for these unfortunate victims. Their destination was Miami, so they had a long trip ahead of them. They arrived in Orlando on Friday afternoon and because the Sabbath was about to begin they interrupted their trip in order to keep the Sabbath. They attended Sabbath services, sang, and worshiped and rested until Sabbath sundown and then they resumed their trip. Meanwhile during that twenty-four-hour period those victims in Miami were suffering, starving, freezing, hurting.

When they finally arrived in Miami much of the relief work had been done. Here time was of the essence, but they chose to keep the Sabbath according to their human formula rather than bring relief to the suffering.

The other side of that story can be seen in the days of Jesus. He was hanging on the cross between two thieves. But it was growing late, the text tells us. It was around 3:00 pm and the Sabbath was approaching at sundown. What would they do if these men on the crosses didn't die before sundown? Their Sabbath started at sundown and they didn't want to be tending to such mundane things as relieving the suffering of men on the crosses.

So, they asked the Roman soldiers to break their legs so they would suffocate and die. Then they could get them off the crosses and into their graves in time for the Jews to keep their Sabbath. Ironic: Let's kill the savior so we can keep the Sabbath!

RELIGION AND HUMAN SUFFERING

We can legitimately ask ourselves what in our religion takes priority over the relieving of human suffering?

> [44] Then they also will answer, "Lord, when did we see thee hungry or thirsty or a stranger or naked or sick or in prison, and did not minister to thee?" [45] Then he will answer them, "Truly, I say to you, as you did it not to one of the least of these, you did it not

to me." ⁴⁶ And they will go away into eternal punishment, but the righteous into eternal life. (Matthew 25:44-46)

I'm not talking about the tsunami, although that underscores this principle. But we don't have to wait for world catastrophes to demonstrate this principle. Our passage in Mark 2 really has little to do with Sabbath-keeping. It has to do with our response to the gospel. Our treatment of each other reveals what we think of God's treatment of us. Religions do not consist of rules and regulations. They were only meant to remind us of our mission.

We worship the Lord of the Sabbath. But let's make certain that we do not put the emphasis on the Sabbath, but on the Lord. The Lord has authority in our lives because he has earned it. The Lord has authority in our lives because he made us, he saved us, he died and lives for us.

CHAPTER EIGHT

Get Up and Begin Again

> "A determination to succeed is the only way to succeed that I know anything about."
>
> —William Feather

EXODUS 3:1-15

¹ Now Moses was keeping the flock of his father-in-law, Jethro, the priest of Midian; and he led his flock to the west side of the wilderness, and came to Horeb, the mountain of God. ² And the angel of the Lord appeared to him in a flame of fire out of the midst of a bush; and he looked, and lo, the bush was burning, yet it was not consumed. ³ And Moses said, "I will turn aside and see this great sight, why the bush is not burnt."

⁴ When the Lord saw that he turned aside to see, God called to him out of the bush, "Moses, Moses!" And he said, "Here am I." ⁵ Then he said, "Do not come near; put off your shoes from your feet, for the place on which you are standing is holy ground." ⁶ And he said, "I am the God of your father, the God of Abraham, the God of Isaac, and the God of Jacob." And Moses hid his face, for he was afraid to look at God.

⁷ Then the Lord said, "I have seen the affliction of my people who are in Egypt, and have heard their cry because of their taskmasters; I know their sufferings, ⁸ and I have come down to

deliver them out of the hand of the Egyptians, and to bring them up out of that land to a good and broad land, a land flowing with milk and honey, to the place of the Canaanites, the Hittites, the Amorites, the Perizzites, the Hivites, and the Jebusites.

9 "And now, behold, the cry of the people of Israel has come to me, and I have seen the oppression with which the Egyptians oppress them. 10 Come, I will send you to Pharaoh that you may bring forth my people, the sons of Israel, out of Egypt." 11 But Moses said to God, "Who am I that I should go to Pharaoh, and bring the sons of Israel out of Egypt?" 12 He said, "But I will be with you; and this shall be the sign for you, that I have sent you: when you have brought forth the people out of Egypt, you shall serve God upon this mountain."

13 Then Moses said to God, "If I come to the people of Israel and say to them, 'The God of your fathers has sent me to you,' and they ask me, 'What is his name?' what shall I say to them?" 14 God said to Moses, "I AM WHO I AM." And he said, "Say this to the people of Israel, 'I AM has sent me to you.'" 15 God also said to Moses, "Say this to the people of Israel, 'The LORD, the God of your fathers, the God of Abraham, the God of Isaac, and the God of Jacob, has sent me to you': this is my name for ever, and thus I am to be remembered throughout all generations.'"

FINDING GEOGRAPHY

I made a quick trip to St. George, Utah, to pick up my grandnephew for a week's visit. Josh[1] was eight years old at the time and wanted to be a geologist, so his Dad, who worked at the Pentagon, took him on a geology trip across America. Their last stop was the Grand Canyon where they rode mules about halfway down and observed the rocks and layers of sediment. Then the rest of their family flew in from Washington and we met them all in St. George for a one-day family reunion.

Josh's maternal grandparents lived in Southern California. They had a new house, one to which I had never been. So, we had to rely on phone instructions. They were from the Middle East and talked with an accent, so when I got the instructions I hadn't written down the details correctly. When I got into their hometown I began driving and turning where I thought they had told me to go. It was a pre-GPS age, so I was going on my own or scribbled notes I didn't understand. I would turn and there

---

1. Name supplied.

would be a cul-de-sac. I would turn on to streets I thought were parallel to theirs and then found them to cross theirs. But eventually we found the house.

Most of us grew up believing we had a map and discovered through trial and error that we had misunderstood some things about the trip. First, we didn't get the instructions quite clear. Second, we discovered that the journey was as important as the destiny. And with any journeys we gradually discovered that there are a lot of dead-end streets and parallel roads and crossing avenues.

JOURNEYS CONTAIN UNEXPECTED ELEMENTS

We had planned to come straight home from Utah. But when we got to Las Vegas we decided to stop to eat. We went into a Circus hotel and found they had a theme park—roller coasters, bumper cars, miniature golf, and a huge buffet. Four hours later we emerged to continue our journey. And our lives were richer for having stopped and played together for a while. That's how the journey of life is. There are Christians whose lives are so intense you can almost hear them squeak when you are with them. Their emotional body tenses with every suggestion of enjoyability. Their lips quiver at the thought of fun. They worry about every thought, every action, every temptation.

I understand that because I have been there. Depending on their confessional orientation, many Christians grow up and move through a legalistic phase of life. The more conservative your background the more intense this may be. It is as if every turn in life is a cul-de-sac. And often they are not equipped to handle these turns in the road.

Often our own children teach us a lot about these things. They can teach us that much of what we believe or tried to teach them they question whether it is really important. And you can doubt your own journey. It may be that we did not grow up with the notion that life is a journey. In my denomination of origin, I was taught that any day the world could end. My parents were loving Christians, but I still went through the legalistic phase and that phase didn't allow for much journeying. In some approaches to journeying you can never make a wrong turn. You get one real shot at life and that's it. And when you blow it you may have some temporary forgiveness, but it will all be recalled when you blow it again. So, each cul-de-sac had another bag of guilt to carry.

Remember the man with the bag of rocks? A little boy saw the old man pulling this huge bag of rocks and asked him what was in there? The old man said, "this is my collection of rocks, but they are getting so heavy—I can hardly walk anymore." And then he died. And when the little boy investigated the bag, it was empty.

MOSES WAS A MAN WHO LEARNED ABOUT JOURNEYING

Moses is one of the great journeymen of all time. Abraham would run a close second. But Moses grows up in an Egyptian home and discovers only later that he is a Hebrew. When he finds an Egyptian tormenting a Hebrew he kills him and buries him in the sand. But as fate always seems to have it someone saw him do it and he had to flee for his life.

Where do you flee from Egypt? To the desert—it will be safe there. So, he goes to the Midianite desert and that is a giant, hot, dry, hostile cul-de-sac. When one looks at pictures of Midian, one should always do it on the hottest day of the summer with the windows closed and the heat turned all the way to the maximum. There you will get the full effect of what Moses was enduring. And you may want to bring in a few rattlesnakes and lizards to complete the picture.

So, what do you do when you started out life in a palace and suddenly found yourself running for your life in the desert? Here you can look at all the avenues to a fresh start and see that Moses learned every one of them.

It is time for rebirth—be born again.
It is time to accept God's forgiveness.
It is time freely to forgive those who put you there.
It is time to learn from your mistakes.
It is time to turn your weakness into strength.
It is time to accept what you cannot change.
It is time to change what you can—for the better.
It is time to put the past behind you.

You can picture Moses in the worst possible kind of desert, wondering in those wee hours of the morning—how did I get here? What wrong turn did I make? Where do I go from here? What to do? And it is time to get up and begin again. If ever a man was ripe for a fresh start, it was Moses in the wilderness of Midian. Getting out of the cul-de-sac becomes a major goal, a major quest, a vision of relief. He is like the little lion in Disney's story of *The Lion King*—alienated, scared, exiled. Something must be about to happen.

GOD NEVER LEAVES US ALONE IN THE CUL-DE-SAC

There are stories in the Old Testament that test our interpretive ability to make God look good. We have quite a different society than that of the ancient Hebrews. But in this setting with Moses God looks merciful as he brings relief. Here is one of God's children who has turned into a dead-end street. Here is a man of great leadership ability who doesn't know it. Here is a man of great learning who is spending his time herding stupid sheep. Here is a man of strategic ability, a man with the greatest military training Egypt could offer, a man who can see no farther than the end of his nose. Here is a man whom God has been training for forty years without his even realizing it.

As Moses tends sheep for one of the citizens of Midian, he notices a strange sight: a bush on fire. When he goes to look at this strange sight he hears a voice:

> ¹ Now Moses was keeping the flock of his father-in-law, Jethro, the priest of Midian; and he led his flock to the west side of the wilderness, and came to Horeb, the mountain of God. ² And the angel of the LORD appeared to him in a flame of fire out of the midst of a bush; and he looked, and lo, the bush was burning, yet it was not consumed. ³ And Moses said, "I will turn aside and see this great sight, why the bush is not burnt." ⁴ When the LORD saw that he turned aside to see, God called to him out of the bush, "Moses, Moses!" And he said, "Here am I." ⁵ Then he said, "Do not come near; put off your shoes from your feet, for the place on which you are standing is holy ground." ⁶ And he said, "I am the God of your father, the God of Abraham, the God of Isaac, and the God of Jacob." And Moses hid his face, for he was afraid to look at God." (Exodus 3:1-6)

At that bush that didn't burn up, God presents a new challenge to Moses. "I want you to go back to Egypt: put the past behind you, turn your weakness into strength, get up and begin again! Go!"

Moses' response is human and normal.

> ¹¹ But Moses said to God, "Who am I that I should go to Pharaoh, and bring the sons of Israel out of Egypt?" ¹² He said, "But

> I will be with you; and this shall be the sign for you, that I have sent you: when you have brought forth the people out of Egypt, you shall serve God upon this mountain." (Exodus 3:11-12)

Moses speaks more out of fear than humility. He has gone from the top to the bottom in a noticeably short time. His concerns are wrapped up in protecting sheep, salving the wounds of the trail, seeing that the wool grows normally for market, pleasing his boss, enduring the heat. He is on the first level of Abraham Maslow's hierarchy of needs[2]—physical needs, safety needs. God is challenging him to get up and begin again.

> [14] God said to Moses, "I AM WHO I AM." And he said, "Say this to the people of Israel, 'I AM has sent me to you.'" [15] God also said to Moses, "Say this to the people of Israel, 'The LORD, the God of your fathers, the God of Abraham, the God of Isaac, and the God of Jacob, has sent me to you': this is my name for ever, and thus I am to be remembered throughout all generations. [16] Go and gather the elders of Israel together, and say to them, 'The LORD, the God of your fathers, the God of Abraham, of Isaac, and of Jacob, has appeared to me, saying, "I have observed you and what has been done to you in Egypt; [17] and I promise that I will bring you up out of the affliction of Egypt, to the land of the Canaanites, the Hittites, the Amorites, the Perizzites, the Hivites, and the Jebusites, a land flowing with milk and honey." (Exodus 3:14-17)

God promises:

> [12] "I will be with you; and this shall be the sign for you that I have sent you; when you have brought forth the people out of Egypt, you shall serve God upon this mountain." (Exodus 3:12)

SCARED OR HUMBLE?

Moses is not humble. Moses is scared. When he killed the Egyptian, he was seen by somebody among the Hebrews. He fled because the Hebrews refused to see him as their leader. And it was only sensible that Moses would now object—what if the Hebrews wouldn't accept him as their leader. And it was only because of the continued, stated, repeated promises of God to be with him, to give him words, that Moses finally ran out of excuses. But Moses' conversation with God in the cul-de-sac of Midian

---

2. Maslow, *Motivation and Personality*.

was one of the longest of any man in the Bible. And it ends with signs. Moses is so scared he must have signs that God is who he claims to be.

No one ever promised that getting up and beginning again would be easy. Each of us has our own cul-de-sac of Midian. Perhaps we wish we could see a burning bush and hear a voice. This represents the restriction of experience. Experience can be a great crippler. We tried it before, and it didn't work so we can't get up the courage to try it again. Moses is in Midian because he demonstrated some extreme behavior—he killed a man. Moses could argue that he was justified by his emotional self that obviously did not accept the argument.

Moses presented every excuse why he couldn't get up and begin again. So, do we. Moses was a good human example. Perhaps we should apply what we already know of Moses from previous study—his unique place in the Hebrew Hall of Fame because of his great diplomatic and leadership ability, his courage and character, his ability to journey through the most difficult circumstances of life, his teachability. None of this was possible by Moses in the cul-de-sac. Only the promises of God gave him the frame of mind necessary to getting up and beginning again.

When God came to Moses in the cul-de-sac, he had already trained him. And that truth is clear today. When God comes to anyone in the cul-de-sac, it is because they are ready to go where he wants them.

CHAPTER NINE

Acting Like Children

"A child is a person who is going to carry on what you have started . . .
the fate of humanity is in his hands."

—Abraham Lincoln

PHILIPPIANS 2:1-13

¹ So if there is any encouragement in Christ, any incentive of love, any participation in the Spirit, any affection and sympathy, ² complete my joy by being of the same mind, having the same love, being in full accord and of one mind. ³ Do nothing from selfishness or conceit, but in humility count others better than yourselves.

⁴ Let each of you look not only to his own interests, but also to the interests of others. ⁵ Have this mind among yourselves, which is yours in Christ Jesus, ⁶ who, though he was in the form of God, did not count equality with God a thing to be grasped, ⁷ but emptied himself, taking the form of a servant, being born in the likeness of men. ⁸ And being found in human form he humbled himself and became obedient unto death, even death on a cross.

⁹ Therefore God has highly exalted him and bestowed on him the name which is above every name, ¹⁰ that at the name of Jesus every knee should bow, in heaven and on earth and under

the earth, [11] and every tongue confess that Jesus Christ is Lord, to the glory of God the Father.

[12] Therefore, my beloved, as you have always obeyed, so now, not only as in my presence but much more in my absence, work out your own salvation with fear and trembling; [13] for God is at work in you, both to will and to work for his good pleasure.

PLANTING A CHURCH

In the spring of 1967, I was called into my supervisor's office and asked to move North and plant a church. All my education up to that point had been classical regarding my ministerial and theological training. I asked him, "What do I do? I've never planted a church." And his reply was also classical, "Give me a report on how it goes!" Not much help, I thought. So, in one last desperate attempt for direction I asked for some advice. He gave me one sentence. "Be a friend of all and a pal of none!"

I was twenty-six years old. I was two years out of graduate school. I had interned under two seasoned pastors whose approach to pastoring was quite different from each other. The church growth movement was not alive. I had no training in planting churches. I had hardly any idea of where to start. So, I drove North and met with the core group of people who wanted a new congregation. There were about twenty-five people at the meeting. At that time, they were driving to at least five different cities to attend congregations but they lived in a city that had no congregational center. They were united on one point: they wanted a church in the town where they lived.

I could give the philosophical backgrounds on theological development. I could show how to design an evangelistic brochure. I could give the historical background of denominationalism in America. But somehow that missed the mark of organizing a new congregation.

THE KEY TO SUCCESS IN CHURCH BUILDING

As we met that evening I was impressed by the diversity of the group. I don't use diversity as I would now. It was the professional diversity that impressed me. There were housewives, doctors, blue collar workers, teachers, bus drivers. They were basically between the ages of 25-50. There was a strong male contingent. I didn't know the importance of this diversity at the time because I had no objectivity in the matter. I just saw a pool of impressive people.

I didn't know whether to "wing" it or "fake" it. Did I tell them I knew nothing about planting a church? Did I tell them that nothing in my graduate training had even given me a class in church finance? Did I invite them to take a Greek or Hebrew class? I could have taught that with ease. Practical training was very weak except for my excellent internship. It became clear that they may have known more about planting a church than I did, so I made this a "listening trip." The venture was amazingly successful.

Today that church is considered important for any pastor in Southern California. It was not because of my expertise that it was successful. But we all learned from the activity and today I still communicate with members of that church. We reminisce, perhaps more honestly, about what really happened.

Within five years we had a net growth of twenty members a year, a rate at which the church has continued to grow over the past fifty years. The community was mobile. I figured once that if we had retained everyone over that five years who had been a member of that congregation we would have over three hundred members over that period.

In the 1960s people moved into the town and out. The growth numbers are not impressive compared to growth in non-denominational churches. Many young people got their training in the area and then moved on to more technical positions. But while they were in town they worked and worshiped in our new congregation. As I have reflected I decided that there was one "secret" or "key" to whatever success we had there: we all acted like children.

ACTING LIKE CHILDREN

The secret of any congregational growth program starts right here. Paul goes on to list the causes of discord and disunity:

> ¹ So if there is any encouragement in Christ, any incentive of love, any participation in the Spirit, any affection and sympathy, ² complete my joy by being of the same mind, having the same love, being in full accord and of one mind. ³ Do nothing from selfishness or conceit, but in humility count others better than yourselves. ⁴ Let each of you look not only to his own interests, but also to the interests of others. (Philippians 2:1-4)

v. 3:   Do nothing from selfishness.

v. 3:   Do nothing from conceit.

v. 4:   Do not be always concentrating on your own interests.

The apostle Paul gives the positive side of this as well.

v. 2:   Be in full accord and one mind.

v. 3:   In humility count others better than yourselves.

v. 4:   Let each look to the interests of others.

It is a hard-learned lesson that church doesn't belong to us. Because this is hard learned, we are brought over the same ground again and again. Hard feeling is a chance to reconcile. Every bad experience is an opportunity to demonstrate growth. Every church fight is a challenge to cooperate. In many churches, members come to every table with a long history. The work at most churches is not altogether like planting a church. Some members have mysterious personalities, some of which have been together for thirty or more years. This can be a negative thing if we let it—in thirty years lines are drawn, opinions toward others can be set in concrete, what masks as Christian cooperation can be undercut by seething frustration and even hatred.

The hope is in acting like children—children of God who love the same things and are joined together in soul with minds set on one thing.

ACTING LIKE CHILDREN IS NOT ACTING IMMATURELY

A lot of material comes across my desk and I have a hard time keeping up with it all because I try to take it seriously. One of the regular visitors to my desk is material on reconciliation. I had a hard time grasping some people's notion of reconciliation. I didn't find much of the material very explicit. But I did find that some of the emphasis was on praying for reconciliation of the races; praying together that racial bigotry and prejudice will be overcome by the human race. That is good. Few would deny that.

The real test of reconciliation comes on a personal level. There are congregations that pray for the reconciliation of the races, but they seethe with ferment in their own locale. Church leaders are interpreted by others in the congregation as being driven by selfish ambition or vain conceit. And the foment eats away at the whole structure of the congregation's witness.

I interviewed at a church where there was a decisive split between the conservatives and the liberals. And control of the Church Board was the football they tossed back and forth each year. I stayed there for three days in that church talking to people about their congregation. And it became clear within hours of my arrival that the liberals had captured the Church Board that year but that the conservatives were grouping and politicking to take over next year.

It also became quite clear that this was destroying unity in the congregation and its days were numbered so far as its future was concerned. In many ways it was a wonderful church—the plant was complete, and the bills were all paid. They had money in the bank. But this undercurrent of discord was making things intolerable for many and the younger people were just leaving. They could not see how they could bring their children up in such an atmosphere.

I suggested to the chairman of the elders that they should disband the Church Board—just not call it for a while, maybe two or three years. At first he was shocked. How could a church function without a Church Board? But he had to concede that the Church Board had become such a political thing that the very functioning of the church was now in danger.

COMMUNION IS MUTUAL PARTICIPATION

Since my church organizational experience, I have received professional training in church planting and church growth. I have been taught by those who have been successful what works and what does not work. And all of them started in the same place: full agreement, loving the same things, joined together in soul, and minds set on the one thing.

No church that seethes can expect to grow. Christian churches participate in the Lord's Supper, a sacrament in the Protestant sense of the word. It is "communion," a Latin word that means "mutual participation." It means we come together, we work together, we participate together, we struggle together, we solve problems together, we are together in soul.

We often read from 1 Corinthians 11 where the apostle Paul talks about the meaning of the Lord's Supper.

> [23] For I received from the Lord what I also delivered to you, that the Lord Jesus on the night when he was betrayed took

> bread, ²⁴ and when he had given thanks, he broke it, and said, "This is my body which is for you. Do this in remembrance of me." ²⁵ In the same way also the cup, after supper, saying, "This cup is the new covenant in my blood. Do this, as often as you drink it, in remembrance of me." (1 Corinthians 11:23-25)

But we usually do not read the full passage. It is scary because it barely stops short of pronouncing a curse on any group of people that participate in communion who have any seething undercurrents of discord among them.

> ²⁷ Whoever, therefore, eats the bread or drinks the cup of the Lord in an unworthy manner will be guilty of profaning the body and blood of the Lord. ²⁸ Let a man examine himself, and so eat of the bread and drink of the cup. ²⁹ For any one who eats and drinks without discerning the body eats and drinks judgment upon himself. ³⁰ That is why many of you are weak and ill, and some have died. ³¹ But if we judged ourselves truly, we should not be judged. (1 Corinthians 11:27-31)

The apostle Paul gives this counsel:

> ¹⁸ For, in the first place, when you assemble as a church, I hear that there are divisions among you; and I partly believe it, ¹⁹ for there must be factions among you in order that those who are genuine among you may be recognized. ²⁰ When you meet together, it is not the Lord's supper that you eat. ²¹ For in eating, each one goes ahead with his own meal, and one is hungry and another is drunk. ²² What! Do you not have houses to eat and drink in? Or do you despise the church of God and humiliate those who have nothing? What shall I say to you? Shall I commend you in this? No, I will not. (1 Corinthians 11:18-22)

He goes on to describe a situation where people eat at home rather than eat with those they despise. Then he pleads with them not to bring God's disapproval upon them by eating and drinking "unworthily" of this sacred ordinance. Congregations can take this counsel with meaning—pulling together. We can examine ourselves to see if we are worthy of having new converts, unchurched people, some of whom only we can reach for the gospel of Christ. We can ask what they will learn if they join us.

It is a frightening thought that God takes us seriously. And it may be even more frightening a thought, that we can take ourselves seriously.

¹ So if there is any encouragement in Christ, any incentive of love, any participation in the Spirit, any affection and sympathy, ² complete my joy by *being of the same mind, having the same love, being in full accord and of one mind.* ³ Do nothing from selfishness or conceit, but in humility count others better than yourselves. (Philippians 2:1-3. Emphasis supplied)

CHAPTER TEN

Finding a Need to Suffer

"Suffering becomes beautiful when anyone bears great calamities with cheerfulness, not through insensibility but through greatness of mind."

—Aristotle

LUKE 22:14-23

¹⁴ And when the hour came, he sat at table, and the apostles with him. ¹⁵ And he said to them, "I have earnestly desired to eat this passover with you before I suffer; ¹⁶ for I tell you I shall not eat it until it is fulfilled in the kingdom of God." ¹⁷ And he took a cup, and when he had given thanks he said, "Take this, and divide it among yourselves; ¹⁸ for I tell you that from now on I shall not drink of the fruit of the vine until the kingdom of God comes."

¹⁹ And he took bread, and when he had given thanks he broke it and gave it to them, saying, "This is my body which is given for you. Do this in remembrance of me." ²⁰ And likewise the cup after supper, saying, "This cup which is poured out for you is the new covenant in my blood. ²¹ But behold the hand of him who betrays me is with me on the table. ²² For the Son of man goes as it has been determined; but woe to that man by whom he is betrayed!" ²³ And they began to question one another, which of them it was that would do this.

CELEBRATING PALM SUNDAY

One morning in church I met a young man and wife, and their children. They were planning to join our congregation and I was delighted. He was handsome, she was pretty, the children were disciplined. Everyone who joins a congregation is special, but this was considered by many a double blessing because of their talent and beauty. They were special in many ways. They immediately enrolled their children in church school. They took advantage of all the young people's activities in the congregation and they helped as their time allowed.

A year later we were talking in church. By now they had become solid members. They were holding some church offices. Everything was going their way. And then life ended as they knew it for that very night the father in the family was killed—just when life seemed the brightest, suffering was looming on the horizon.

Every year Christians celebrate Palm Sunday—a day that seemed the brightest in the experience of Christ and his disciples. Chants of victory, cheers of hosanna, laughter, and happiness, that the Lord was king, that the Lord was riding into Jerusalem on a donkey, in the tradition of the humble kings of Israel. This had to be an announcement of better things to come. This had to be what Israel had been expecting for all these years. And this had to be the happiest moment in the life of any Israelite who had ever lived.

The palm branches lined the streets and graced the hands of those who held them. This was a symbol of victory and praise and the children who had been healed and who had heard his stories waved them. And the parents who had thrilled at their children's healing waved them.

PASSION WEEK STARTED WITH A VICTORY MARCH

The disciples were sent to find the proper animal and when it was found Jesus mounted it. Imagine who might have been in that victory march. Lazarus whom Jesus had raised from the dead after he had been in the tomb for three days: some scholars believe he led the donkey! How about the man who was healed by the pool? Can't you imagine he was walking there with his bed rolled up on his shoulder. What a happy occasion for him!

Do you think maybe people he had healed on the Sabbath were there? We have record of at least seven of them, and probably there were more. I can't imagine that if they were in town they weren't there for they had something to praise Jesus about. How about those guys filled with devils who came out of the tombs in Galilee? Don't you think they might be in the parade? They had evangelized the whole Decapolis by the time Jesus returned there a year later. If they could get to Jerusalem for the Passover we can suspect that they were in this entourage.

Of course, the disciples were there and the different Marys were there and behind the scenes Nicodemus was there and probably Joseph of Arimathea, both good Pharisees, not sure yet where this strange teacher would ultimately lead them. Victory celebrations are a part of the human experience. They are good for the human spirit and soul. They keep some important things in focus—they remind us of significant events, important people, great times we have had and how all these have affected us and what we have become.

Do you feel for people who can't celebrate? People who have found a need to suffer beyond what God ever intended or wished? A simple celebration is a gift of God—the ability to recognize the time for celebration is part of God's schedule. There is a time to suffer. There is a time to celebrate. Some Christians in their super conscientious delusion feel that celebration is worldly and evil. This parade was not for them. This parade was for Jesus' believers and followers. It was a responsive celebration.

ON THIS EARTH VICTORY IS OFTEN SHORT-LIVED

When we read the record in the Gospels of the triumphal entry of Jesus into Jerusalem on that Palm Sunday we just can't believe that the tide could turn. There is the story of Shoeless Joe Jackson. He was a star outfielder for the Chicago White Sox in 1919. The kids worshiped Shoeless Joe. Kids wanted to be like him.

The kids followed him wherever he went and then something horrible happened. When the White Sox were in the World Series, heavily favored to win because they had a steel strong team, the tide turned, and the Sox lost. Rumors spread, people talked, investigation was pursued and eight men on the Sox were found guilty of accepting bribes from gamblers who wanted to win a lot of money. Those all-star players had thrown the game.

It was a serious charge, a severe claim. So critical was it that these eight baseball players were banned from professional baseball for the rest of their lives. At the end of the season as Shoeless Joe, probably the biggest star on the Sox team, was walking to his locker, a little kid ran up to the fence, suffering marked his face, concern colored his skin, and in desperate tones he cried out, "Say it isn't so, Shoeless Joe! Say it isn't so!" A great experience had turned to powder in the little boy's mind. His great hero had fallen.

The Passion Week, or Holy Week, can be viewed in a similar light. Here is the great parade at the beginning of the week, and then the rumors start, the trial begins, Jesus is condemned for his "crimes" and here is the entourage crying for understanding, "Say it isn't so, Jesus! Say it isn't so!" But unlike Shoeless Joe, Jesus is suffering for our sins not his own. And he walks silently those last few days, letting people figure things out, letting the ax fall where it may, letting people be led or directed by the Spirit of God or the spirits of their own surmising.

This may be confusing because somehow we often act like we think that with God there can be no suffering. Others think there can be no celebrating either. Both are wrong. There is a time to suffer and there is a time to celebrate and to a large degree we choose our need to suffer and we choose our need to celebrate. God will give us direction.

THE LAST NIGHT WITH JESUS

In the above passage we have traveled to the end of the week. It has been a week of tremendous work, many healings, many sermons, and much personal ministering to people. Marked by the exhilaration of the first day of the week, Jesus and his disciples work tirelessly through the week doing God's work.

Some things are not so much to the liking of leaders. Cleansing the temple undoubtedly topped the list. Here was an invasion of the temple administration that would not be welcomed. The encounters with the leaders increased throughout the week until decisions were made that this matter should be settled before Passover. And so, the pressure is on and Jesus senses all that is happening. But he is not able to communicate all that is happening in a way that the disciples understand it.

As they gather around the table in the upper room for the Passover meal, as good Jews, they are unaware that Satan has entered as well. He has entered the heart of Judas. The deals were made sometime during that triumphant week. Imagine, the highly trusted and admired, Judas, the trusted administrator and treasurer of the disciples, out during this busy week, while the disciples are winning souls and touching broken lives, perhaps even the best educated of the disciples, Judas, that sterling character in the eyes of the disciples and the public alike, Judas, the man who dared to correct Jesus from time to time, Judas, was making deals with the enemy.

Judas helped with the plot. Judas found a need to suffer. It didn't make sense. But he twisted it around to make it all fit. He would make a little money but that was not the important element here. Jesus would not allow himself to be taken. He felt that Jesus would be forced to set up his kingdom and Judas would oversee the treasury of the new government.

Suffering in life is normal but some people have to exacerbate their suffering. Sometimes we have to find a need to suffer so we can feel important. That's normal but it is not productive, and it is not nearly as fun as celebrating. Suffering comes on its own. We really don't need to find it. Perhaps what we need is to recognize what is worth suffering for.

CELEBRATION IN OUR INNOCENCE

By the end of the week all the disciples would suffer. Jesus would suffer and die. The excruciating pain that would come to the believers just five days after Palm Sunday is not something to seek. The source of their suffering was their belief that Jesus was Savior, that Jesus was the long-awaited Messiah, that Jesus was the fulfillment of the prophecies of all time.

Palm Sunday leads to the Lord's Supper and then out to the Garden of Gethsemane, to the court, to the trials, to the hill called Golgotha and suffering for the human race. But on this day we are entitled to celebrate in our ignorance as the disciples did.

On Palm Sunday we are entitled to celebrate in our innocence as the disciples did. But we know that suffering will come, and that suffering can make us strong and urgent, understanding and patient with others. The suffering that will come can make us serious, conscientious, and concerned. It can give us focus and direction and help us identify our mission in life as a church as well as a member of the church. It can make us positive and strong. It can make us reach out to those who visit us and encourage them to come back and find a home where they can learn what it is to love.

[19] This is my body which is given for you. Do this in remembrance of me. [20] This cup which is poured out for you is the new covenant in my blood. [21] But behold the hand of him who betrays me is with me on the table. (Luke 22:19-21)

Breaking the body causes suffering. Draining the blood causes suffering. Being betrayed causes suffering. Which of these are necessary?

CHAPTER ELEVEN

No God, No Hope

"God is perfection, and nothing that we could ever bring would in any event satisfy the perfection of God."

—William Barclay

EPHESIANS 2:11-22

[11] Therefore remember that at one time you Gentiles in the flesh, called the uncircumcision by what is called the circumcision, which is made in the flesh by hands—[12] remember that you were at that time separated from Christ, alienated from the commonwealth of Israel, and strangers to the covenants of promise, having no hope and without God in the world. [13] But now in Christ Jesus you who once were far off have been brought near in the blood of Christ.

[14] For he is our peace, who has made us both one, and has broken down the dividing wall of hostility, [15] by abolishing in his flesh the law of commandments and ordinances, that he might create in himself one new man in place of the two, so making peace, [16] and might reconcile us both to God in one body through the cross, thereby bringing the hostility to an end. [17] And he came and preached peace to you who were far off and peace to those who were near; [18] for through him we both have access in one Spirit to the Father.

¹⁹ So then you are no longer strangers and sojourners, but you are fellow citizens with the saints and members of the household of God, ²⁰ built upon the foundation of the apostles and prophets, Christ Jesus himself being the cornerstone, ²¹ in whom the whole structure is joined together and grows into a holy temple in the Lord; ²² in whom you also are built into it for a dwelling place of God in the Spirit.

THE ATTITUDE OF A SECULAR AGE

As I talked with a young man after class, he made it clear that God was not a part of his thinking. "I live my life and enjoy it. What comes after this I don't care about. As far as I am concerned, I have no interest in anything religious, anything having to do with God, anything having to do with anything other than the life I am enjoying right now. Religion? I'm not interested in anything that has to do with religion."

This attitude is not unusual in a secular age. The adage goes, "you only go around once, so live it to the hilt." And "living" for many today simply means taking advantage of whatever happens in your life. Wherever your life leads, go there. Whatever happens, accept it. "Eat, drink and by merry, for tomorrow you die." This is a common attitude in a secular age. It presents the greatest challenge to the Christian who does believe in God, who does believe religion is part of our very being, and who recognizes that death is not a logical end to life.

Paul urges believers to remember when we were "Gentiles."

> ¹¹ Therefore remember that at one time you Gentiles in the flesh, called the uncircumcision by what is called the circumcision, which is made in the flesh by hands—¹² remember that you were at that time separated from Christ, alienated from the commonwealth of Israel, and strangers to the covenants of promise, having no hope and without God in the world. (Ephesians 2:11-12)

In a nutshell he presents the gospel as the only hope, as the only future, as the only stabilizing factor in a life of separation, alienation, and estrangement from God.

IN THE JEWISH MIND A GENTILE WAS OUTSIDE GOD'S MERCY

"You were called the uncircumcision," and as such you were outside the realm of salvation. Mixing with the Gentiles had brought the Jews great grief. Samson played with the Philistine ladies and was eventually destroyed. The kings of Israel and Judea periodically strayed from the true faith and took the nation with them into perdition.

Wherever the Gentiles were, there was iniquity and confusion. Gentiles were enemies of God. Gentiles were the seat of corruption, persecution, and debauchery. Within this mindset the Jews became an exclusive group, sometimes blind to corresponding evil within their own midst. The Gentiles were an object of contempt. They were a barrier to righteousness. Jewish boys who married Gentile girls, Jewish girls who married Gentile boys were ceremonially buried. Such apostasy was commemorated by a ceremonial funeral. Such a Jewish boy or Jewish girl was pronounced dead.

In the ancient stories that went into the contemporary popular play, *Fiddler on the Roof*, this kind of association is immortalized. Tevye the milkman, the father of five girls, sees his first daughter marry a boy of her own choosing. That in itself was a break with tradition where the matchmaker had been hired by the parents to arrange the marriage. But Tevye finally gives permission to this marriage. When the second daughter responds to a proposal from a young Jewish man without even consulting her parents, Tevye bends a little more. And while it was painful in both instances at least both men were Jews. But when his third daughter takes up with a Russian Gentile, the pain is more than Tevye can bear. He utters the words, "How far can I bend before I break?" And he disowns his daughter for her relationship with this Russian Gentile. In his mind, this daughter is dead, and he moves on with life after his mourning period ends.

The Jews considered that the Gentiles were unclean. Gentiles were cursed by God. And so, there could be no mixture of Jewish and Gentile blood. It was outside the natural order of things set up by God. It was not part of God's plan. Gentiles, said the Jews, were created by God to be fuel for the fires of hades because God loves only the Jews. The barriers were up in this Jewish mindset.

Until Christ came the Gentiles were an object of contempt to the Jews. The barrier between them was absolute. If a Jewish boy married a Gentile girl, or if a Jewish girl married a Gentile boy, the funeral of that Jewish boy or girl was carried out. Such contact with a Gentile was the equivalent of death. Even to go into a Gentile house rendered a Jew unclean. Before Christ the barriers were up; after Christ the barriers were down. Before Christ there was no hope of unity; in Christ the new unity had come.[1]

THE JEWS HAD HOPE

From the beginning of the scriptural account of history, God's people had hope. When our first parents sinned, God gave a promise that the great deceiving serpent would eventually be destroyed—that God would send a deliverer who would crush his head and bring things back to their original purpose in nature, in life, in ethics, in spirituality.

> [15] I will put enmity between you and the woman, and between your seed and her seed; he shall bruise your head, and you shall bruise his heel. (Genesis 3:15)

That seed was one anointed by God, he would restore all faithful humanity to God's original purpose, and he would deliver humanity from the bondage of sin. As the scriptural account proceeds, God watches humanity fall over and over again, straying from whatever plans he laid out.

While there were righteous men and women in ancient times, the majority represented a godless bunch. Finally, God comes with a plan that can produce a people who are faithful. He will create a group, a family, a clan, that breaks the cycle of sin and undoneness. He finds Abraham, a faithful man in a faithless generation and he promises to make of him a great nation, a multitude of descendants more numerous than the stars of heaven. In Abraham, God starts over. He had started over with Noah's family, but they had strayed away. Now he starts with Abraham and his family.

The whole Hebrew scripture is the story of that family. Jesus came as a member of that family and now a new message is preached by Jesus.

> [18] And Jesus came and said to them, "All authority in heaven and on earth has been given to me. [19] Go therefore and make disciples of all nations, baptizing them in the name of the Father and of the Son and of the Holy Spirit, [20] teaching them to observe all

---

1. Barclay, *The Letters to the Galatians and Ephesians*, 125.

that I have commanded you; and lo, I am with you always, to the close of the age." (Matthew 28:18-20)

How does one relate to something new? How can we ever reframe reality so that we do things we have never done before? How could a Jew mingle with a Gentile when only uncleanness could result? It was a message they largely rejected. Hope was something to which only Jews were entitled. Hope was not something to offer Gentiles. Gentiles were essentially perceived as subhuman. It might be compared to offering salvation to a herd of cattle. And yet even the cattle of the field could receive God's grace more readily than a Gentile. We often do not realize how hard it is to change attitudes and mindsets. Routines bring us stability and equilibrium. And we need that.

THE GOSPEL IS FOR JEWS AND GENTILES

There is a curious experience found in Acts 10 that indicates how God was breaking down the barriers. Cornelius was a Roman centurion—a Gentile of the worst kind in Jewish thinking. He was working for the great antigod power of Rome, the suppressor of the Jews, the clear enemy of righteousness. Cornelius was a God-fearer. He was one who worshiped and prayed to the Jewish God, Yahweh, and God had plans for him. He was an unchurched believer. And God was about to bring him into contact with the church. God appeared to Cornelius and commanded him to take his men and visit a man named Peter. Meanwhile, as Cornelius was on his way to see Peter, God had a job to do with Peter, a good Jew who believed that all Gentiles were unclean, evil, separated, something to be avoided.

In Acts 10 there is the record of God sending a vision to Peter in which he sees a sheet dropped from heaven filled with "unclean" animals.

> [12] In it were all kinds of animals and reptiles and birds of the air. [13] And there came a voice to him, "Rise, Peter; kill and eat." [14] But Peter said, "No, Lord; for I have never eaten anything that is common or unclean." (Acts 10:12-14)

A Jew would not eat these animals in compliance with the covenant they had with God. Yet here Peter is commanded to eat everything on the sheet. Peter is appalled. There is no way he could eat the creatures on that sheet, for he was a good Jew.

¹⁵ And the voice came to him again a second time, "What God has cleansed, you must not call common." (Acts 10:15)

This was a conundrum to Peter. He did not understand why God would invade his mind in such a way as to change this clear tradition of his life. And then Cornelius entered his life—a Gentile, an unclean man who, unbeknownst to Peter wanted to hear the gospel. Peter stood in the face of Cornelius who immediately bowed.

RESPONDING TO GOD'S CALL

God ordered Peter to accept Cornelius as a fellow believer in Christ. Here was a man who was a God-fearing man—upright, well-spoken of even by the Jews, and brought by an angel of God to teach and baptize.

> ²⁵ When Peter entered, Cornelius met him and fell down at his feet and worshiped him. ²⁶ But Peter lifted him up, saying, "Stand up; I too am a man." ²⁷ And as he talked with him, he went in and found many persons gathered; ²⁸ and he said to them, "You yourselves know how unlawful it is for a Jew to associate with or to visit any one of another nation; but God has shown me that I should not call any man common or unclean. ²⁹ So when I was sent for, I came without objection. I ask then why you sent for me." (Acts 10:25-29)

Peter ponders that strange vision. Jews are gathering around, appalled by what they see. Peter attacks their mindset as well. Cornelius testifies that God has led him to be instructed.

> ³³ So I sent to you at once, and you have been kind enough to come. Now therefore we are all here present in the sight of God, to hear all that you have been commanded by the Lord. (Acts 10:33) We see that old Jewish mindset broken when Peter utters these words:
> ³⁴ And Peter opened his mouth and said: "Truly I perceive that God shows no partiality, ³⁵ but in every nation any one who fears him and does what is right is acceptable to him." (Acts 10:34-35)

It is a moment of truth. From then on the gospel went to the hopeless, godless, fearful, separated, "evil" Gentiles. Those without God would now have hope. Such was the beginning of the "churching" of the "unchurched." Such was the beginning of bringing hope to the hopeless.

What kind of message do we have here? Is it not the same message Peter and Paul had? Is it not the same fire that burns within us? And who is out there who wishes to break our exclusivism? Where are the unchurched without God and without hope in this world?

Why would we expect to find them in any other way than the way explained here? Praying to be used by God, Peter received a new revelation of himself—he now saw himself caught in his own routines and his own traditional ruts, exclusively sharing his belief in God with others who believed like he did. But out in the estrangement of life Cornelius prayed for mercy from God and God led him to the Christians.

CHAPTER TWELVE

Eat, Drink, Bread, Blood

> "Be such a man, and live such a life, that if every man were such as you, and every life a life such as yours, this earth would be God's paradise."
>
> —Phillips Brooks

JOHN 6:51-58

[51] I am the living bread which came down from heaven; if any one eats of this bread, he will live for ever; and the bread which I shall give for the life of the world is my flesh."
[52] The Jews then disputed among themselves, saying, "How can this man give us his flesh to eat?" [53] So Jesus said to them, "Truly, truly, I say to you, unless you eat the flesh of the Son of man and drink his blood, you have no life in you; [54] he who eats my flesh and drinks my blood has eternal life, and I will raise him up at the last day. [55] For my flesh is food indeed, and my blood is drink indeed. [56] He who eats my flesh and drinks my blood abides in me, and I in him.
[57] As the living Father sent me, and I live because of the Father, so he who eats me will live because of me. [58] This is the bread which came down from heaven, not such as the fathers ate and died; he who eats this bread will live for ever."

READING THE QURAN

I ONCE ENGAGED IN a two-hour discussion with one of my students who was a Muslim about our two religions: Christianity and Islam. It was an amiable discussion. We talked about ethics, theology, philosophy, and the various practices of the two religions. He said he had great appreciation for Jesus Christ of Nazareth. He spoke of Jesus' teachings and his life and how much Muslims appreciate the work that he did.

"Jesus was the Messiah," he told me. "The Jews rejected Jesus the Messiah," he continued. "Jesus was sent to be their 'anointed one' but they refused to accept him." For the most part our conversation was relaxed and informative.

Much of what he had to say I could concur with. But it was clear, as the discussion progressed, that we would never agree on the position of Jesus in our universes. Jesus was a great teacher, a great prophet, a great spiritual leader, he told me. Jesus came with great insights for humanity, and he stood in the line of the great prophets. The first prophet was Adam, and the second was Abraham. And then came Jesus, the "third prophet" to stand out. There were other prophets, but these were the great ones. Jesus was to be imitated under most circumstances. But the greatest prophet of all was Muhammad. He was to be the supreme exemplar under all circumstances.

Muhammad had come to clear up all the distortions of truth, he said. His superiority was that he gave us the Quran, a holy book that gives the true interpretation of all the prophets and clears up all the distortions. If you want to understand the Bible, read the Quran. It will give you the true meaning of all of Jesus' statements. "You must know," he said, "that the Bible is Pauline and Paul got everyone off track."

JESUS' CLAIMS ARE THE STUMBLING BLOCK

Throughout human history there have been those who liked Jesus but did not accept his claims. My Islamic acquaintance answered all my questions the same way: Muhammad was sent by God to clear up all the mistakes of the Jews and Christians with regard to religion, life, and more specifically, Jesus. The Jews had misunderstood Jesus and so they rejected him. Christians misunderstood Jesus and so they made him their God. It is just that simple. On what authority? The authority of the greatest prophet of Allah, Muhammad and the Quran, the Islamic holy book.

This messianic thinking did not start with Muhammad. It started on that hillside in Galilee and later in the synagogue of Capernaum as Jesus was teaching. At first the Jews sought to make Jesus king and then as they perceived what he was saying, they sought to destroy him.

After this great "bread of life sermon" found in John 6, the record tells us that:

> [1] After this Jesus went about in Galilee; he would not go about in Judea, because the Jews sought to kill him. [2] Now the Jews' feast of Tabernacles was at hand. [3] So his brothers said to him, "Leave here and go to Judea, that your disciples may see the works you are doing. [4] For no man works in secret if he seeks to be known openly. If you do these things, show yourself to the world." (John 7:1-4)

The word spread fast as to who Jesus claimed to be. There was only one way to deal with a blasphemer (one who claimed the priorities of divinity): Kill him.

My student claimed that Muhammad said Jesus never claimed to be God. He was a great prophet but only his followers came up with those ideas about his being God. So, Jesus is not God, never claimed to be, and the whole New Testament, without the writings of Paul, needs to be filtered through the interpretation of the Quran, he said.

"Well," I responded, "you will never convince a Christian of what you are saying. Built into the New Testament record is the warning that anyone who says what you are saying is a false teacher." No one is coming, I said, to reinterpret the Christian scriptures, except what Jesus called, "false prophets." And furthermore, it is clear, that "if you truly have so great an admiration for Jesus, as you claim, you will take his teachings at face value. But then we would have a clear problem, for you would be a Christian by definition, and not a Muslim."

THE CLAIMS OF CHRIST ARE THE DEMARCATION LINE

Few people have problems with Jesus' teachings about ethical behavior. Few people have problems with Jesus' life and example of service and humility. Few people have problems with Jesus' willingness to bring ease to human suffering, or sight to the blind, or strength to the weak, or food to the hungry, or clothing to the naked, or freedom to the oppressed.

Those are not only worthy causes; Jesus is the prophet for all who wish to make them their cause.

If these were the uniqueness of Christ then Christianity would triple its membership. If Christians and Muslims agreed on the nature of Jesus then both groups would be Christians. But that demarcation line is scattered with the claims of Christ. And that is a line that many people cannot get around.

In John 6 Jesus once again drives the point home.

> [51] "I am the living bread which came down from heaven; if any one eats of this bread, he will live for ever; and the bread which I shall give for the life of the world is my flesh." (John 6:51)

The Islamic would say there is no claim to be God here; Jesus is speaking metaphorically. How can one eat Jesus' flesh? This is a metaphor, not literal. And what did the Jews say?

> [52] "The Jews then disputed among themselves, saying, 'How can this man give us his flesh to eat?'" (John 6:52)

This was not a point that escaped Jesus' listeners. There has been no advancement in understanding to dispute what Jesus said. It doesn't take a sixth century "prophet" to unpack this. Jesus unpacked it.

> [53] So Jesus said to them, "Truly, truly, I say to you, unless you eat the flesh of the Son of man and drink his blood, you have no life in you; [54] he who eats my flesh and drinks my blood has eternal life, and I will raise him up at the last day." (John 6:53-54)

No simple "prophet" ever spoke like Jesus.

> [55] "For my flesh is food indeed, and my blood is drink indeed. [56] He who eats my flesh and drinks my blood abides in me, and I in him. [57] As the living Father sent me, and I live because of the Father, so he who eats me will live because of me. [58] This is the bread which came down from heaven, not such as the fathers ate and died; he who eats this bread will live for ever." (John 6:55-58)

WHAT DOES IT MEAN TO EAT, DRINK, BREAD, BLOOD?

The only way to get around these claims is to depreciate the source. The Gospel of John has perhaps been under more attack than any other book in the New Testament. Maybe the writer was not hearing things right. Over and over, he records the insistence of Jesus that life is not possible without Christ. Over and over, he insists that Jesus is preaching total commitment to him as the source of all life, both present and future.

According to this source Jesus leaves no out.

> [57] "As the living Father sent me, and I live because of the Father, so he who eats me will live because of me. [58] This is the bread which came down from heaven, not such as the fathers ate and died; he who eats this bread will live for ever." (John 6:57-58)

How do we get around these claims? Only by saying the source is faulty and untruthful and unreliable, only by saying that the record needs reinterpretation or a new understanding.

That is what men do. When the saying gets tough, some run away. Some reinterpret. Some look to another prophet and ask, "What does this mean?" For those who listened to Jesus in the synagogue of Capernaum,

> [60] Many of his disciples, when they heard it, said, "This is a hard saying; who can listen to it?" [61] But Jesus, knowing in himself that his disciples murmured at it, said to them, "Do you take offense at this? [62] Then what if you were to see the Son of man ascending where he was before? [63] It is the spirit that gives life, the flesh is of no avail; the words that I have spoken to you are spirit and life. [64] But there are some of you that do not believe." For Jesus knew from the first who those were that did not believe, and who it was that would betray him. [65] And he said, "This is why I told you that no one can come to me unless it is granted him by the Father." (John 6:60-65)

Jesus reasons with them, what if you were to see me ascending back to heaven? Who would you believe then? Only God can help a person believe these claims. And many no longer followed him because the claims were too hard. It did not fit into their belief system. So, when we find something that doesn't fit and we refuse to change, we either reinterpret, or depreciate the sources, or simply leave. And that's what most did.

Eating and drinking, bread, and blood, was the great test that came to all who claimed to see something unique in Jesus Christ. Eating and drinking, bread, and blood, was a call for commitment. But for those who refused to commit, the answer was usually reinterpret, make it say something more palatable, or reject it. And most of his disciples left at that point.

JESUS IS GOD INCARNATE

Many congregations come to church each week to eat, drink, bread, blood. Most of us believe this is metaphorical language. That is not our problem. We are not expected to eat the literal flesh and drink the actual blood of Jesus Christ. Few of us are confused about that. While some have insisted that when the bread hits our tongues it becomes the tangible flesh of Jesus, and when the cup enters our physical digestive system it becomes the real blood of Jesus, most of us would object that this misses the point.

Jesus is talking about dependence and recognition of who he is: God incarnate, God come in the flesh to fulfill the whole sanctuary service recorded in the Hebrew scriptures. Here is an understanding that makes all the sacrifice sensible. Here is the pascal lamb preaching in the synagogue of Capernaum: Just as you depended on manna in the wilderness to sustain you and keep you alive when there was no food available, your eternal sustenance depends on "what you do with me." Jesus is saying, I am not a simple prophet. I am not simply here to make more fishes and more bread out of your barley loaves. I am here to call upon you to accept me as your Savior.

> [57] "As the living Father sent me, and I live because of the Father, so he who eats me will live because of me." (John 6:57)

Let no one deceive you, a Christian is defined by what he/she does with Christ. To what extent are we going to accept his inescapable claims? Peter stepped forward as the people were fleeing in the wake of these claims.

> [66] After this many of his disciples drew back and no longer went about with him. [67] Jesus said to the twelve, "Do you also wish to go away?" [68] Simon Peter answered him, "Lord, to whom shall we go? You have the words of eternal life; [69] and we have believed, and have come to know, that you are the Holy One of God." (John 6:66-69)

What Peter was saying was, though I may not know exactly, at this point in my life, what you completely mean, I do know what I have seen and heard, and it all rings true! To whom will I go? The same question confronts us today. Is Christ our sustenance? Do we depend upon him for our very life? Do we extol him as we eat, drink, bread, blood? Not just in the communion service, but in what it represents? The inescapable claims of Christ? This is where life begins.

CHAPTER THIRTEEN

TASTE OF NEW WINE

"To adorn our characters by the charm of an amiable nature shows at once a lover of beauty and a lover of man."

—Epictetus

JOHN 2:1-11

¹ On the third day there was a marriage at Cana in Galilee, and the mother of Jesus was there; ² Jesus also was invited to the marriage, with his disciples. ³ When the wine gave out, the mother of Jesus said to him, "They have no wine." ⁴ And Jesus said to her, "O woman, what have you to do with me? My hour has not yet come."

⁵ His mother said to the servants, "Do whatever he tells you." ⁶ Now six stone jars were standing there, for the Jewish rites of purification, each holding twenty or thirty gallons. ⁷ Jesus said to them, "Fill the jars with water." And they filled them up to the brim. ⁸ He said to them, "Now draw some out, and take it to the steward of the feast." So, they took it.

⁹ When the steward of the feast tasted the water now become wine, and did not know where it came from (though the servants who had drawn the water knew), the steward of the feast called the bridegroom ¹⁰ and said to him, "Every man

serves the good wine first; and when men have drunk freely, then the poor wine; but you have kept the good wine until now."

[11] This, the first of his signs, Jesus did at Cana in Galilee, and manifested his glory; and his disciples believed in him.

DYSFUNCTIONS

One of the characteristics of being human is the phenomenon that often plans do not turn out as we thought they would. Each of us can point to plans we have made that didn't turn out right. And usually, it is because we didn't make allowance for extenuating events.

Some events in our lives are unexpected. Sociologists refer to these expected or unexpected turn of events as "dysfunctions." When our children are small we plan to chronicle their lives by taking movies or pictures and the next thing we know we are out of film or the camcorder dysfunctions. We plan to set up the perfect home, but other factors enter that interfere. And so, we must reframe things.

As children we are given a certain picture of God, what God is like. And then some tragic event occurs that interferes and shatters our best made plans. A man once talked to me about his divorce. He had never figured that he might be divorced someday, but then one day his wife ran off with another man and he was shattered. My advice was that he become very actively involved with raising his two children. But then his seven-year-old boy came down with leukemia and he called me and said, "Now what am I supposed to do?"

Events, prayers, hopes, dreams, all are subject to dysfunctions that we do not anticipate. Our expectations do not always match our plans. The events in this story from the Gospel of John were some of those unforeseen dysfunctions. The setting: a wedding festivity—a joyful occasion, a time of feasting—and then something happens, not planned.

A WEDDING—ONE OF THE MERRIEST OF EVENTS

In Jewish tradition the wedding was one of those marvelous occasions when you could let all your joy show. The bride and groom did not go on a honeymoon like they do in our custom. Rather, when the merriment of several days was over, the bride and groom stayed home and "were treated like a queen and a king." They wore crowns, they were waited upon, they were praised and coddled. There was feasting and drinking. Drinking wine was not to excess. For the Jew it was unlawful to drink "red" wine because that broke their covenant with God.

> [31] "Do not look at wine when it is red, when it sparkles in the cup and goes down smoothly." (Proverbs 23:31)

"Red wine" was simply that wine that has fermented to its fullest level to around 12% alcohol. Because of the covenant, drunkenness and alcoholism were virtually unknown among the ancient Hebrews. But there were times during the year when fermentation could not be avoided.

Drunkenness was in fact a great disgrace, and they actually drank their wine in a mixture composed of two parts of wine to three parts of water. At any time the failure of provisions would have been a problem for hospitality at a wedding would be a terrible shame for the bride and the bridegroom. That indeed would have been a humiliation.

To stay within the covenant, Jewish tradition required cutting fermented wine with water. Eventually, however, the alcohol had an effect and people were merry and probably a little dull. Jesus attended one of these feasts at the beginning of his ministry. In fact, it was only three days after he had called five of his closest disciples according to John. The feast was in Cana, a sleepy little town about halfway between the Sea of Galilee and Mt. Carmel in the Roman province of Galilee.

Commentators have made much of the fact that this scene demonstrates the sociability of Jesus and his desire to be with people in a time of happiness. This is important to our view of Jesus for there have been times in our history when anything connected with fun was considered evil or worldly. So, we have the picture of Jesus being with people in all aspects of their lives. He blesses marriage by attending this feast. But something happened that was not planned. It may have been that he brought five extra people who were not invited—these new disciples of his¬ which added more people to the attendance role. If this is true there can be little doubt that they were all drinking the wine. But the details of this story are not clear. We just know that there was a dysfunction in plans: the wine ran out.

DETAILS THAT SHOULD NOT DISTRACT US

As we read the Gospel of John there are characteristics that jump out at us in almost every chapter. Whenever there is a Jewish custom mentioned, the writer explains it or gives details about it that are self-explanatory. This has led commentators to the conclusion that John was not primarily writing to a Jewish audience but rather to a Gentile one. If we were writing a letter to someone who knew nothing about Western customs in America we might include a number of parenthetical statements. For example, we might write, "We celebrated Christmas last week with the family members who live in Southern California, viz., Christmas is a Western holiday when we celebrate the birth of Jesus."
John does this often in his Gospel. So, as we read this passage we see those kinds of clarifying details. Notice for example:

> ⁶ Now six stone jars were standing there, for the Jewish rites of purification, each holding twenty or thirty gallons. (John 2:6)

Most of those attending the feast would not have needed that explanation. They knew that it was out of those jars that their feet were washed after the dusty trip to Cana. They knew that it was out of those jars that their hands were washed before they ate together. And they also knew that these jars were never used for wine, only water for these acts of cleansing. For those of us who are far removed from Jewish custom and tradition these details are helpful. But we need not get bogged down in them.

I have heard vigorous discussions about whether the wine at Cana was fermented. And those who are teetotalers insist that "the best wine" saved till last refers to the pure, unfermented grape juice that was transformed by Jesus from the water in the big purification jugs. Today the "best wine" usually carries a higher price and comes from a "good year." I have friends who are members of wine clubs, and they talk about the "bouquet", and they sniff the open wine glass to check the fragrance and then they taste the wine and moan in ecstasy over its goodness. We can get so bogged down in such details that we miss the point of the whole incident. So, reader beware!

JESUS CHANGES THINGS

Jesus was invited, with his disciples, presumably by Mary, Jesus' mother, to this cheerful occasion. And for whatever the planning, the wine ran out. Jesus' mother, demonstrating her trust in Jesus gives some of the best advice you will find anywhere in the Bible. She says to him, ³ "They have no wine." And then she calls the servants, introduces them to Jesus and orders, ⁵ "Do whatever he tells you!"

When dysfunction occurs what better advice could we have as disciples of Christ than that? "Do whatever he tells you!" All the great men and women of faith have followed this advice. They have studied to see what Jesus says and they have sought to obey him. Obedience is the great response to the gospel. If we honestly believe we obey. Obedience to Jesus is the evidence of our faith. It shows that we have some grasp of the circumstances, the issues involved in life.

I had a little boy who was not really good at obeying when he was only two. He learned a little more each day that not obeying leads to heartache. Once we were at Sears and he was walking through the TV department turning off all the television sets that were on display. I told him, "You may walk around here and look at everything, but if you touch anything I will strap you in your stroller. Do you understand?" He smiled and said, "Yes." Then he went over and turned off another TV set. So, I strapped him in his stroller. After a few minutes I asked him if he wanted to try again and he said "yes" again, and I reiterated the conditions and he agreed to them. And he walked over and turned off a radio. So—back to the stroller.

Two-year-old children learn by conditioning. But if we are thirty-five years old and are still learning simply by conditioning we are dysfunctional. As we grow in our faith we should see clearly that obeying is a result of believing, that belief that goes untested is tenuous, and that disobedience is a clear evidence of a lack of trust. So, Mary tells the servants, "Do whatever he tells you!" Jesus instructs them to fill the jars with water—not the wine jars but the water jars—the purification jars. There can be no question that this was not wine held back, but wine that was new, and they were about to taste it.

WINE FROM THE PURIFICATION JARS

As the guests at the wedding dip into the water that fills the purification jars, they all marvel at the wine that pours forth. It was the custom to put out the best wine first because as time goes on and the wine takes effect no one really notices if the quality of the wine goes down.

> [9] When the steward of the feast tasted the water now become wine, and did not know where it came from (though the servants who had drawn the water knew), the steward of the feast called the bridegroom [10] and said to him, "Every man serves the good wine first; and when men have drunk freely, then the poor wine; but you have kept the good wine until now." (John 2:9-10)

Now we can do a little temperance lesson here. The original language does not establish anything on a level of modern wine. "Wine" in Greek does not mean fermented or unfermented—it means juice. So, we can insist that this is a picture of pure Welch's grape juice, miraculously appearing in answer to a major dysfunction at the feast. But John's Gospel characteristically presents incidents and facts in a way that the reader is expected to draw deeper lessons the more it is read.

The first picture we should get here is that the presence of Christ at social gatherings should help us understand our own participation on such occasions when real human things are occurring.

The second picture is a little deeper. Jesus is beginning his ministry and he does it in a miraculous way—religious events are important for believers in that they remind us of the power of God. Just as the people looked to the sacrifice of Isaac by father Abraham, and the Exodus from Egypt, and the work of God in appointing a king and later freeing Israel from bondage in Babylon, so Christian believers look back to the ministry of Christ as a long series of his miraculous events to relieve human suffering.

There is a third picture we can grasp. When Jesus steps into the picture, new things appear. New perspectives, new ways of facing problems, new life of power, new hopes and new optimism that challenges and problems can be met and overcome. Every group of believers faces its Red Sea. Every set of believers suffers its bondage. Every crowd of believers runs out of wine. But the same Jesus who appears as an angel in the old era and as a Savior in the new era, continues to minister to our hearts and minds as we allow him access. It is the recognition that he is at work that demonstrates our trust.

As the text says,

> [11] This, the first of his signs, Jesus did at Cana in Galilee, and manifested his glory; and his disciples believed in him. (John 2:11)

CHAPTER FOURTEEN

THE RESURRECTION OF JESUS CHRIST

"Money is not required to buy one necessity of the soul."

—HENRY DAVID THOREAU

1 CORINTHIANS 15:1-11

¹ Now I would remind you, brethren, in what terms I preached to you the gospel, which you received, in which you stand, ² by which you are saved, if you hold it fast—unless you believed in vain.

³ For I delivered to you as of first importance what I also received, that Christ died for our sins in accordance with the scriptures, ⁴ that he was buried, that he was raised on the third day in accordance with the scriptures, ⁵ and that he appeared to Cephas, then to the twelve.

⁶ Then he appeared to more than five hundred brethren at one time, most of whom are still alive, though some have fallen asleep. ⁷ Then he appeared to James, then to all the apostles. ⁸ Last of all, as to one untimely born, he appeared also to me. ⁹ For I am the least of the apostles, unfit to be called an apostle, because I persecuted the church of God. ¹⁰ But by the grace of God I am what I am, and his grace toward me was not in vain. On the

contrary, I worked harder than any of them, though it was not I, but the grace of God which is with me.

[11] Whether then it was I or they, so we preach and so you believed.

THE ISSUE OF RESURRECTION

In college we were taught to memorize great chapters of the Bible. If we wanted to know the bulk of the material on the creation of this earth we went to Genesis 1-3. If we wanted to dwell on the highest expression of scripture on the topic of love we were directed to 1 Corinthians 13. If we wanted to understand the millennium we would go to Revelation 20—all that is said about the topic in the scripture is in that chapter. The great parables of grace are found in Luke 15. The sufferings of the Messiah in prophetic and typical forms we read Isaiah 53. The shepherd's psalm is found in Psalm 23. The great teachings on the resurrection of Jesus and its relevance for disciples of Christ are found in 1 Corinthians 15.

I doubt that any of you have experienced or been eyewitness to a resurrection. In a scientific age, resurrection is reinterpreted as symbolic rather than literal. In a post-scientific age, people should have fewer problems with believing in a resurrection. For the Christian resurrection has never been a problem. The resurrection of Jesus Christ has always been a cornerstone of Christian faith. Christians take the resurrection of Christ literally. It is the great evidence that Jesus was the Christ prophesied throughout the Hebrew scriptures. "The empty tomb" was the central evidence of the apostles' preaching in the New Testament and was recorded as the hope of this world and salvation.

FIRST CORINTHIANS IS A LETTER

There are several types of literature in scripture. The prophets of old delivered oracles to the people. The poets of scripture praised God through their symbolic and metaphoric writings. The historians of scripture record events that are important in our understanding of sacred history. There are great sections of laws that God lays out for his people as they seek to fashion a life of meaning on this earth. In the New Testament we have personal messages of Jesus' closest disciples in which they give an account of events in Jesus' life. We call them the "Gospels." But perhaps the most famous of all the writings of the Bible are the letters, most of which were written by the apostle Paul, a convert to Christ from a very combative and sincere Judaism.

There is something personal about a letter. And the letters in the New Testament were not what you would commonly refer to as business communications filled with politically correct niceties. They were rather filled with personal references, concerns, and greetings. They also contained moral admonitions of theological substance and practical instruction. You can find both technical treatises and friendly conversations in the letters of the New Testament. We learn more about St. Paul from his letters than we do from his biography in the historical book of Acts of the Apostles.

Many times, these letters, or epistles as we call them, were products of emergency. Few of us sit down and compose a letter the way we would write an article or organize a research paper. The letters of Paul are like that. Paul probably wrote more letters that were lost but a few of them were polished products of his thought. He spoke to the situations in the church. The value of these products of his pen is found in the fact that the church through the ages has faced the same kinds of problems he was speaking to in the infant church in Jerusalem and Asia Minor. As we read these letters we find material that is as valuable for us as it was for the original recipients. There is order to Paul's letters. He has primary concerns and the main concern that emerges in all of them is the crucial question, *How can a person be righteous before a holy God?*

PAUL'S THEMES ARE TIMELESS

In his letters Paul is not concerned with chronological orders of things. He is concerned with the order of Christian experience. The letter to the Romans, for example, answers the question of how a person can be righteous before God by presenting Christ as the answer given by God to that question. In Christ God displayed both his justice and his love by bearing the penalty he himself had set up for sin. This vindicates the law of God and answers the sin problem. When we accept Christ as our substitute, our representative and our surety of salvation, we are forgiven and given the status of a person in right relation to God.

As a result, the letter to the Romans appears first in our canon. It has become known as the great epistle of salvation—not because it is the only letter to talk of salvation but because it is the closest to an organized treatise on the subject. One of the great spiritual experiences of my life has been to sit down with the book of Romans and read it through in one sitting as a willing recipient of its message—letting it speak to my undoneness and need for a Savior.

The next epistles speak more to the needs of specific churches. The letters to the congregation in Corinth reveal that there are some serious misunderstandings with regard to what should be called the teachings of Jesus or Christianity in general. Here is the beginning of the great counsels to the church.

The Corinthians were careless believers. They did not take the law of God seriously. For whatever the reason they viewed salvation as a license to sin. And therefore, the church was filled with aberrant behavior—people behaved as though they were unconverted, unchanged, still in their immorality, from which they had theoretically been delivered. In such living there is no evidence of the power of the gospel at all. If Christians live like anyone else in the community, argue about the same things, perform the same behavior, envy and gossip at the same rate and live the same sexually immoral lives, then where is the power that is supposed to deliver the Christian from evil? Paul speaks to this in hard-hitting ways through the letter to the Corinthians.

FIRST CORINTHIANS IS CONCERNED WITH OUR STANDING BEFORE GOD

The City of Corinth has been called the vanity fair of the ancient world. It has been likened to the London, Paris, New York, and Tokyo of the first century. It was the world's center of licentiousness. And the problems Paul speaks to in this congregation reflect this society. If anyone has trouble joining the church for its hypocrisy, they should read this letter to the Corinthians.

This church had factions. There were people practicing incest. There was litigation being carried out between members. Some were continually getting drunk—elders called in, not able to serve, drunk. By today's standards there probably would have been drug problems. And on top of this there was false teaching to justify this kind of living. You name it, Corinth may have had it. Try to imagine what kind of church fights must have gone on in the Church Board. What kind of political struggles to capture power accompanied this kind of life? And what possible hope could there be for congregational growth?

Paul speaks to this situation not with handwringing, or anger, or despair or unveiled passion. The report he got about Corinth must have been like hearing that a 747 with many of your relatives and friends had crashed. But it was not a fatal crash and there was hope that many would get out. The emotional impact would be intensified by not knowing who they may be.

F. W. Farrar, a cleric of the Church of England (Anglican), schoolteacher and author quotes a "great statesman" who once wrote: "I do not know what is meant by painful responsibility. I do the best, the wisest, the utmost thing I can; and no man can do more. My moral responsibility ends with the use of my best endeavors."[1] That is what Paul did. He wrote in the most powerful way he knew how. He directed his instruction to their problems, but he couched everything he said in reference to the cross of Jesus Christ. In no other epistle is Christ mentioned so many times. His appeal to love, his moral instruction, his plea to drop the lawsuits. Everything is wrapped in the cross. And then he goes on to the master argument of all: the resurrection of Christ. He appeals to the fact that so many people were witnesses of the resurrection at the same time—at one point five hundred people together saw him.[2]

RAISED FROM THE DEAD

Paul gives the logic of the gospel. He appeals to the fact that without the resurrection there is no gospel message.

> [12] Now if Christ is preached as raised from the dead, how can some of you say that there is no resurrection of the dead? [13] But if there is no resurrection of the dead, then Christ has not been raised; [14] if Christ has not been raised, then our preaching is in vain and your faith is in vain. . . .
>
> [17] If Christ has not been raised, your faith is futile and you are still in your sins. [18] Then those also who have fallen asleep in Christ have perished. [19] If for this life only we have hoped in Christ, we are of all men most to be pitied. (1 Corinthians 15:12-14, 17-19)

---

1. Farrar, *The Messages of the Books Being Discourses and Notes on the Books of the New Testament*, 219.

2. 1 Corinthians 15:5.

Paul argues that there can be no logical way out of the resurrection for the Christian. Contemporary liberal theology has done a real number on this New Testament teaching, explaining it to the detriment of our own faith. Some theologians have the notion that God, if there is a God, has given them license to recompose the gospel—to put it into such contemporary terms that the plain teachings of scripture are obsolete, outdated, time-warped and irrelevant. Paul's words stand here to judge that kind of thinking.

The fact of the resurrection of Jesus Christ is the promise of our own resurrection. I sat in the living room one night with a lady I had known most of my life. Her mother, ninety-two years of age, was there. She had been a friend of my parents some fifty years before. Our conversation was on the father in this family who had just met his untimely death, one month after his sixtieth birthday. He was lighting his wood stove, unaware that there was a propane leak. The instant the match struck the house blew up. Windows were blown seventy feet out into the yard. He had second and third degree burns over eighty percent of his body. He lived through the night and died the next morning.

As we watched the memorial service on video Friday night, we reminisced about his life. He and I had gone to college together. We were fellow travelers on the road of life. We ministered together, attended Seminary together and had kept in contact through the years. Now he was gone. And then we heard once again the great assurance in the passage where our text is found for this chapter:

> [54] When the perishable puts on the imperishable, and the mortal puts on immortality, then shall come to pass the saying that is written: "Death is swallowed up in victory." [55] "O death, where is thy victory? O death, where is thy sting?" (1 Corinthians 15:54-55)

The resurrection of Jesus Christ is the assurance for every believer that eternal life has been purchased.

CHAPTER FIFTEEN

THE PRIVILEGE OF MATURING

"There is no royal road to anything. One thing at a time, and all things in succession. That which grows slowly endures."

—JOSIAH G. HOLLAND

EPHESIANS 4:1-32

[1] I therefore, a prisoner for the Lord, beg you to lead a life worthy of the calling to which you have been called, [2] with all lowliness and meekness, with patience, forbearing one another in love, [3] eager to maintain the unity of the Spirit in the bond of peace. [4] There is one body and one Spirit, just as you were called to the one hope that belongs to your call, [5] one Lord, one faith, one baptism, [6] one God and Father of us all, who is above all and through all and in all. [7] But grace was given to each of us according to the measure of Christ's gift. [8] Therefore it is said,

"When he ascended on high he led a host of captives, and he gave gifts to men."[9] (In saying, "He ascended," what does it mean but that he had also descended into the lower parts of the earth? [10] He who descended is he who also ascended far above all the heavens, that he might fill all things.) [11] And his gifts were that some should be apostles, some prophets, some evangelists, some pastors and teachers, [12] to equip the saints for the work of ministry, for building up the body of Christ, [13] until we all attain to the unity of the faith and of the knowledge of the Son of God, to mature manhood, to the measure of the stature of the fulness of Christ; ¹⁴ so that we may no longer be children, tossed to and fro and carried about with every wind of doctrine, by the cunning of men, by their craftiness in deceitful wiles.

¹⁵ Rather, speaking the truth in love, we are to grow up in every way into him who is the head, into Christ, ¹⁶ from whom the whole body, joined and knit together by every joint with which it is supplied, when each part is working properly, makes bodily growth and upbuilds itself in love.

¹⁷ Now this I affirm and testify in the Lord, that you must no longer live as the Gentiles do, in the futility of their minds; ¹⁸ they are darkened in their understanding, alienated from the life of God because of the ignorance that is in them, due to their hardness of heart; ¹⁹ they have become callous and have given themselves up to licentiousness, greedy to practice every kind of uncleanness.

²⁰ You did not so learn Christ! — ²¹ assuming that you have heard about him and were taught in him, as the truth is in Jesus. ²² Put off your old nature which belongs to your former manner of life and is corrupt through deceitful lusts, ²³ and be renewed in the spirit of your minds, ²⁴ and put on the new nature, created after the likeness of God in true righteousness and holiness.

²⁵ Therefore, putting away falsehood, let every one speak the truth with his neighbor, for we are members one of another. ²⁶ Be angry but do not sin; do not let the sun go down on your anger, ²⁷ and give no opportunity to the devil. ²⁸ Let the thief no longer steal, but rather let him labor, doing honest work with his hands, so that he may be able to give to those in need.

²⁹ Let no evil talk come out of your mouths, but only such as is good for edifying, as fits the occasion, that it may impart grace to those who hear. ³⁰ And do not grieve the Holy Spirit of God, in whom you were sealed for the day of redemption. ³¹ Let all bitterness and wrath and anger and clamor and slander be put away from you, with all malice, ³² and be kind to one another, tenderhearted, forgiving one another, as God in Christ forgave you.

VISION AND MISSION

Congregations these days talk about their vision and mission. In talking about vision, they are dealing with where they would like to be ten years from now. Businesses look at who they are and where they would like to be. Does it surprise you that Home Depot stores have sprung up all over America, almost overnight? How long ago did you see your first Home Depot store? It was founded in 1978. And now I pass at least three on my way to work each day.

Home Depot's management sat down, when the firm began, and discussed: What do we want to do? Where do we want to be ten years from now? How many stores do we want to open in the next ten years? And they decided they wanted to be the most complete home store in America. They wanted to have the most lumber available for the do-it-yourselfer; they wanted to have the most tools available, the most screws, nails, wire, screwdrivers, wood, and plants. They wanted to be able to supply the do-it-yourselfer with all he needed when he walked into their store. They didn't want him/her (fifty percent of Home Depot's customers are women) to have to go anywhere else. Today there are over 2200 Home Depot Stores in America.

What did McDonald's sit down and strategize? They wanted to be the most popular fast-food restaurant in America and the world. They wanted to open seven new McDonald's restaurants a day—2500 new restaurants a year. Today there are 40,000 restaurants in the world.

Starbuck's Coffee stores are appearing everywhere. Did that just happen? All of a sudden all wanted Starbuck's Coffee. Probably most of us never heard of Starbuck's Coffee forty-five years ago. The firm opened in 1971. Today there are about five new Starbuck's Coffee stores opened every day in America. A total of 30,000 stores in the world. Was that just some natural law that Starbuck's would all of a sudden appear? No. A group of people sat down and visioned.

That is *vision*.

VISION MEANS PLANNING WHAT YOU WANT TO BE

Without a vision we don't know what we want to be. If you are in a congregation your church probably has said it wants to be responding to the love of God. But that doesn't state what you would like to see in ten years. Did your congregation sit down ten years ago and state on paper where it would like to be today? If you didn't then you have no plan even now. If you don't do that now then you may be no farther along in ten years than you are today. A grim reality!

One church I studied sat down twenty years earlier and stated that their vision was to be "a biblically functioning community." When they wrote that vision they had twenty members. Next they studied their Bibles intensely to understand the meaning of "a biblically functioning community." They never thought of numbers. All they talked about was doing God's will. They had almost no idea how to carry out the implications of their vision.

They concluded that God might choose to keep them small because in an age of secularism how could they expect to grow? If they had only twenty members forever, they were determined to do God's will and function as the New Testament described a congregation should. That was their vision. Growth was not part of their vision statement—only function.

Come hell or high water they would be a church that studied the word of God for direction. No matter what the consequences, they would be a congregation that followed as best they could all the patterns of the New Testament church. In all their planning, they determined to secure the vision that at all times and in all places they would act like Christians and they would take care of each other as they understood the early church did.

They did not plan for numerical growth. They planned for spiritual maturity. They saw the privilege of maturing in Christ to be their diamond in the rough, their pearl of great price, their priceless gem. All their purpose and mission were centered in their vision which was to be the best example on earth of "a biblically functioning community." They would take it from there. If they grew they would adjust. If they didn't grow they would enjoy what they had. But numerical growth, they determined, was in God's hands not theirs.

UNITY AS A VISION FOR THE CHURCH

In the epistle to the Ephesians the apostle Paul outlines a constitution for the biblically functioning community. In Ephesians 4 he begins by talking about oneness. The Spirit brings unity. Those who are truly church are eager to maintain unity—they do not insist on their own way. They do not lord their authority over others in the congregation. They do not strike out on their own. They work together humbly, trying to do and say and be what is best as they represent God on this earth.

> [1] I therefore, a prisoner for the Lord, beg you to lead a life worthy of the calling to which you have been called, [2] *with all lowliness and meekness, with patience, forbearing one another in love,* [3] *eager to maintain the unity of the Spirit in the bond of peace.* [4] There is one body and one Spirit, just as you were called to the one hope that belongs to your call, [5] one Lord, one faith, one baptism, [6] one God and Father of us all, who is above all and through all and in all. (Ephesians 4:1-6. Emphasis supplied)

Paul made it clear that there is but one God, one Christ, one Spirit, one hope, one goal, one body, one faith, one baptism, one father, one son. The church seeks to represent this oneness. But what a poor job it has done. As you look around the nation you don't see much oneness. You see scores of denominations. You see liberals and conservatives and fundamentalists and evangelicals and neo-evangelicals and neo-orthodox and new liberals and neo-liberals.

With some you would think that the gospel means to fight abortion, or to accept homosexuals or to fight for women's rights, or to eat healthfully, or to judge those who wear jewelry. There are so many versions of the gospel today it is no wonder that people are confused—not just unchurched people are confused, but many churched people are confused as well.

Paul talks of oneness, unity, pulling together. When some Christian communities were established in early America, it was the dream of its founders to produce a biblically functioning community by stressing the oneness. A new land, a new chance not to repeat what had happened in Europe where there were state churches and persecution and pain inflicted by those churches.

Creeds had a lot to do with the persecution. And so, the early American Christians condemned creeds because of how they had been used. Creeds did not mature the church but made it political, they maintained. My church of origin taught the same thing. Their position was that there was a progressive movement when you adopted a creed: first you made the creed, then you used the creed to test fellowship, then you tried members by the creed, then you denounced as heretics all who didn't subscribe to your creed, and finally you persecuted the heretics who didn't subscribe to your creed.

UNITY IS A GOAL OF GROWING CHURCHES

As part of your vision, you need to state clearly that you plan to be the clearest demonstration of unity of any church in America that claims the name of Christ. If you are fighting and griping and complaining and threatening to leave when you don't get your own way, you will never be that kind of demonstration that Paul talks of in his description of a biblically functioning church community.

God gave gifts to help the church attain this. Paul wrote,

> [11] And his gifts were that some should be apostles, some prophets, some evangelists, some pastors and teachers, [12] to equip the saints for the work of ministry, for building up the body of Christ, [13] until we all attain to the unity of the faith and of the knowledge of the Son of God, to mature manhood, to the measure of the stature of the fulness of Christ. (Ephesians 4:11-13)

These gifts are to equip us, to provide for the work of ministry, and to build up the body of Christ so that we will have a unity of faith and knowledge of Christ and bring us to maturity. It is the privilege of every church member to mature in Christ. Any congregation that claims the name of Christ must have within its infrastructure a method by which it helps new members to mature. And this maturity must first be demonstrated by the church members themselves from the top on down.

Every cunning attempt by a secular society will be used to stop any community of faith that attempts to unify. Paul counseled,

> [14] So that we may no longer be children, tossed to and fro and carried about with every wind of doctrine, by the cunning of men, by their craftiness in deceitful wiles. (Ephesians 4:14)

God's people know what they believe and where they are going with the gospel. God's people study the Bible to make sure that what they are and what they do is in harmony with the concept of a biblically functioning community.

For this reason, those churches that have caught the vision set up small groups, they make church their priority, and they make study a necessity. They provide ministries for their own group first and then for the community. The church I studied had twenty members. They envisioned themselves being a biblically functioning community. They knew not what that would imply or how the unchurched would relate. But today, years later, they have over 20,000 members!

IDENTIFYING THE VISION

I have never read a vision statement for a business that says, "the vision of this company is to make money and become rich." I have never read a vision statement for a church that says, "the vision of this church is to become numerically the largest church in the world." Size and money are not visions. They can be the result of vision. The church's vision is to influence lives, and to provide a place for people to grow to maturity. This is impossible where people are not unified. No congregation can grow either numerically or spiritually if there is misunderstanding undealt-with, or if there are growing hard feelings.

Again, Paul warns us about living like the Gentiles. In the Lord, he says, you have forsaken that path. That was the path of darkness, or politics, of controlling other people's minds, of becoming callous and licentious, greedy, and cruel. It is the old nature, as he calls it, living on in the new creation. It is the old perspectives on life, and they must be replaced by the oneness of the Spirit—"the new nature" which has the privilege of maturing.

> "Behold, how good and how pleasant it is for brethren to dwell together in unity?"—this is the Scriptures' praise of life together under the Word. But now we can rightly interpret the words "in unity" and say, "for brethren to dwell together *through Christ.*" For Jesus Christ alone is our unity. "He is our peace." Through him alone do we have access to one another, joy in one another, and fellowship with one another.[1]

Paul helps us.

> [25] Therefore, putting away falsehood, let every one speak the truth with his neighbor, for we are members one of another. [26] Be angry but do not sin; do not let the sun go down on your anger, [27] and give no opportunity to the devil. [28] Let the thief no longer steal, but rather let him labor, doing honest work with his hands, so that he may be able to give to those in need.
>
> [29] Let no evil talk come out of your mouths, but only such as is good for edifying, as fits the occasion, that it may impart grace to those who hear. [30] And do not grieve the Holy Spirit of God, in whom you were sealed for the day of redemption. [31] Let all bitterness and wrath and anger and clamor and slander be put away from you, with all malice, [32] and be kind to one another,

---

1. Bonhoeffer, *Life Together*, 39.

tenderhearted, forgiving one another, as God in Christ forgave you. (Ephesians 4:25-32)

A new purpose statement could read for your congregation—this will be a center where people will be equipped and given the opportunity to mature. This is a worthy purpose, for maturing is a privilege of the believer in Christ.

CHAPTER SIXTEEN

How to Escape Temptation

"Every moment of resistance to temptation is a victory."

—Frederick William Faber

1 CORINTHIANS 10:1-13

¹ I want you to know, brethren, that our fathers were all under the cloud, and all passed through the sea, ² and all were baptized into Moses in the cloud and in the sea, ³ and all ate the same supernatural food ⁴ and all drank the same supernatural drink. For they drank from the supernatural Rock which followed them, and the Rock was Christ. ⁵ Nevertheless with most of them God was not pleased; for they were overthrown in the wilderness.

⁶ Now these things are warnings for us, not to desire evil as they did. ⁷ Do not be idolaters as some of them were; as it is written, "The people sat down to eat and drink and rose up to dance." ⁸ We must not indulge in immorality as some of them did, and twenty-three thousand fell in a single day. ⁹ We must not put the Lord to the test, as some of them did and were destroyed by serpents; ¹⁰ nor grumble, as some of them did and were destroyed by the Destroyer.

¹¹ Now these things happened to them as a warning, but they were written down for our instruction, upon whom the end of the ages has come. ¹² Therefore let any one who thinks that he stands take heed lest he fall.

[13] No temptation has overtaken you that is not common to man. God is faithful, and he will not let you be tempted beyond your strength, but with the temptation will also provide the way of escape, that you may be able to endure it.

HOW SALVATION WORKS

As a youngster I had a very thin understanding of how salvation worked. I thought that if my sins were forgiven and I tried hard to be good, something would click, and God would take pity and maybe he would save me when I got good enough. As long as I was faithful I was safe. I often went forward in an altar call.

As a youngster I was taught to be honest. But in my honesty I had to admit that there were times I was not honest. I did pretty well sometimes. But other times I did miserably. I was cranky, selfish, and certainly not faithful. How could any of us ever go to heaven if we were not faithful? "Are you ready for Jesus to come? Are you faithful in all that you do?" That's how the chorus went.

THE UNIVERSALITY OF TEMPTATION

Too often older people think temptation is something young people face generally under three categories: sex, drugs, and rock and roll. And too often young people think of temptation as something that older people don't face. Both views are right, and both views are wrong. Both views are shallow because temptation is something that is always tailor-made for every person, whether old or young.

Dr. Laura Schlesinger used to end her radio show each day with the words, "Now go and do the right thing!" But no one does. And so, we sang, "Are you ready for Jesus to come? Are you faithful in all that you do?" And my answer was: No. Some days I did better than other days. And that was true as a young person as much as it is now as an older, more mature person. In a previous chapter we mentioned that it is Jesus' right-doing that saves us. It is his perfect life and undeserved death that results in our acquittal before the tribunal of God. His right doing is credited to our account and on the basis of his work and his righteousness we are declared righteous. All of this is ours through faith.

In this chapter we incorporate the same principle. As it is Jesus' right doing that saves us, so it is God's faithfulness to us that we have assurance of salvation. I still remember how my life began to change when I read a verse no one ever taught me to repeat by memory.

> [10] Therefore I endure everything for the sake of the elect, that they also may obtain salvation in Christ Jesus with its eternal glory. [11] The saying is sure:
> If we have died with him, we shall also live with him;
> [12] if we endure, we shall also reign with him;
> if we deny him, he also will deny us;
> [13] *if we are faithless, he remains faithful—*
> for he cannot deny himself.
> [14] Remind them of this, and charge them before the Lord to avoid disputing about words, which does no good, but only ruins the hearers. [15] Do your best to present yourself to God as one approved, a workman who has no need to be ashamed, rightly handling the word of truth. (2 Timothy 2:10-15. Emphasis supplied)

I was so struck by the meaning and freedom this verse brought me that I could hardly believe it. Then I had my daughter etch the verse in calligraphy and I hung it on my study wall to think about it. I made a huge banner and hung it in my classroom, and someone came to me and said, "I don't know where you got that saying but it's not true, you know." I said, "Really?" And I knew then that I wasn't alone in my misunderstanding. I gave him the reference source in 2 Timothy, and he went out confused. Everyone knew that we had to be faithful in order to be saved and when we are faithful then the Lord would be faithful and save us. But the order was different.

GOD'S FAITHFULNESS IN TEMPTATION

So, Paul starts his passage on temptation.

> [13] God is faithful, and he will not let you be tempted beyond your strength, but with the temptation will also provide the way of escape, that you may be able to endure it. (1 Corinthians 10:13)

Talk about a promise to believers? When was the last time you honestly said, "You know I just can't resist that cake—I know my gut is growing, but I just can't resist this temptation!" Not true—God is faithful. "He will not let you be tempted beyond your strength!" When we are faithless, he is faithful. There is the marvelous power of the gospel brought right into your life.

Part of our failure to resist temptation in areas that count is our misunderstanding of the source of temptation. Flip Wilson and his tee-shirt in the 1960s said, "The Devil Made Me Do It!" We all know that is an excuse and the devil cannot make us do anything, but the devil surely is a source of temptation. We see the devil coming as "an angel of light" to Jesus in the wilderness seeking to win his allegiance.

> [14] And no wonder, for even Satan disguises himself as an angel of light. (2 Corinthians 11:14)

The devil may be the least of the tempters in this world. The most common source of temptation is simply our own human condition. We excuse sin, we justify it, we rename it, we rationalize it, we desensitize it, we make it sound less than serious. In short, we redefine it. We do it through our philosophy, our psychology, our science, our objectivity. We all think of temptation as something external, packaged to fit us. Food, drink, drugs, illicit love, pornography, acts of rebellion, anger, cruelty, selfishness, you know the lists. Paul gives catalogues of sins in his letters. But there is no temptation where there is no awakened desire in a person.

These sinful natures of ours exhibit sin when we don't even know it. You may remember the story of the lady who came to Charles Spurgeon, the famous English preacher. She said to him, "I enjoyed your sermon against sin, you know it's been two years since I have sinned." And Rev. Spurgeon realized immediately his sermon had failed, so he commented, "You must be quite proud that you haven't sinned in two years." "Oh," she said, "Indeed I am! Very proud!" Renaming sin doesn't solve the temptation problem.

HOW GOD IS FAITHFUL TO HIS PEOPLE

There is nothing that is so powerful that it can destroy your faith in God. Nothing. God is always faithful. "He will not let you be tempted beyond your strength." Young people have temptations in their inexperience. Many powerful temptations come to them through their friends—to begin smoking, to take drugs, to have illegitimate sex, to risk their youth through disease, self-depreciation, and esteem issues. Young adults have identity and career problems to work out and temptation to leave

God behind is greater than ever. Yet even as the children of Israel hiked through the miserable wilderness of Sinai, God fed them, God provided cool water whenever they needed it.

How could a million people survive in the middle of the desert without a well, without food? God was faithful. He remained faithful to them by providing for their needs and many times it was despite their unfaithfulness. When the people escaped the wilderness, many sat down in their new land and drank with pagans.

> [8] We must not indulge in immorality as some of them did, and twenty-three thousand fell in a single day. (1 Corinthians 10:8)

When they deliberately tested the Lord there were serious consequences. Some were attacked by snakes. Some grumbled when God gave directions, and others were killed by destroying factors. Yet through it all, God was there giving them his faithfulness. He was faithful when they were faithless. The temptation of older people to complain and criticize young people is not a temptation that God's faithfulness cannot overcome. The temptation of older people to be set in their ways when they could use their experience to rejoice and teach the rewards of faithfulness to God and of God, is not a temptation that cannot be defeated. Temptation can be overcome through the power of God. The temptation not to live by faith is not a temptation that cannot be overcome.

OVERCOMING TEMPTATION

The temptations of young people can be overcome. The temptations of adults can be overcome. The temptations of older people can be overcome. They are all temptations to be and think and act short of the way God intended for the human spirit to think and act. I often compare our circumstances with the Israelites. They were comfortable in Egypt, but God wanted them to be a free people, to occupy their own land. And finally, they left. Then they got to the wasteland and God wanted to take them into the promised land. But they got comfortable in the desert and forgot why they left Egypt. They came to the place where they said they didn't even want to go into the promised land. They would just as soon stay in the rough country.

So, we have some of the same chances. It is time to let go of our temptations to fear, to vegetate, to become comfortable again, to lose any vision we have. We all got out of Egypt (put in our own challenge) but now we are tempted to let the backwoods become comfortable. It was such a big step that maybe we shouldn't take the other one. Believe it. God is faithful. He will not let you be tempted to a greater degree than you can handle. Instead, he will provide a way of escape from every temptation.

We all face temptations to be morose, to wallow in our pain and question the course of our life. We sometimes wish for more years, or experiment in areas that our own natures will deceive us. Young people often enter into suicidal actions that make risk too great. They may rebel against parents or act selfishly and judgmentally. As we grow older we often create an atmosphere where our employees or our customers, or our friends, or our nephews, nieces, children, wives, husbands, are made to feel less worthy of God's faithfulness than they should!

Temptation is not static. It is always tailor-made to our situation, either by our own human condition or by the skillful devil who comes as "an angel of light," never as a pitch-forked, hoofed, pointed tailed little imp. But when we are unfaithful, God is faithful. This is our encouragement.

CHAPTER SEVENTEEN

The Resurrection Body

> "Life's more than a magazine in which we flip the pages and enjoy the pictures."
>
> —Ralph Boyer

1 Corinthians 15:1-11

¹ Now I would remind you, brethren, in what terms I preached to you the gospel, which you received, in which you stand, ² by which you are saved, if you hold it fast—unless you believed in vain.

³ For I delivered to you as of first importance what I also received, that Christ died for our sins in accordance with the scriptures, ⁴ that he was buried, that he was raised on the third day in accordance with the scriptures, ⁵ and that he appeared to Cephas, then to the twelve.

⁶ Then he appeared to more than five hundred brethren at one time, most of whom are still alive, though some have fallen asleep. ⁷ Then he appeared to James, then to all the apostles. ⁸ Last of all, as to one untimely born, he appeared also to me. ⁹ For I am the least of the apostles, unfit to be called an apostle, because I persecuted the church of God. ¹⁰ But by the grace of God I am what I am, and his grace toward me was not in vain. On the

contrary, I worked harder than any of them, though it was not I, but the grace of God which is with me.

¹¹ Whether then it was I or they, so we preach and so you believed.

FLYING OVER MICHIGAN

A young family boarded a nine-passenger charter plane in Chicago to fly to the family retreat in Michigan. Father was already at the vacation home and would meet them at the little landing strip on an island in northern Lake Michigan. On board: George, the family macaw; Barney, the family mutt; a daughter, two sons, mother, and two pilots. The plane was full. Interestingly, father was an experienced pilot, but when John Kennedy, Jr.'s plane crashed he had given up flying at the pleading of his wife. Now the family was on a similar flight around the same kind of day, over a large body of water.

Father was working on plowing a clear path through the mud and snow when he heard the little plane fly over. It was incredibly low. He said, "It banked a little to the right, then it came back and banked to the left. They flew over, and I thought, 'they don't know where they are. They're lost.'" The sky was overcast, the visibility was poor, and the plane disappeared into the fog. Father figured the two pilots had decided to land at a larger airport which had more facilities for incoming planes. So, he waited for a phone call.

When the plane was reported missing, father just sat in the cottage living room and kept waiting for the phone to ring. The weather was turning worse—driving rain, thirty-four-degree air. It was clear that there would be a heavy snow soon. Those who have lived through a Michigan winter will understand. Father continued waiting for the phone to ring. On board—everything in this world of worth to him. Imagine yourself in that position. What would go through your mind? What would you do? Suddenly his position in business, his status in the community, his money in the bank—all this was put on hold.

PAUL AND THE RESURRECTION

When the apostle Paul wrote of the resurrection he wrote about something that was every bit as real to us as this experience was to this father. Knowing nothing about the future one craves assurance. To this young father the phone became a lifeline. At this point the phone could ring at any time and the news would be one of two things—good or bad.

Since this father had four loved ones on board that news could be good *and* bad. Two alive, two dead. Two alive, one dead, one seriously injured, not expected to live. You can figure out all the alternatives. He is waiting for the phone to ring. For Paul, Christ has been resurrected. But all of us are facing death. The message is crucial. Are we going to believe in our own future? Will Christ resurrect us? This is that life issue that Paul speaks to in this passage.

1 Corinthians 15 is the most complete treatment of resurrection in the Bible. Not all of the Jews in Jesus' day believed in a resurrection. The Pharisees were progressive enough to believe in a resurrection. But the Sadducees did not believe in it. They claimed it was nowhere to be found in the writings of Moses and so, being the conservatives that they were, not willing to see any light having come from the throne of God since Moses, they denied that resurrection could occur. Christ came down on the side of the Pharisees on this one. He taught a resurrection and Paul later elaborated on it in this chapter to the congregation in Corinth. He builds on Christ's resurrection that he claims establishes the fact that ours will occur. If Christ has not been raised, he argues, then we will not be raised.

It is difficult for us to put our minds back into the first century and understand who all that Paul is addressing. You don't hear much about these things today outside of church. I don't hear students at school arguing about whether our bodies will be spiritual or physical. Howard Stern deals with physical bodies on his TV show. *Meet the Press* does not debate the metaphysical makeup of the resurrection body. In fact, you probably have to go to a funeral to hear any reference to the resurrection at all.

RESURRECTION A HOT ISSUE IN PAUL'S DAY

You cannot discuss the early church without recognizing that Greek philosophy was flourishing. This was a period of Roman culture, but Rome had inherited much of its thought from Greece and its philosophers. While things were politically a Roman world, things were culturally a Greek world. And Greek philosophy was considerably hostile to biblical religion.

The Greek philosophers believed that matter was evil and immaterial things were the habitation of the soul. The "soul" was eternal, and it was necessary for that soul to be separated from the matter of the body in order for any goodness to occur. In fact, we are being punished as "souls" by having to inhabit these physical bodies for a while. True freedom is found in escaping from these bodies. If you die you are free, for your spirit or soul has escaped from this prison house known as the body.

This view of death was considerably different from that of the Hebrews. The Hebrew scriptures taught that death was a sleep and that there was no soul apart from the body. The matter, or dust, plus the spirit, or life-giving principle of God, *became* a living soul.

> ⁷ Then the Lord God formed man of dust from the ground and breathed into his nostrils the breath of life; and man *became* a living being [soul]. (Genesis 2:7. Emphasis supplied)

When the body died the soul was gone. A person was whole, not partitioned. A person was not three things (like body, soul, and spirit) or two things (body and spirit) put together. A person was a person. Modern psychology supports this Hebrew view from a scientific standpoint. While there are aspects of the being that we refer to as the mind or the body, these are not to be separated. Only in Christian theology influenced by Greek philosophy do we find such divisions.

Paul presents the future of humankind in quite simple terms if you come at it from the angle he was—as a believer in Hebrew revelation. He is not speaking as a pagan philosopher. He is using the Greek language with Hebrew definitions. He is using the language of the pagan philosophers (Greek), but he gives those words Hebrew meanings. Death for the Greek equaled life. Death for the Hebrews equaled sleep. Same word in Greek (*thanatos*) but two different ways to understand what is meant. He died? Alive? Asleep?

DOES IT MATTER WHAT YOU BELIEVE?

If you recognize Paul's issues here in 1 Corinthians 15, how you believe about the resurrection shows whether you are a believer at all. That makes this a central doctrine of the Christian church. The gospel message includes the following elements: the life of Christ, the death of Christ, the resurrection of Christ. The life of Christ was a life of sinless existence. In order to inherit eternal life, we must be sinless. The only way that can happen, according to the gospel teaching is if Christ, as the second Adam, succeeds where Adam failed, lives the perfect life, and then imputes that sinless life to the believer.

The death of Christ was a death of final punishment for sin. God told Adam and Eve that they would have to die for their sin. He warned them before it happened. He warned them while they were in their sinless condition. But they sinned anyway. So now they must die. Every person who sins must die. And death is final—it is the end of the human race. Christ came as the lamb of God, lived a sinless life and therefore was not worthy of death. But he died. And so just as that righteous life was imputed to our sinful record, so his death is imputed to us and by believing in that death for us we are acquitted for our sins and relieved of the eternal punishment.

The resurrection of Christ is the guarantee that all this is true. When I went to buy my first house I had to show records of my income, check stubs of my last couple of months of salary, and that wasn't enough; I had to put down a pile of money to demonstrate my good faith that I was serious about this transaction.

So, God tells us through Paul, Christ lived for you . . . Christ died for you . . . and if you are not clear on that, Christ was raised from death. It is impossible to live for someone else. It is impossible to die for someone else. But perhaps the impossibility of coming back to life will help you believe the first two impossibles! When Jesus healed people, he first forgave their sins. Why? Because anyone could say "I forgive you," but how many people could give evidence by physically healing someone?

THE HOPE OF THE CHRISTIAN

Here is the hope of the Christian: the resurrection promise. But what about all this body stuff? Let me take you back to the young father who is still sitting by the phone. What he doesn't know is what happened to the airplane with everything of value on it: his wife, his three kids, their dog and bird. And he wouldn't know for fifteen hours.

CHAPTER EIGHTEEN

Is "Father" the Best Term?

> "What a father says to his children is not heard by the world,
> but it will be heard by posterity."
>
> —Jean Paul Richter

EXODUS 20:12

¹² "Honor your father and your mother, that your days may be long in the land which the Lord your God gives you."

COMMANDMENT SUBJECT MATTER

This text comes from the middle of the Ten Commandments that was given to the Israelites through Moses in the wilderness. As you look at the first four commandments you see that they have to do with our relationship to God. And the last six commandments have to do with our relationship to each other. How we treat each other as believers in God has a lot to do with the society we create here on this earth. We are to respect life, we are to respect truth, we are to respect marital relationships. We are to respect honesty; we are to respect integrity. Even in a secular society these principles, when followed, create a civilized society, but they are especially important for the person who claims to follow God.

As a youngster I was required to commit these Ten Commandments to memory. In camp meetings, youth retreats and Vacation Bible Schools I can remember our teachers having us repeat all Ten Commandments word for word as a group. I won little stars and prizes for doing so. For the last six commandments that was easy. They are short, to the point, and all six occupy less space than the second commandment in its entirety. It was a real challenge to memorize that one. The fourth commandment was another long one, but we tackled it in record time because we wanted the picture of Jesus or the sticker on our card. The fifth commandment was one of the longer of the last six, but it was a snap next to those big ones in the first four.

IS "FATHER" THE BEST TERM?

In the Hebrew scriptures we have a patriarchal society. That means that the father was considered the representative of the family and was answerable to God for the spiritual life of the family. It is not an enviable position. And it has largely been neglected in today's secular society. Not only that, but the whole idea of "father" has been so ridiculed, laughed at, downgraded, and attacked that you can't help wondering if "father" is a good term at all anymore.

In many families today, the mother is the one person who seems concerned about the values of the family. The pictures I see displayed on the TV screen show the guy drinking beer with his buddies or racing in a new car or in the magazines, demonstrating a new cigar or brand of cigarettes. And in a society that sees its ethics from a standpoint of what works best, the mother seems the logical person to be the spiritual leader of the family. After all, many mothers are with the children more, they see things that fathers don't see, they spend the time out of necessity, teaching children how to behave and how to respond to negative positive stimuli.

Our society talks about children as *belonging* to mothers—out of her body the children emerged, and therefore these must be her offspring. Where does "father" fit in? In today's society, rooted as it is in naturalism, it is easy to look at the father as simply the sperm donor. And by the time the sit-coms get done with him he is the neighborhood buffoon, the great blunderer, the judgmental, out-of-date-disciplinarian whose clever little children should be able to outsmart him most of the time—all in the name of "negotiation." As the Duke of Windsor said, "The thing that impresses me most about America is the way parents obey their children."[1]

Today, where the frequency of divorce competes with that of weddings, it too often seems natural to look to the mother as the nurturer and caretaker of the children. It should come as no surprise then that our society knows little of "honor your father." But in the Hebrew economy, God held the father responsible for discipline, education, indoctrination, and guidance of the children. And as the inheritor of the promises given originally to the Jews, Christians should pay more attention to this instruction, "Honor your father."

THE COMMANDMENT WITH A PROMISE

The musical play, "Shenandoah," tells the story of a man during the American Civil War who is left with several children to rear after his wife dies in childbirth. The family realizes the pain and difficulty of having only one parent. The Civil War descends on this Virginia family and the father sings to his daughter, as things are falling apart: "Papa's gonna make it all right!"[2]

As life crushes in, and the children are forced into a war that makes no sense to him, it becomes clear that Papa can't "make it all right." There is no Papa who does everything right, nor is there any Papa who can correct the ills that touch his children. With Mama gone, the children grow up and begin to realize that Papa may have done his best, but the best is not always enough and as adults they must fill in many of the cracks in life.

Here is a microcosm of the fifth commandment. Children, as they grow up, have a choice when it comes to "honoring" their fathers. They can continue their pedestrian, awe-inspired, original attitude toward their fathers, that here is a man who is superhuman, never makes a mistake, never does anything wrong, never stumbles in life. Or they can mature and realize that they too will be cast in a new role. This new role will give them the same place that Papa once had in the early years of their lives.

I am no longer convinced that we live in a society that takes this commandment very seriously. Not only do families depreciate Dad, but contemporary society tends to come down on him awfully hard. One

---

1. Goodman, ed., *The Forbes Book of Business*, 281.
2. Geld and Udell, *Shenandoah*.

can always find a good reason to do this, but our society is changing from a family-oriented society to a utilitarian society in which everyone must work to keep up their standard of living. A too common notion is the suggestion that "it takes a village." "Groups" have formed to equalize the power. Such groups seldom "equalize" anything because of the nature of reality—if something has been abused, we generally have to swing the pendulum far over the goal in order to equalize, and then we have a largely new society. And so, you wonder, "is 'father' the right term?" To what extent should "father" be honored? Some say, "only so far as he is 'honorable'" and so they have a mighty big escape route.

CHANGING LIVES WITH AGING

I have had many years to think about my relationship with my Dad. He died over forty years ago. I was in graduate school with two small children. Few of us could even attend his funeral. My mother and brother and I spent a week going through his stuff, reminiscing, and remembering his life. We watched home movies. We went through his desk and discovered things meaningful to him. We laughed, we cried, we suffered, and we appreciated. It was a time to celebrate a life in a new way. In the good time we had together for the first time in many years, we realized that part of us was missing. Dad was gone. Dad had always been there. He had always pulled things together. He had usually had to take guff from us when he did so, and seldom did we express our appreciation adequately.

I found myself embarrassed over my lack in honoring him. Everything I was, everything I had—my outlook on life, my concern for others, my education, my value system—was directly attributable to him. He was my vision. He was always willing to share his thoughts on life, and they were usually deep thoughts. My events of the day, and comings and goings of people—gossip, if you will—looked thin by comparison. He was interested in going deeper, looking at meanings behind the obvious.

My Dad was the kindest man I ever knew. He was concerned with my development. He was also the smartest person I ever knew. He could converse on any topic with intelligence. He had a large library and he read the books. Before his conversion to Christianity, he was an electrical engineer student in Stockholm, Sweden. After his conversion he moved into the caring professions, ministering to people as a nurse and later as a publisher and artist.

He served as a backboard to toss my ideas against as I grew up. And then he became the reason for my mistakes. I blamed him for stuff that wasn't his fault. But his love and acceptance were unfaltering. At one point in my life, he told me that he had "lost" me. And it brought him great pain. It took a divorce for me to recognize how cruel I had been to him. I recognize now that any good my life has produced was also largely to his credit. In my mistakes he had supported and loved me. And his refusal to force me at any step of the way was what made me human.

HONOR THROUGH OBEDIENCE

As children we honor our parents by obeying them. We learn the basics of disciples and authority from them. Without intact parents this part of our development may never be normal. As teenagers we can honor our parents by gradually learning to apply the principles they have taught us. That means we become independent. We rebel, and we strike out. As young adults our honor takes on a new cast. Now we begin to weigh what Papa did to make it all right and we begin to appreciate what he did to protect us—sometimes it was an overprotection. And yet as maturing adults we have the ability to see all sides of the issue and Dad becomes important once more. We form our own opinions as free moral agents before God.

Few of us cherish the place of our fathers. Life is often kept on the surface—daily events, sort of a family news show. But there is depth for Dad, because he gets to play with the grandchildren, and he can reminisce that his days with his own children were profitable. Without this privilege there is no honor and the promise of the long life of satisfaction will never be fulfilled. "That your days may be long" is a promise of quality not longitude. How we treat our fathers when we are young adults will largely set the stage for how our children will treat us when they are young adults.

Some people speak glibly about honoring only the honorable. They claim their father has done something dishonorable, so they don't have to keep the commandment. But that has never been the standard for us. The Christian turns the other cheek and in so doing, wins the enemy, in some cases, her own father. Christians honor their parents unconditionally because they know that perceptions and facts seldom line up. This commandment is the only one with clear condition: *Your days will be long* in proportion to the honor you bestow. We honor our fathers, living or dead.

Nobody had a perfect father, but no one had a father who didn't have perfect motives. And that is the truth that can bind us together as fathers and sons, fathers and daughters.

CHAPTER NINETEEN

Our Father in Heaven

> "Get the pattern of your life from God,
> then go about your work and be yourself."
> —Phillips Brooks

MATTHEW 6:7-15

⁷ "And in praying do not heap up empty phrases as the Gentiles do; for they think that they will be heard for their many words. ⁸ Do not be like them, for your Father knows what you need before you ask him. ⁹ Pray then like this:

Our Father who art in heaven,
Hallowed be thy name.
¹⁰ Thy kingdom come,
   Thy will be done,
   On earth as it is in heaven.
¹¹ Give us this day our daily bread;
¹² And forgive us our debts,
   As we also have forgiven our debtors;
¹³ And lead us not into temptation,
   But deliver us from evil.

¹⁴ For if you forgive men their trespasses, your heavenly Father also will forgive you; ¹⁵ but if you do not forgive men their trespasses, neither will your Father forgive your trespasses."

AVOIDING EMPTY PHRASES

As a Christian I cannot remember a time when I did not know "the Lord's Prayer." Somewhere in my development I realized that it came in two versions. I surmised that one was Catholic and the other Protestant, but I can't say anyone taught me that. In one you asked for forgiveness of "your debts" and in the other you asked for forgiveness of "your trespasses." In one you asked for forgiveness of "your debtors" and in the other one you asked for forgiveness for "those who trespassed against you."

In some congregations it is customary to repeat the Lord's Prayer somewhere in the worship service. Have you ever thought of singing it at the end of the worship service? Or perhaps singing it instead of repeating it at the end of the pastoral prayer? Perhaps that would fit better if you were in a more liturgically minded congregation.

The Lord's Prayer is a treasure in Christianity. It is a prayer every believer knows by heart. It is a prayer that is woven into the fabric of the Christian tradition. It is a prayer that believers repeat with their families, in their liturgy and sometimes even in their personal devotions. But with some it becomes a Christian icon, perhaps even in our own way, a "heaping up of empty phrases," the very thing Jesus warned us against.

What does this sacred icon teach us about God? How is it different from other prayers? Why have we learned to repeat it so often? When was the last time we really thought about what we were saying?

THE LORD'S PRAYER

William Barclay has suggested that the Lord's Prayer is really the Disciple's Prayer. It is not a prayer that is readily understood by children. It is not a personal prayer. It is not a family prayer unless you think of the congregation as the family. It is a prayer that only makes sense to believers. It is the *Disciple's* Prayer.

The Lord's Prayer is a prayer which only a disciple can pray; it is a prayer which only one who is committed to Jesus Christ can take upon his lips with any meaning. The Lord's Prayer is not a child's prayer, as it is so often regarded; it is, in fact, not meaningful for a child. The Lord's Prayer is not the family Prayer as it is sometimes called, unless by the world *family* we mean *the family of the* Church. The Lord's Prayer is specifically and definitely stated to be the *disciple's* prayer; and only on the lips of a disciple has the prayer its full meaning. To put it in another way, the Lord's Prayer can only really be prayed when the man who prays it knows what he is saying, and he cannot know that until he has entered into discipleship.[1]

Perhaps this is startling that unbelievers can't utter this prayer with any meaning. Children can learn it, but they will do it by rote. It is in the children's mode of that food blessing we all learned: "God is great, God is good, let us thank him for our food. Amen." Let's eat! It's one thing to say words, it is quite another to understand meanings.

I once had a pet myna bird. She was given to me by a friend who had heard me say in a sermon once that I would love someday to own a myna bird. The bird's name was *Sweetie Pie*. She had been housed in the living room by a door that made a blood-curdling squeak every time the door closed. *Sweetie Pie* could reproduce that squeak so perfectly that you looked around to see what door was opening and who was entering the room.

She also had a congested cough because my friend was a smoker. She could whistle the paint off the door molding. She could talk so clearly that you wished some people you knew could do as well. I put her cage in the window of my study, which was on the front of my house.

One morning I was working in the flowerbeds in front of my house when two teenage girls walked by. When they got within hearing distance *Sweetie Pie*, who was enjoying the fresh air that flowed in through the open window of my study let out a shrill wolf whistle. I was in the direct line between the window and the girls and I never looked up. I'm not sure how the kids took it—I hoped they were flattered.

I didn't know that my next-door neighbor had taken it all in. And later he would tell me what he had thought at the time. Not knowing that I had a bird that had whistled he confessed that he had laughed and said to himself, "Well, old Ed is frisky this morning!"

But if I were to ask *Sweetie Pie* what she meant by her words or her wolf whistle she would never have had anything to explain. For her those words and that whistle, the cough, and the squeak of the door were simply more sounds she could replicate. They had no meaning to her in the way they had to us.

A child can be taught the Lord's Prayer but have nothing to say of its meaning. A worship service can include the Lord's Prayer but be devoid

---

1. Barclay, *The Gospel of Matthew*, 1:198-199.

of understanding. And so, Jesus' warning should apply as well to the Lord's Prayer as it does to "the Gentiles"—Jesus' term for the unchurched.

IN PRAYING DO NOT HEAP UP EMPTY PHRASES AS THE GENTILES DO

Why? Because many Gentiles believed that a multiplication of words was needed to get their gods' ears. Prayer wheels were erected so that every time the wheel went around in the wind, their god would hear the prayer. And when the wind blew, that wheel could go around many times, each time delivering that prayer.

Their gods were like the owner of a new chariot and they were the rattles in the door. And if the rattle made enough noise the owner might stop the chariot and pay attention to the rattle because it was driving him crazy. Perhaps some Christians have the same idea in a different form.

So, the Lord's Prayer is really the Disciple's Prayer. Jesus was educating the disciples in answer to their request that he teach them to pray. It may be that Jesus never intended for them to repeat this at all. But repeating it does no harm if we examine and understand its meaning. It should not take the place of our own daily prayers.

OUR FATHER

For many people "God" is a swear word. In everything Jesus said, taught, and did, we were to understand and appreciate God in a new light. Christians would do well to examine how big their God is. What phrase could Jesus use to help his disciples grasp God in a meaningful way? How could he depict God as one who had only our best interests at heart? How could he separate his God from the gods around? How could he undo those small views of God?

Even among the Jews there was a fear of God that was more like terror than respect and loving appreciation. For the Gentiles, the gods were more like tools in their hands. When the rain refused to fall, and the crops dried up in the seed they saw their gods were angry. When earthquakes struck, and volcanoes erupted, they saw their gods were vindictive. Even today we hear talk of tornadoes and hurricanes as acts of God. Insurance companies may not insure your house against such events because God is too powerful for them to maximize the value of their companies to their stockholders. God is out of our reach when he gets mad—no telling what he will do. Respect for God is often skewed to mean the emotions of human beings. When parents discipline their children in anger those children may interpret that discipline as the way God is—out of control and cruel.

Jonathan Edwards preached about "sinners in the hands of an angry God."[2] And that, more than perhaps any other sermon ever preached has enjoyed exposure in our literature books. We are like a spider being dangled over the flames of God's wrath and at any moment we could be dropped into the flames of eternal torment. Jesus had a formidable task on his hands to change our perceptions of God. And to do it he started with this simple little phrase, "Our Father."

If you had a father who was just, merciful, fair, loving, and honest, perhaps you can relate to this phrase with warmth and positive appreciation. If your father was an alcoholic who beat you and your mother to a pulp when he got drunk perhaps this phrase would give you more trouble. But for Jesus, "Our Father" was a relational description. Jesus continually talked about God as his Father, giving direction, looking out for his best interest.

MEMBERSHIP HAS ITS PRIVILEGES

When I was little the high school where my brother was a student had a fair. My brother worked on the school grounds crew and drove a tractor. I stood in awe as I saw him drive. I was just a little boy and that was my big brother on that big tractor. During this fair the powers-that-be had decided to put together a little train and they asked my brother to decorate the tractor so it looked like a locomotive. He was then asked to drive the tractor and pull the train.

Whoever wanted a ride would pay a dime to ride in the little cars behind the train. And much to my excitement, my brother told me I could ride with him in the locomotive! I can still remember climbing up into the big seat next to him as we pulled the train around the campus of the high school.

Late in the afternoon of the fair a lady came up to my brother and said she wanted her little boy to ride in the locomotive. My brother informed her that no children were allowed to ride in the locomotive. The

---

2. Edwards, July 8, 1741.

dime they paid was for a ride in a train car. The lady became irate—she pointed to me sitting in the locomotive, about the same age as her little boy, and I still remember the rancor in her words as they spilled from her mouth. Bitterly she pointed at me, and said, "So who is that kid? A big shot?" My brother never missed a beat, he answered her, "That's my brother—he's the assistant engineer!" I felt so good—I *was* a big shot—I was the assistant engineer!

God is "our" Father. That makes us brothers and sisters. The implications of that phrase are eternal. We come to God, not as one who acts against us, not as one who works against us, not as one who demonstrates that he is out of control, not as a swear word in our depraved vocabulary, not as one who desires our worst, not as one who is keeping us from anything of benefit in our lives. We come to God as "our" Father.

We come as a community of faith to recognize that he does not belong to one of us. This is not "my" Father for me to use against you. This is not "a" Father who has no regard for this group or that. This is not "some" Father who shuts us off from blessing. This is "our" Father. This is a person who may be big enough to run the universe, but personal enough to relate to his people as a responsible and loving Father.

OUR FATHER IN HEAVEN

This Father of whom Jesus speaks dwells in heaven. I have found it a curious fact that in the first century Christians were condemned by Roman officials as atheists. You could go into a Christian home and find Christians worshiping—nothing! There was no god there.

Go to a Roman pantheon and you would find a house for "all gods." And they were there—in image form: Caesar, animals, dragons, cattle, fire, serpents. In Pergamum there was a temple that housed a living snake that the people came and worshiped. But if you went to a Christian house of worship you found people worshiping a God who was not there.

"Our Father in heaven." There is objectivity about God in this truth. God is separate from us in a specific and important way. You can talk about your experience with God, but I know that God is in heaven, not in your living room or bedroom. I can be protected from your view of God and you from mine.

You are surely aware that we are presently being deluged with novels and religious speculation about the millennium and the antichrist and the rapture and other subjects from the book of Revelation. Movies and books and pundits have slowly become the evangelists of the day. There is a fever out there where every earthquake or middle east activity is used to divert us from the truth of God's gospel. The good news is not that God is doing something in Israel. It is not that we are in a new millennium. The good news is that God is faithful to us as "our Father in heaven." Nobody has a corner on God.

There was a time when some Christians denied communion to those who were not members of their denomination. The Scottish Presbyterians, for example, held to a tradition that practiced restricting the Lord's Supper to those who had gone through a human investigation to see if they were worthy to participate. And if they were they were given a little medal token to present to the elders at the table. If they didn't pass they were denied the Communion Supper.

Americans started new churches, some of which rebelled against this practice. God is "our Father," they said, not "their Father," and any examination that needs to go on is between us and our Father not between us and the elders. And so, churches began to stand for open communion. Those who claim Jesus to be Lord and have accepted him as their personal savior were welcome and invited to partake of the full benefits of membership. Many churches follow that tradition today. Our Father is in heaven not exclusively in a denomination or a movement of religious excitement here on earth.

WHAT KIND OF GOD

Many people today lay claim in some way to God. Some make him sectarian. Some make him a policeman. Some make him a moralist. Some declare him dead. Others use him for colorful language. And still others politicize him.

Jesus saw him as, "Our Father who is in heaven." Jesus' teaching can straighten out how we look at other people. It can straighten out how we relate to nature, how we relate to society and how we relate to believers of other spiritual communities.

It will transform our natural penchant to judge and criticize. It will reframe our own corner on God. It will solve our own questions about ourselves as people of so much importance that God would become incarnate to give us status and worth.

There is an old Roman story about an emperor who was enjoying the triumph of his victories. Parades and celebrations attended him as he marched his troops and captives through the streets of Rome to the shouting and adoration of the people. At one point in the triumphal entry to the city sat the empress and her family. Next to her sat their little son. But the son got so excited when he saw the parade approaching with the emperor leading that he got up off his little throne, jumped down into the crowd and weaved his way around people and through their legs to get to the road where his father's chariot was about to pass.

A legionary stooped down to stop him and swung him up in his arms and exclaimed, "You can't do that, boy! Don't you know that's the emperor in that chariot?! You can't run out to his chariot!" And the little boy laughed to the big legionary, "He may be your emperor," he said, "but he's my father!"[3]

> [7] And in praying do not heap up empty phrases as the Gentiles do; for they think that they will be heard for their many words. [8] Do not be like them, for your Father knows what you need before you ask him. [9] Pray then like this: Our Father who art in heaven. (Matthew 6:7-9)

---

3. Barclay, *The Gospel of Matthew*, 1:203.

CHAPTER TWENTY

Hallowed Be Thy Name

> "Too often a sense of loyalty depends on admiration, and if we can't admire, it is difficult to be loyal."
>
> —Aimee Buchanan

LUKE 11:1-4

¹ He was praying in a certain place, and when he ceased, one of his disciples said to him, "Lord, teach us to pray, as John taught his disciples." ² And he said to them, "When you pray, say:

"Father, hallowed be thy name. Thy kingdom come. ³ Give us each day our daily bread; ⁴ and forgive us our sins, for we ourselves forgive every one who is indebted to us; and lead us not into temptation."

A SIMPLE PRAYER AND A SIMPLE PARABLE

No matter how old we get, many of us feel that we never get a handle on prayer. Often it is in crisis that this question of praying becomes a reality. But when we only pray in a crisis we may intuitively feel that something is missing.

Here is a man facing bankruptcy, praying fervently for deliverance. But he entertains a lingering suspicion that such a prayerful interest might not have occurred had he not found himself facing financial disaster. Here is a husband facing the infidelity of his spouse, praying for God's intervention. But what kind of praying has he done in his own life up to this point? Is he not simply an opportunist in prayer—a fairweather friend of God? Here is a student facing a final test who suddenly realizes he has not studied adequately for this moment and he prays for knowledge. Is there not the emptiness that he has only called upon God because of this crisis?

Regardless of how we might feel in such situations, we may pray. Our God is in heaven. Our God is big enough to understand all the shallowness and the opportunism that may plague our inner thoughts as we come to him with our felt needs. When the disciples ask Jesus to teach them how to pray, he accommodates them with a sample prayer and a simple parable. We traditionally call this, the Lord's Prayer.

WHAT DOES IT MEAN TO BE "HALLOWED?"

When I was a kid there were two holidays I looked forward to. The first was *Christmas*. That was the queen of holidays. We got together with the cousins. One year we drove to Burbank. The next year they came to Riverside. It was an event to see that part of our family pull up into our driveway and begin unloading presents. When the gifts were safely deposited under the tree we kids would sneak a look at the little tags, anxiously hoping that the big present might be ours. No question about it, Christmas was a kid's holiday. Every Christmas I was glad Jesus had been born!

There was another holiday that ran a close second. It was the candy fest of the year: Halloween. We went door to door promising tricks if we didn't get treats. I don't remember ever delivering a trick myself, though I knew some bullies in the neighborhood who looked forward to that aspect of the holiday. I just cherished the thought of those bags of candy. I would bring the bag home, dispense with the apples and the whole wheat cookies and popcorn balls and nutritional stuff, and then I would pile up the stash of good candy victuals—the Tootsie Rolls and Almond Joys, Snickers and Hershey bars—the Bazooka bubble gum and Double Bubble were also cherished.

Here was my introduction to "hallowed" days, and these days were special, happy, positive, exciting experiences. Little did I realize that the same meaning was in the Lord's prayer: "Our father in heaven, may your name be hallowed." May your name be special. May your name be holy. May your name be separate from all other names. Just like Christmas is separate and special. Just like Halloween to a kid is special and separate. So, Jesus instructed his disciples that they were to remind themselves every time they prayed, that God was holy, God was special, God was different, God was separate—and they were to act accordingly.

I got a human foretaste of that when I started dating a freshman in high school. I was a junior and she was special. There could be a whole group of girls walking along (I noticed they usually traveled in packs) but if she was in the group there was a glow in that spot that she occupied. Her very name had an essence about it. Seeing her across the campus produced an adrenaline fix. She was special. She was different—separate from all the rest.

THE NAME OF GOD IS HALLOWED

To "hallow" something meant to treat it differently, separately, specially. A temple was a hallowed building—a different building. A holiday was a special day—a "holy day." A priest was a separate person, serving a different function than other men—a holy purpose. An altar was something different. God, by his very nature, was hallowed. But Jesus taught more: The name of God was separate. The name represented the character, the very essence of what a person was.

We had a saying, "Sticks and stones can break my bones, but names will never hurt me." Not true of course. To be called "a name" was an attack on who we were. That's worse than sticks and stones. The saying should have gone, "Sticks and stones can break my bones, but names will hurt me more."

I heard about a guy once who thought it was cool to take an ice cream sandwich from the grocer's freezer and eat it while he walked around the store. Then he would throw the wrapper in the trash before leaving without paying for the ice cream sandwich. If he had kept his mouth shut about it no one would ever have known, and he could have had an ice cream sandwich every day for free. But he found the activity to be a little sport and he would brag about it with his friends.

Everyone would laugh and finally they began calling him "sticky fingers." He took little pride in that. Before long, the name was shortened to "Fingers." Then it dawned on him—this was not an especially endearing name either. When people had renamed him, new friends would ask—"why do they call you 'Fingers?'" He worked at inventing reasons why he was called "Fingers." "Sticks and stones can break my bones, but names can make me feel important."

Today parents are more careful about what names they give their children. Many parents buy books listing children's names and carefully pick names that will represent what they want their children to become. People often want to pick names that can't be "nicked." They don't want nick names hung around their children's necks that may develop bad suggestions or reputations. They want that name to be prominent and authentic. To the ancients, names were even more crucial. If you knew a person's name you knew his character. You knew what he was. The name was the very essence of the person. So, in scripture "the name of God" was hallowed—"set apart."

The psalmist wrote,

> [10] And those who know thy name put their trust in thee, for thou, O Lord, hast not forsaken those who seek thee. (Psalm 9:10)

This didn't mean that those who knew that God is called Jehovah would trust him. Rather it meant that those who knew what God was like, those who knew the nature and the character of God, would know that they could trust him.

> [7] Some boast of chariots, and some of horses; but we boast of the name of the Lord our God. (Psalm 20:7)

Here is someone who knows that God is a person of greater power and compassion than anything humanity can invent. If you truly "know his name" you don't just call on him when you're in trouble. You respect him because he is a person of character and integrity. He is different. Jesus puts two aspects together here: "Hallowed be thy name." We are to respect God as different. We are to treat him as separate.

THE MEANING OF REVERENCE

If we were to sum up this whole thought in one word it would be "reverence." Jesus taught his disciples that they were to reverence God—that means they were to pray to be enabled to reverence him. This is the petition: "Our Father in heaven, enable us to reverence you."

William Barclay lists some essentials for this to happen.[1] You can only reverence God if you believe he exists. Remember when you took philosophy or mathematics in school? You learned that there were axioms—self-evident facts that did not need to be proved. Barclay gives examples: "a straight line is the shortest distance between two points." That is an axiom. It is the basis of all other proofs. In Algebra you learned that "two parallel lines, however far produced, will never meet."[2] You don't have to prove that you simply need to know it. You can look for evidence, but it would be a waste of time to spend much time on this because it's an axiom.

So, with God, you reverence God only if you believe God is. The Bible writers accepted God's existence as an axiom. They saw no point in trying to prove God because they believed they experienced God every moment of their lives. For those who need it there is ample evidence to believe that God exists—from the world, from ourselves, from the way we function morally—these are all evidence, but they are not proofs. If you spend time trying to prove your axioms in math you will never get any math problems solved. So, you accept that they are true and demonstrate the evidence by successfully doing the math.

For the Christian, God exists. He has revealed himself in his word. And that is the beginning point of all faith, not the five philosophical proofs for God's existence calculated by Saint Thomas Aquinas.[3] You can only reverence God if you have some idea what he is like. The ancient Greeks believed in gods, but they didn't reverence them. They tried to trick them, and their gods tricked them back and tricked other gods. They tried to use them; they tried to play their gods off against each another.

Our God has three great qualities: holiness, justice, and love.[4] If you truly know, that is believe, these qualities, you will reverence God. Otherwise, he may just be a swear word for you. If you take these qualities

---

1. Barclay, *The Gospel of Matthew,* 1:206-210.
2. Barclay, 1:206.
3. Aquinas, *Summa Theologiae,* Article 3, 67-70.
4. Barclay, 1:208.

of God seriously you cannot tolerate an age that obviously doesn't know him. You will have dissonance in this age that doesn't know him. How do we understand this age that doesn't know what he is like? Because it does not reverence him as it should. With many today it is not normal to reverence God.

To accept his existence and the facts about him intellectually is still not enough for reverence. You can be scared without being a disciple. You can only reverence God if you obey him. Reverence is not just believing God exists. It is not just accepting what he is like. It is not even simply being constantly aware of him. All of this is possible without reverence. Reverence includes all this plus obedience and submission to him. Martin Luther wrote, "How is God's name hallowed amongst us? When both our lives and our doctrine are truly Christian."[5] By that he meant our intellectual convictions and our practical actions are all in submission to the will of God.

A LORD IS IN CHARGE

As disciples we make the profession that we have accepted Jesus as Lord. Proclaiming him as Lord means we submit to him in humble obedience. A Lord calls the shots. A Lord points the direction. A Lord is in charge. We don't have to do any of this of course, but if we don't we will not see this petition fulfilled in our daily life. And the Lord's Prayer will be lost on us. It will be just a ritual we repeat occasionally or regularly in our worship services. "Hallowed be thy name," Jesus insisted, Let God be given the reverence that his nature and character deserve.

---

5. Barclay, 1:209-210.

CHAPTER TWENTY-ONE

Thy Kingdom Come, Thy Will Be Done

> "If we need of a strong will in order to do good,
> it is still more necessary for us in order not to do evil."
>
> —Thomas Mole

MATTHEW 6:10

> ¹⁰ Thy kingdom come,
> Thy will be done,
> On earth as it is in heaven.

THE BEAUTY OF POETRY

Have you ever noticed how you like to say things over and over, only in different ways? Somewhere in your schooling you heard or read or even memorized the immortal Sonnet No. 43 by Elizabeth Barrett-Browning from her *Sonnets from the Portuguese*, written in 1850 to her husband Robert Browning:

> How do I love thee? Let me count the ways.
> I love thee to the depth and breadth and height

My soul can reach, when feeling out of sight
For the ends of being and ideal grace.
I love thee to the level of every day's
Most quiet need, by sun and candle-light.
I love thee freely, as men strive for right.
I love thee purely, as they turn from praise.
I love thee with the passion put to use
In my old griefs, and with my childhood's faith.
I love thee with a love I seemed to lose
With my lost saints. I love thee with the breath,
Smiles, tears, of all my life; and, if God choose,
I shall but love thee better after death.[1]

Here is a beautiful work, world-renowned for its style, feeling and grace—a classic example of Victorian poetry by a dazzling lady. Probably it is the best known of poet Elizabeth Browning. Perhaps a little-known fact about her is that she knew enough Hebrew to read the entire Old Testament from Genesis to Malachi. She was brilliant and persevering.

In this romantic piece of literature, she tells us the same thing in several different ways. We call it poetry. In English and American literature, we learned that poetry had meter and much of it had rhyme. As a kid, I concluded that if you could rhyme you could write poetry—I don't know that anyone taught me that—there are just some things you educate yourself to believe. My mother saved my first poem. You won't remember that poem because it never made it into the literature books. But then I was only six and I knew it was a poem because it rhymed!

Hebrew poetry was not known for its rhyme. Hebrew poets didn't rhyme. But that doesn't mean the Hebrews had no poetry. Their way of writing poetry was to say the same thing in different ways. It was called parallelism. My Hebrew professor in Seminary never tired of pointing out to us fledging linguists that the first poetry found in the Bible is in Genesis 2:

> [21] So the LORD God caused a deep sleep to fall upon the man, and while he slept took one of his ribs and closed up its place with flesh; [22] and the rib which the LORD God had taken from the man he made into a woman and brought her to the man. [23] Then the man said,
>
> > "This at last is bone of my bones
> > and flesh of my flesh;

---

1. In the public domain.

> she shall be called Woman,
> because she was taken out of Man."
>
> ²⁴ Therefore a man leaves his father and his mother and cleaves to his wife, and they become one flesh. (Genesis 2:21-24)

In ecstasy, my professor would then add, Adam utters these immortal words as he sees this beautiful new creation (Eve) for the first time: a woman!

JESUS GOES POETIC

These are ways of saying the same thing in different ways. And that is the style in much of Hebrew parallelism.

> ²³ Then the man said,
> "This at last is bone of my bones
> and flesh of my flesh;
> she shall be called Woman,
> because she was taken out of Man." (Genesis 2:23)

Remember Psalm 27:

> ¹ The Lord is my light and my salvation;
> whom shall I fear?
> The Lord is the stronghold of my life;
> Of whom shall I be afraid? (Psalm 27:1)

Or Psalm 23:

> ¹ The Lord is my shepherd, I shall not want.
> ² He makes me lie down in green pastures;
> He leads me beside still waters;
> ³ He restores my soul.
> He leads me in right paths for his name's sake. (Psalm 23:1-3)

Or Psalm 24:

> ¹ The earth is the Lord's and all that is in it.
> The world, and those who live in it.
> ² For he has founded it on the seas,
> And established it on the waters. (Psalm 24:1-2)

In saying it poetically, the writers of scripture or any other literature can demonstrate that aspect of humanness that other animals don't have. Cats are not poetic, but poets write poetry about cats. Pigs can see "white," but they do not comprehend "whiteness." There is something advanced and unique about looking at life poetically.

In this passage Jesus says the same thing in different ways.

> [10] Thy kingdom come,
> thy will be done,
> on earth as it is
> in heaven. (Matthew 6:10)

God's will and God's kingdom are the same thing. It is a hard saying—when God's kingdom comes into your life, God's will becomes the priority in your life. Suddenly a new perspective is gained, and a new outlook becomes dominant in your mind. The original Greek uses the word for kingdom, *basileia*, a word that can mean a visible kingdom in which you have a king, castles, palaces, territory, and subjects. But the central issue in a kingdom is "king*ship*." And so, we may pray for God's kingship in our lives—his ruling power, our recognition of his authority to rule and guide in our lives.

Shortly after my son was born one of my new church members died. She was eighty-nine years old a week before she died. I had just visited her that week. We talked together and had a delightful visit. One of the first questions she asked me was, "How's the baby?" I had never met her before that visit. But she wanted to know how my baby was. I just happened to have some pictures with me. She took the pictures, held them, and said the right words, "Oh, he is so cute." And then she added, "I have been so anxious to meet you." And then I shared that I would bring him the next time I came to visit her. And she liked that.

She asked about other members in the congregation and she told how much she missed them all. Her mind was clear, and we planned to visit again. I prayed with her. What would you have prayed? For her to get well? For her to regain her strength and come back to church? Would you pray for God's will to be done? That is a common request. So, what would God's will be in this case? I got a call three hours later that she had died. She will not meet my son now. I never had a chance to take her a church bulletin or the latest church newsletter. The new address for her in her apartment served no purpose just three hours after I visited with her.

WHAT IS THE *WILL OF GOD*?

Christians have all had experiences where we asked the question: What is the will of God? But we are infamous for asking the wrong question. I stand by the widow whose husband has just been killed in a tragedy and she asks, "Was this God's will?" I stand by the father of a little boy who has just died of cancer and he looks at me through swollen eyes and puffy tear-stained cheeks and he asks, "Was this the will of God?" I stand outside my university office after getting the message that I will be terminated after thirty-four years of what I thought was faithful, committed, thoroughgoing service and I ask, "Where is God's will here?"

There are a few ways we can repeat this phrase from the Lord's Prayer, "Thy will be done." William Barclay suggests at least three ways to utter these words.[2] We can say it in a tone of defeated resignation, he says. A person may not want to say it but can't get out of it. God is too strong and there is no other explanation. So, whatever happened must be his will. And so, we are resigned. We are defeated. Not happy about it—just resigned. Who can argue or fight with God? We can say it in a tone of bitter resentment. We may feel trampled by the "iron feet of God." God sometimes appears to be the enemy. And the worst things in life get chalked up to "God's will." And so, we may say those words with rancor, anger, and bitterness.

We can say it in perfect love and trust. One of my first funerals, as a young preacher fresh out of Seminary, involved a ninety-five-year-old lady. She had no pain; she just went to sleep. At the casket she was flanked by her two sisters, both in their nineties. There were no tears; these two sisters were almost boisterous. Not because they were glad she was gone, but because they were glad she had lived.

"It is God's will," they said, "that our sister rests now!" They saw God's will in terms of wisdom and love. They knew they too would soon be joining their sister. They were also in their nineties. They were sad, but they did not show any tone of defeat or bitterness. They had faith. And they expressed that faith in understandable tones. But "thy will be done" has haunted humankind throughout the ages. How do we know the will of God? And we usually relate this question to ourselves. Students: What should my life work be? Who does God want me to marry? Should I move to Minneapolis? What is God's will?

---

2. Barclay, *The Gospel of Matthew*, 1:212-214.

NONE OF THESE ARE CONCERNS OF THE LORD'S PRAYER

When Jesus' disciples asked him to teach them to pray, Jesus said,

> 9 "Pray then like this: Our Father who art in heaven, Hallowed be thy name. 10 Thy kingdom come, Thy will be done, On earth as it is in heaven." (Matthew 6:9-10)

How do I count the ways? I love thee freely. I love thee purely. I love thee with passion. There's three ways. In this case Jesus is saying: "the kingdom" and "the will of God" are synonyms.

When the kingdom came to this earth in the person of Jesus Christ, God's will was done. Everything connected with the gospel constitutes the will of God. This explains how the New Testament can speak of the kingdom of God as being present—here, now, through the work of Jesus Christ. He has reclaimed the territory of this earth from the hands of the usurper. And God the Holy Spirit actively carries on the work of the kingdom on earth in our lives.

When the kingdom comes into the heart of the believer, the will of God becomes a personal concern. As we saw earlier, "kingdom" means "kingship"—it means that God becomes your "king." I had a friend once who took issue with this idea. He said, "My God is not my king. My God is my friend." And he quoted Jesus where he had said: 14 "You are my friends if you do what I command you."[3] That's okay if you don't dismiss the big picture: that kingship involves a whole new set of principles by which a spiritual person lives who is in Christ.

Maybe we could look at it that God is a king of the people. There is that intimacy of friendship that Jesus tried to get across to us because we have such remoteness in our thinking about God. Some people have seen so total a separation between us and God that God doesn't even care. God wound up the world like a clock and left. He is seen as the "absent landlord." So, we do need to remember this closeness, this intimacy, this eminence, this friendly God. We can also remember that if we are drowning we want a friend to save us but a friend who doesn't swim is not much help. There must always be that "kingly" edge.

God's will is his rulership in our lives. There is a sense of resignation, but it is only as we see God's wisdom and love. We don't just blurt out that

---

3. John 15:14.

everything that happens is God's will. Many things that happen in our lives and in this world and in this evil age are not God's will.

Was death ever a part of God's plan? Death is sometimes merciful. Was pain ever a part of God's plan? Pain sometimes teaches and strengthens us. Were trials ever a part of God's original will? Trials are sometimes like workmen who do a job in our lives to make us humbler or kinder, or more understanding, or more tolerant, or more reasonable, or more intelligent or more compassionate. Maybe even communicable for the first time.

GOD'S RULERSHIP

Sometimes we say the same thing in many ways. "Thy kingdom come, thy will be done." Same thing, two ways of saying it. The Hebrews call this poetic style, "parallelism." The Psalms are full of it. It is said to help us understand hard things. Was it God's will that my mother died? I don't think so. Was it God's will that my church member died? I don't think so. Was it God's will that 30,000 people died in an earthquake? I don't think so. Was it God's will that a plane with 300 people crashed? I don't think so.

These may be the wrong questions to ask. Is it God's will that his kingdom rules in our lives? Yes. Do you want to know God's will according to this prayer? Then check your life and ask to what extent has the gospel taken root in your thinking? In your values? In your treatment of other people? In your compassion for those who irk you or tweak your worst side? In your understanding of those who "push your buttons." In your honesty in family or business dealings.

God's will is to transform every life on this planet. God's will is to bring about a world of kindness and service. This is not talking about living a sinless life. Nowhere does the Bible support such an idea and your life and mine provide the evidence. Those who preach the sinless life are sometimes the cruelest people when it comes to their treatment of others.

Jesus came to bind up the brokenhearted. He came to heal the fractured lives. He came to bring hope to the hopeless and life to the unmotivated. He came to give new life to the downtrodden and new courage to the depressed. He came to live out that kind of rulership in each of his people. That is the will of God. This is the kingdom of God. They mean the same.

You wonder what is the will of God? Look to the Lord's Prayer—it will lift you above the electric train and other gifts from Santa Claus. You will never look at prayer the same way again when you grasp the message of this prayer—it is indeed the "Disciple's Prayer."

There is evil in this world, but that doesn't mean it's God's will. My father didn't want me to buy baseball shoes when I was in high school because he thought I might break my ankle. He didn't stop me from buying them. And in the first game of the season, I broke my ankle because of my carelessness regarding those shoes. Was it Dad's will that I break my leg? No. But he loved me, and he let me make some decisions that ultimately taught me something through pain and hardship.

When the kingdom, *the kingship* of God enters our life, God's will is done on earth as it is in heaven.

CHAPTER TWENTY-TWO

Give Us This Day, Our Daily Bread

> "Let never day nor night unhallow'd pass,
> but still remember what the Lord hath done."
> —William Shakespeare

MATTHEW 6:7-15

⁷ And in praying do not heap up empty phrases as the Gentiles do; for they think that they will be heard for their many words. ⁸ Do not be like them, for your Father knows what you need before you ask him. ⁹ Pray then like this:

Our Father who art in heaven,
Hallowed be thy name.
¹⁰ Thy kingdom come,
   Thy will be done,
      On earth as it is in heaven.
¹¹ Give us this day our daily bread;
¹² And forgive us our debts,
     As we also have forgiven our debtors;
¹³ And lead us not into temptation,
     But deliver us from evil.

¹⁴ For if you forgive men their trespasses, your heavenly Father also will forgive you; ¹⁵ but if you do not forgive men their trespasses, neither will your Father forgive your trespasses.

THE RULERSHIP OF GOD

God is our Father. He is here but he is also there, i.e., in heaven. He is imminent—close, but he is also transcendent—far away. He cares about details, but he can see the big picture in a way that is infinitely different from the way we look at things. Hence he is wise, and his judgment and perception are clearly superior to ours. A true disciple thus surrenders the will to this God.

The kingdom is the *rulership* of God in our lives. The will of God is really the same as the kingdom of God—God's rulership in our hearts (on earth) and in heaven (throughout the universe). When we confess that Jesus Christ is our personal Savior and allow that confession to take root in our lives, the kingdom, the will of God has arrived in us and will make itself known in special ways.

And now, "give us this day, our daily bread." It is better translated, "give us today bread for the coming day."[1] It is a basic request. It acknowledges that God is involved in our little lives, and that makes him big in our lives.

THE BREAD THAT WE REQUEST OF GOD

The study of interpretation is intriguing. When you have a person sitting in front of you, you can see meaning in the way he or she says something. You can take one sentence with five words and get a different meaning every time you hear it stated. For example, notice the difference in this one sentence when the emphasis is adjusted. Sentence: "I think you are cute."

>*I* think you are cute. What does that mean? "Others may think you are ugly, but *I* think you are cute."
>I **THINK** you are cute. "I'm not really sure but I *think* so."
>I think **YOU** are cute. "There are others who may be cute, but I am talking about you. I think *you* are cute."
>I think you **ARE** cute. "No matter what others are saying I think you *are* cute."

1. Barclay, *The Gospel of Matthew*, 1:215.

I think you are **CUTE**. "You may not be pretty, but you are *cute*."

The implications that can be drawn from simple statements that are open to our reflective moods, our inflections, and even our polar feelings at the time, are infinite. No wonder life is so complicated after we reach eighteen. No wonder there are so many denominations in the world all claiming to have the true understanding of religion or the Bible. Carving away our personal elements is a science all to itself when it comes to interpreting the Bible.

Picture Jesus sitting there with his disciples teaching them to pray, at their request, and he says: "When you pray, say . . . give us this day our daily bread"—and the disciples going out and discussing what he meant—for the next two thousand years debating what this meant. Some said, he means the Communion Service. Every time we get together we should have communion—"our daily bread." The Lord's Supper is where the bread is eaten.

Others said, he means himself. Jesus is the "bread of life." We are to eat his body and drink his blood—that means we are to digest his word. He means we should ask that each day we will be filled with this bread. His presence becomes our presence. And others said, he means the bread we will eat together at the great feast of the bridegroom in heaven. And still others said, he means the spiritual bread that he offers. We should ask Jesus for spiritual bread every day. This lets God know that we want his spiritual nourishment—daily devotions, daily worship.

WHAT IS THIS BREAD?

In the Gospel of Matthew, we have the word "daily." [1] "Give us . . . our daily bread."[2] But it was not a commonly used word. In fact, scholars at one time thought Matthew made up this word. That's part of the confusion. But then one day someone dug up a piece of papyrus in the holy land that had this very word on it.[3]

Papyrus was a common form of paper that was used when Jesus was on earth. We get the word "paper" from this—*papyrus*. It was not durable and so much of it has simply deteriorated into the ages. But in some of the warmer zones, like parts of Palestine and Egypt, a lot of fragments have been found.

2. Matthew 6:11.
3. Barclay, 1:217.

A fragment from a lady's shopping list was found that had this rare word on it, the word that scholars have traditionally interpreted, translated "daily." The word was only used this one time in the New Testament, but we now know from the secular world that the word had to do with an ordinary shopping list. Just like when you go to Safeway or Kroger. It simply referred to the things on that list that were needed to keep life going.

It appears that this is the re/al meaning of Jesus' prayer. "Give us this day our daily bread" is simply saying, "Help us, Lord, to get everything we need that is on our shopping list." It is a way of saying, "We acknowledge that you are the giver of all good gifts." Regardless of what good things come into our lives, they are eventually attributable to the Lord.

I read a book on avoiding debt. It gave one insight in one sentence: *Quit spending more than you earn.* But no one would pay $24.95 for one simple sentence, so the author elaborated on that thought. One of the major points he made was in his analysis of your present situation. He asked, "Have you ever gone without a meal?" If you haven't, he said, "dwell on that." I had to acknowledge, No, I have never gone without a meal. And I was not going without any meals at the time I read the book. Furthermore, I had stored up a few meals in my body cupboard just in case.

"Our daily bread." Our daily needs. Everything on the shopping list that is necessary. Whatever is necessary for our physical and mental well-being. That is the request Jesus suggests his disciples make each day. That is a petition that is legitimate and worthy of those who wish to learn to pray. He doesn't launch into what is a need. He figures we know that.

WHAT OUR "DAILY BREAD" SUGGESTS

God has a place in our shopping cart. All this prayer suggests is that we take that seriously each day. It is human nature to see God as a last resort. It is divine insight to understand that God is a part of our ability to make a living, our ability to choose wisely to balance the budget, and a part of our understanding of needs and a fulfilling of those needs.

On Thanksgiving most of us sit down to a tasty meal of traditional foods—turkey and all the trimmings. But at the same time some people sit down to nothing. And that's okay. There are times when we have no control over some things. And there are times when we need to feast to the glory of God. But Thanksgiving is one day that America acknowledges

God, at least ceremonially, with a short grace. The Lord's Prayer teaches us to make every meal a Thanksgiving dinner. God cares about our shopping cart and he deserves thanks.

THINGS TO BE HAPPY ABOUT

It is time for us to think about those simple things that bring a natural high. We can refer to these as part of "our daily bread."[4]

   Falling in love
   Laughing so hard your face hurts
   A hot shower
   No lines at Wal-Mart
   A special glance
   Getting mail
   Taking a drive on a pretty road
   Hearing your favorite song on the radio
   Finding the sweater you want is on sale for half price
   A long-distance phone call
   Giggling
   A bubble bath
   Lying in bed listening to the rain outside
   A chocolate milkshake
   Hot towels out of the dryer
   A good conversation
   The beach
   Finding a $20 bill in your coat from last winter
   Running through sprinklers or walking in the rain
   Friends
   Falling in love for the first time
   Laughing at yourself
   Midnight phone calls that last for hours

The rest of the list is for you to make up. How long can you make it at any time of year when you have the chance to acknowledge naturally from whom all good gifts come?

   [11] "What father among you, if his son asks for a fish, will instead of a fish give him a serpent; [12] or if he asks for an egg, will give him a scorpion? [13] If you then, who are evil, know how to

---

4. This list below is just a sample. For more items on our "daily bread" list see Kipfer, 14,000 *Things To Be Happy About*.

give good gifts to your children, how much more will the heavenly Father give the Holy Spirit to those who ask him!" (Luke 11:11-13)

William Barclay reminds us:

> We must note that Jesus did not teach us to pray: "Give *me my* daily bread." He taught us to pray: "Give *us our* daily bread." The problem in the world is not that there is not enough to go round; there is enough and to spare. The problem is not the *supply* of life's essentials; it is the *distribution* of them. This prayer teaches us never to be selfish in our prayers. It is a prayer which we can help God to answer by giving to others who are less fortunate than we are. This prayer is not only a prayer that we may *receive* our daily bread; it is also a prayer that we may *share* our daily bread with others.[5]

Our Father in heaven, give us this day our daily bread. And we will acknowledge and thank you for it.

---

5. Barclay, 1:219.

CHAPTER TWENTY-THREE

Truth is in the Tasting

> "Purity of soul cannot be lost without consent."
> —St. Augustine

GALATIANS 6:1-6

¹ Brethren, if a man is overtaken in any trespass, you who are spiritual should restore him in a spirit of gentleness. Look to yourself, lest you too be tempted. ² Bear one another's burdens, and so fulfil the law of Christ. ³ For if any one thinks he is something, when he is nothing, he deceives himself. ⁴ But let each one test his own work, and then his reason to boast will be in himself alone and not in his neighbor. ⁵ For each man will have to bear his own load.

⁶ Let him who is taught the word share all good things with him who teaches.

THE TRUTH BUSINESS

Christianity claims to be in the truth business. We claim to be in a search for truth, all the time. And yet it may be that nothing scares us more than truth. All through history we read the great Christian writers and feel their intensity for wanting to find the genuine article of truth. For some it came in the form of searching for the nature of God. For others it was less ethereal—they wanted to know how we could live strong and victorious lives because of finding truth.

> [32] "And you will know the truth, and the truth will make you free." (John 8:32)

Men and women have pondered as to what that meant. One day as I was giving that some thought, a congressman from the state was pummeled with whether he had had an affair with his female intern who had disappeared a month before. Finally, by the end of the week he "told the truth." He had indeed had a long-standing sexual affair with this intern. And not her alone—but at least five other women as well. Here was a politician who had voted to impeach the president because "he had not told the truth" about having an affair with his intern.

It is amazing how slippery this word "truth" is. For most of us truth means "facts." And yet facts are seldom connected with truth as we practice. Stories that are accepted as truth are too often devoid of facts and because of that innocent people have gone to their death, executed by the state based on "truth" but not facts. For most of us truth is what we happen to believe at the time. For us it is truth whether it matches the facts or not. And that causes chaos in our society because what is truth for many of us is filled with biases and assumptions that are separated from facts.

UNFACTUAL MATERIAL

I once had a student in a college theology class. He had real trouble with the philosophical view of God. After class he would come to my office and want to argue with me that if there was a God he was a "flawed" God. His argument was that everywhere we look in the world there is chaos and disorder. Rather than look for the positive evidence for the existence of God, he turned the tables around and looked for the negative evidence against the existence of God.

"Flaw" was something he couldn't get around. And so, he chose to pick my brain in an effort to prove his "truth" that there really was no righteous God. If God is "flawed" then he is not God because the very definition of God does not allow any "flaw." Two years later I was surprised to find this same young man arguing theology with the community and contending that I was a heretic, one who taught error in an effort to mislead people in their spiritual walk. He put out flyers attacking my teaching and the teaching of others on the faculty. And these flyers caught the attention of the powers that be and within a few months I, along with my colleagues were viewed as risky and questionable professors.

The controversy grew to the point that people began to believe that the Religion Department at the college could not be trusted. The stories became so outlandish that at one point I was publicly accused of being a Jesuit in disguise and one student even testified that I had brought a Catholic priest into the basement of the men's residence hall to perform a midnight mass. One story led to another until things became chaotic.

All these rumors, and there were some spinoffs, fused together eventually and became "truth" and I, along with several of my colleagues, were forced out of our employment because we were not "safe." When I resigned and moved to the West Coast and sought other employment, the story had developed that I had sued the college and received a $7,000,000 settlement from the college administration because of my heretical teachings. Astonishing enough, *none* of these stories were factual but they had grown to the point where they were considered "true" and the college had to "clean up its act" by forcing several of us to resign.

TRUTH IN FAITH

This experience was the beginning of my gradual slide. I found that wherever I went, to speak for weeks of spiritual emphasis, or camp meeting convocations, or to give seminars for pastors, all of which had been my specialty and part of my job description, I would always run into someone who would question my faithfulness to "the truth."

One man, after hearing me speak at a special meeting with church members, and after hearing me answer questions for over an hour about these things, stood up and confessed, "I have never met you before today, but I have talked about you all over the region. I have shared the things I heard about you and I have proclaimed them as true. But after hearing you today I want everyone here to know that I am truly sorry to you, for what I have said. You are nothing like what I had heard, and I think you have gone on record here as a 'truth-loving' Christian. I humbly apologize to you before this gathering that I have been wrong, and I hope you will accept that apology."

As I stood there in the podium, listening to his confession I realized a moment of truth. When all is said and done, truth is revealed in the tasting. By that I mean, somewhere in our experience we demonstrate the truth, and it is that truth that makes us free. I thought of this biblical passage:

> ¹ Brethren, if a man is overtaken in any trespass, you who are spiritual should restore him in a spirit of gentleness. Look to yourself, lest you too be tempted. ² Bear one another's burdens, and so fulfil the law of Christ. (Galatians 6:1-2)

Here was a man tasting the truth. And the tasting was in giving me, a person he thought was deep in transgression, the time to talk, by listening to what I had to say. And when he had done that he treated me with "gentleness." I could hardly harbor any hard feelings toward this man. I could hardly feel devastated or violated by such treatment, in spite of whatever he had said or done or thought. His tears demonstrated to me that he was tasting Christian truth in this act.

THE TEST OF TRUTH

The test of truth in the church is a gracious spirit. When the Holy Spirit touches a Christian heart, that heart becomes gracious. That means that the same grace that melted that heart at one point in his or her experience is now demonstrated toward someone else who he thinks of as a sinner. This word that the apostle Paul uses to describe sin is not the normal word for willful sin. ¹ "If a man is overtaken in any trespass."[1] Paul is talking about the common mistakes that all of us make even when we are committed to Christ. The truest of intentions are often wrought with mistakes. But the truth in the tasting is our willingness to encourage each other in spite of these mistakes. That includes forgiving and exhibiting a spirit of understanding.

How else can a community of faith succeed in its witness to the world than to be filled with people who exhibit the same kind of grace toward others that Christ exhibited toward them? The spirit of getting even, the disposition of vengeance, the feelings of pseudo-justice that say everyone who has hurt me needs to be hurt in return is not the spirit of Christ. It is surely not the exhibition of grace. Grace allows a person who has made a mistake to correct that mistake without being thrown to the wolves.

1. Galatians 6:1.

In the life of God, his dealing with us, the philandering human beings in this world, is illustrated here. He has stayed with us regardless of how bad it made him look. He has remained faithful to us even when we were unfaithful to him. And until we taste that truth we will not know truth. Until we exhibit the same kind of grace toward each other, we are not there.

FINDING GRACE

Every congregation may have some people who think they find no grace there. So, they may have demonstrated their own rush to judgment or their own frustration or their own lack of grace. We need not judge them. We don't know their motives. But we must learn from what they consider to be "truth." Truth is not always connected to facts. The disconnection is part of the human condition. We call it *original sin*. Church people have in some cases felt violated, misjudged, ill-treated, and misunderstood. It is time to get off of our feelings of victimization and learn that our only reason for existence as a faith community is to demonstrate the grace that God has demonstrated to us.

None of us deserves eternal life. None of us can hold up a life of perfect righteousness. None of us can claim to be an example of what everyone should be. But these are, after all, not the issues of life. What we hold up is the grace of God. What we hold up is the righteousness of Christ. What we hold up is the gentleness with which we can treat each other and bear each other's burdens, and help others bear their back-breaking load of life.

We will often fail to do this perfectly. We will forget the facts of the matter in favor of our own take on truth, but like the man in the meeting we must be willing to stand up and say, "I was wrong, please forgive me." This is what Paul means when he says,

> [6]"Let him who is taught the word share all good things with him who teaches." (Galatians 6:6)

At the heart of the truth is tasting it—allowing the grace of God always to permeate our attitudes toward and our treatment of each other.

CHAPTER TWENTY-FOUR

Happy Are the Thankful

> "As bread is the staff of life, the simple sustenance of the body,
> so appreciation is the food of the soul."
>
> —Priscilla Wayne

PSALM 66:1-20

1 Make a joyful noise to God, all the earth;
2 sing the glory of his name;
   give to him glorious praise!
3 Say to God, "How terrible are thy deeds!
   So great is thy power that thy enemies cringe before thee.
4 All the earth worships thee;
   they sing praises to thee,
   sing praises to thy name." *Selah*
5 Come and see what God has done:
   he is terrible in his deeds among men.
6 He turned the sea into dry land;
   men passed through the river on foot.
   There did we rejoice in him,
7 who rules by his might for ever,
   whose eyes keep watch on the nations—
   let not the rebellious exalt themselves. *Selah*
8 Bless our God, O peoples,

>   let the sound of his praise be heard,
> ⁹ who has kept us among the living,
>   and has not let our feet slip.
> ¹⁰ For thou, O God, hast tested us;
>   thou hast tried us as silver is tried.
> ¹¹ Thou didst bring us into the net;
>   thou didst lay affliction on our loins;
> ¹² thou didst let men ride over our heads;
>   we went through fire and through water;
>   yet thou hast brought us forth to a spacious place.
> ¹³ I will come into thy house with burnt offerings;
>   I will pay thee my vows,
> ¹⁴ that which my lips uttered
>   and my mouth promised when I was in trouble.
> ¹⁵ I will offer to thee burnt offerings of fatlings,
>   with the smoke of the sacrifice of rams;
>   I will make an offering of bulls and goats. *Selah*
> ¹⁶ Come and hear, all you who fear God,
>   and I will tell what he has done for me.
> ¹⁷ I cried aloud to him,
>   and he was extolled with my tongue.
> ¹⁸ If I had cherished iniquity in my heart,
>   the Lord would not have listened.
> ¹⁹ But truly God has listened;
>   he has given heed to the voice of my prayer.
> ²⁰ Blessed be God,
>   because he has not rejected my prayer
>   or removed his steadfast love from me!

LISTING IMPORTANT EVENTS

Several years ago, a friend of mine told me that when you come to the place in life where you are mildly depressed, try writing out your blessings. So, I tried it. His formula was this: for the next ten days write out ten things each day for which you are thankful, but never repeat anything. I found that the first day I wrote out things like

1. I am thankful for life.
2. I am thankful for family.
3. I am thankful for church.

4. I am thankful for a job.

5. I am thankful for friends, and so on.

On the second day I still had a lot of noticeably big and visible things.

As the ten days proceeded (and I couldn't repeat any of those previous blessings) an interesting phenomenon occurred. I began thanking God for smaller and smaller things. I began to be aware that being thankful may even have to do with unlikely things like lessons learned and trials endured. I couldn't believe that I began thanking God for trouble because of the affect it had on my character. The upshot of this exercise, which I have repeated a number of times and continue to do when things get rough, was that I began to see how much happier I was when I concentrated on those areas of gratitude.

Barbara Kipfer's book illustrates what small reasons we have for which to be thankful.[1] The book is strictly "stream of consciousness." The author appears to have just closed her eyes and written anything that came into her mind. It is a great answer to the propensity to complain and gripe. Rather than analyzing your gripes, she suggests listing your blessings. Never in my wildest imagination did I think I could keep writing in my ten-day exercise until I had 14,000 things to be happy about, but this book really hit the mark and I keep it next to my desk at all times.

A LIST OF THINGS IN PSALM 66

In Psalm 66 we see some obvious things that can make us happy if we spend time applying them.

- v. 2: Sing the glory of God's name.
- v. 2: Make God's praise glorious.
- v. 3: How awesome are God's deeds.
- v. 3: How wonderful that God's enemies cringe in his presence.
- v. 5: Come and see what God has done.
- v. 6: God turned the sea into dry land.
- v. 6: God made Israel pass through the waters on foot.
- v. 6: This is cause for thanksgiving.

---

1. Kipfer, *14,000 Things To Be Happy About.*

v. 7:   God rules by his power.

v. 7:   God's eyes watch everything that occurs on this earth.

v. 9:   God preserves our life.

We sit down to that much anticipated meal each year: cranberry sauce—jellied or preserved—take your pick; the butterball turkey cooked dry or moist—take your pick; the mashed potatoes—with or without onions or leeks or garlic—take your pick; the candied sweet potatoes or yams with the marshmallows and sugar and cinnamon; the fresh or frozen peas or carrots or cauliflower or rutabagas or the rice pilaf —take your pick; the corn in a bowl or on the cob—take your pick; the fresh rolls, the butter, the pumpkin pie, the ice cream. It goes on and on and we are thankful. It is a feast to celebrate gratitude.

Such obvious good things. We saw *Harry Potter and the Sorcerer's Stone*. Harry is the 12-year-old "wizard." I don't believe in wizards. He was searching for a stone with incredible power, guarded by a ferocious three-headed monster dog. He fought his way through tremendous odds with the belief that his wizard powers could bring him victory. What a delightful story of persistence and faith. Not scriptural, just fantasy. The power of love brought him through it all. TV evangelists are carping on the story, criticizing the influx of new age and demonism into our society. It was entertaining, fun, and reminded us of how much enjoyment life can bring. The good win, the bad are beaten.

Most of us are negligent. Most of us take things for granted. Maybe we don't intend to appear ungrateful but if we were to write a thank you note to Jesus everyday wouldn't we be more sensitive to those things that are going on? So many things to be happy about. With time I imagine that all of us could think of 14,000 things. And we could write a second volume!

THIS IS NOT THE ONLY LIST GIVEN IN PSALM 66

I've listed the easy things. Now look at the hard ones. The writer continues:

v. 10: God tests us.

v. 10: God refines us like silver.

v. 11: God put us in prison.

v. 11: God laid burdens on our backs.

v. 12:   God let people oppress us.

v. 12:   God let us go through fire and water.

Now think about this: Thank you God for imprisoning us. Thank you God for laying burdens on us from day to day. Thank you God for the oppression we suffer, the hard times that come our way, the fiery trials we face and the tough times that challenge us. Be serious. These we view as curses. It is here that my philosophy kicks in and I start reasoning and talking and complaining and griping. Where are you God? What kind of life did you introduce here? If you are a God of love why am I suffering? And on and on it goes.

In one of my classes on a Friday afternoon my students were to present a project. The class divided into four groups and each presented a project. When I graded them, it became apparent that they had all done a lot of work, a lot of research, a lot of hard digging. I passed back the papers. Three out of the four projects got 0/100. They sat soberly as they looked at their papers. All that work. All that time and effort—no credit. And I explained, each of these papers was ten pages long. Each of these papers was highly technical. Each of these papers represented many hours of labor on their part and they got no credit. This was a technical writing class. Ten percent of their grade rested on the results of this project. And out of a class of twenty, fifteen came away with no credit. One student finally feebly and daringly challenged me: "I came to this school to learn computers not to learn to write." No one else said anything.

When no one was willing to talk anymore I explained, "You all worked hard, you presented meaningful stuff, what went wrong?" No comments, no questions, just silence. "Did you dream all this up yourself? Is this all your own work?" One paper had so many formulas and so much technical data that the writers single-spaced the material to get it down to ten pages.

"You're going to tell me that you could write that much material and never use a source? Not one reference to sources in two of the papers and only one reference in the third." And then I dropped the bomb. "Since you presented material that was obviously not your own and yet you passed it off as your own, giving no references, no sources for your work, I have to conclude that this was plagiarism."

I then told of two college presidents recently in Ivy League colleges. One gave a commencement address in which he took the points from an anonymous source on the internet but failed to tell his audience that he got it off the internet. The other gave a brown-bag luncheon talk to a small group of graduate students and presented material he had gotten off the internet anonymously but never bothered to tell the group. Both presidents were forced to resign their positions because of this seemingly innocent infraction. For the same reason three projects in my class earned 0/100.

Should they be happy about this? Should they be thankful to me for doing this? Yes, they should. Wasn't it better for them to learn this lesson now than when they become college presidents someday? Wouldn't it be better to understand the seriousness our society places on such behavior now than to wait until they are presenting a report to a group of potential investors and lose the account or their job or their career? The psalmist recognizes insightfully that God, who sees all and understands all, puts people in prison and takes them through trials and fire and sword, so they can learn these important lessons—probably through no other way. Happy are the thankful when they suffer!

HAPPY ARE THE THANKFUL

So, we have the clear word of scripture: Because I have learned all of this from a loving, all-seeing God, I will come to the temple and offer my sacrifice. Because I now see that God cares about my character development I will carry out the vows that I made while I was in trouble. Is there anyone who hasn't made the promise? "O God, if you will get me through this I will reform my life." "O Lord deliver me from these trials, and I will be more faithful." The psalmist has that divine insight that while there are those smooth things to thank God for, there are the rough roads as well. And when the road smooths out I will work harder to bring my life into harmony with God's law.

Here is the great truth that happy are the thankful:

> [16] Come and hear, all you who fear God,
> and I will tell what he has done for me.
> [17] I cried aloud to him,
> and he was extolled with my tongue.
> [18] If I had cherished iniquity in my heart,
> the Lord would not have listened.
> [19] But truly God has listened;
> he has given heed to the voice of my prayer.

[20] Blessed be God,
> because he has not rejected my prayer
> or removed his steadfast love from me! (Psalm 66:16-20)

There are hard things in life that can cause us depression, despondency, heartache, disgust. But happy are the thankful. Happy are those who see these things as God's workmen to move us into a better life. Happy are those who recognize the hand of God in his providence to mold us and make us better people. Happy are the thankful. They see that even the hard things are reasons to be happy. As we recognize this we can be incredibly happy over the smoother roads when they come.

CHAPTER TWENTY-FIVE

Removing the Cup

"After the ship has sunk, everyone knows how she might have been saved."

—Italian Proverb

LUKE 22:39-46

> [39] And he came out, and went, as was his custom, to the Mount of Olives; and the disciples followed him. [40] And when he came to the place he said to them, "Pray that you may not enter into temptation." [41] And he withdrew from them about a stone's throw, and knelt down and prayed, [42] "Father, if thou art willing, remove this cup from me; nevertheless not my will, but thine, be done." [45] And when he rose from prayer, he came to the disciples and found them sleeping for sorrow, [46] and he said to them, "Why do you sleep? Rise and pray that you may not enter into temptation."

THE INCARNATION OF JESUS CHRIST

Advent is that time each year when we are reminded of the incarnation of Jesus Christ, the central teaching of the Christian faith. This time of year is one of great symbolic meaning to believers. It is a time when, despite all the secular aspects of our society, we look again at that touching story of the birth of Jesus and why he came to this earth from heaven.

The stores have already begun to capitalize on it. Frosty the Snowman is back, Rudolph the Red-Nosed Reindeer will be sung about, over, and over. Occasionally we hear the gospel story in the classical Christmas carols. Even on the most secular radio stations and television specials we will hear an occasional "Silent Night" and "Hark! the Herald Angels Sing."

Following September 11, 2001, there was more religious talk about holidays. We heard more about the parallel holidays of Ramadan and Hanukkah in our nation. The terrible tragedy that happened at the World Trade Center spearheaded such talk. People seemed a little more willing to mention God. Signs connecting patriotism with religion are typical in times of tragedy and in times when we are forced to face our destiny.

DIFFERENCE BETWEEN HOLIDAYS

In spite of the fact that three religions emphasize their unique elements of faith in this period of time each year, we still hear no Ramadan carols or Hanukkah hymns. A news reporter, out of respect or out of political correctness, will often close his or her segment with "Happy Hanukkah," and yet there is little question whose holiday season this really is in our society.

We don't know much about Hanukkah presents, or whether Ramadan has a parallel to the Christmas tree. But some Jewish and Muslim homes may feel threatened by the predominance of Christmas practices at this time of year. I am happy for the God-talk. I was listening to a talk radio show as I drove through the rain. The caller was praising God and the talk show host was praising the universe. The radio host was a self-proclaimed atheist trying to emphasize that the "universe," this nebulous, symbolic collection of stars and constellations, was somehow personal enough to care about the caller's concern. The caller kept talking about the "big G," to counter the impersonal talk. It was an unashamed witness to that higher power who takes a personal interest in our little world and our little concerns while running the universe.

Christians have always separated the universe from God. For the Christian, God is the superintendent of the universe. The universe is always a creation of this God whose omniscience includes the ability of caring about human tragedy and celebration. The contrast was encouraging, and it seemed to me that the talk show host was out of his league even though it was his show. I liked that.

To call God "the universe" is too simplistic. It is to say, "I really don't want the responsibility of facing my life before a person. I really prefer to see things that happen here in a fatalistic way." It is the effort of many to downplay the fact that there is a personal God who cares about us and who expects accountability. Yet to the Christian, nothing else makes sense. To stand before a superior being who reads and evaluates our motives is too stunning for many people today.

JESUS AND THE PERSONAL GOD

Throughout the event we call "the incarnation," when God was in Christ reconciling the world to himself, we have a person relating, not to the universe as his guiding light, but to God the Father. And this is, in itself, a great revelation encapsulated in the Christian religion.

In the Gospels we will never find Jesus referring to God as "the universe." Jesus gives no evidence that we live in a fixed existence where everything is decided, though he does intimate on a regular basis that God has a "plan" for his creation. God is always allowed final decisions. God is the creator of the universe; he is never identified as "the universe." He reminds his followers, as well as those who balk at God's authority, that someday all will stand before a judge who knows all and is all righteous.

Jesus' attempt to negotiate with God in this passage is a prime example of this. As he kneels in the garden he pleads with God, "Can I get out of this? Is there another way to accomplish this mission?" But he acknowledges the superintending status of God. He does not superimpose his human understanding of life on that divine knowledge of God.

> [42] "Father, if thou art willing, remove this cup from me; nevertheless not my will, but thine, be done." (Luke 22:42)

He likens his mission to drinking from "a cup" of suffering. This mission represents everything that the religion of the Hebrew scriptures had been demonstrating from the very beginning of its days—the lambs and bulls that had been slaughtered in substitution for human estrangement. The whole sanctuary service that had been meticulously followed by the Hebrews in the wilderness, and later in the temple in Jerusalem—these were all at stake.

Without this act of Jesus giving his life, none of these other things would have any meaning. And yet his human nature, yearning for those basic needs of acceptance and reconciliation, pleads to the Father, "Are you sure there is no other way?" He was not praying to the stars. He was not invoking the wisdom of wizards. He was not laying out the tarot cards. He was not seeking the instruction of witches as King Saul did. He was seeking the direction of a personal, intelligent person to whom he was totally committed.

WHAT JESUS FACED

While there are some parallels to our own struggles with temptation, especially the temptation to question the existence of God at times when things go wrong, it is not a perfect picture of our temptation. None of us must deal with the fact that if we make the wrong decision the whole human race is in trouble. Those were the issues for Jesus.

What began at Christmas was about to end at Easter and the universal issue was whether Jesus would go through with the final battle of the great plan of God for the salvation of the human race. None of us ever will face that. Adam faced it and failed. Jesus was now facing it. We can see the crucial nature of a battle with sin that must be won.

I used to work for a beekeeper. It wasn't always a pleasant job. Along with the routine work of extracting honey and moving hives around the country to pollinate crops and collect the rewards of honey to sell, I had the job of answering phone calls from people in the city who were freaking out because a swarm of bees was camping in their trees or walls. So, I would get my gear—face net, empty hive, smoker, and drive over to their house.

What most of the people did not understand was that this swarm of bees, sometimes a foot in diameter and hanging down two feet, was not there because of the honey. And they were not there to freak anyone out. They were not there to attack anyone. They were there to protect and show loyalty to the queen bee. So, my job was relatively simple—just scoop them out of the tree, into a box, and take them home. Every time I picked up a swarm I started a new hive, if . . . if I succeeded in getting the queen. If I did not get the queen when I scooped the bees into the box, the box would be empty by the next morning. The loyalty to the queen, while instinctive, was their crucial issue.

The ancient kings knew this principle. When they invaded a country, if they did not kill the king, they had not won the battle. In Jesus' case the battle over evil and the enemy king, had to be final. It could not be a bandage on a wound. It involved life and death.

> ⁴¹ And he withdrew from them about a stone's throw, and knelt down and prayed, ⁴² "Father, if thou art willing, remove this cup from me; nevertheless not my will, but thine, be done." (Luke 22:41-42)

GOD AND THE TRIAL

Wrapped up in these words "remove this cup" are all the issues in the great conflict between good and evil. Evil is of the nature that unless it is totally defeated it will continue to spread and undo the good life God intended for all to have. Jesus had free will. He could have said, "I've had enough. Why is it all worth this?" But instead, he left it in his father's hands. "If you can remove it, if there is another way to carry out this mission of salvation please show me now. But if not, I'm going through with it!"

While there is no direct parallel to anything we face, it is a fact that every day we face some kind of trial that we wonder the same thing. In times of hardship, in times when understanding is confusing us, in times when temptation seems so terribly overwhelming, in times when we wonder if there is a God and why doesn't he act in a different way in our lives, we too utter those words, "Can you remove this cup, Lord?"

It is at those times when we can look at Jesus' decisiveness there in the garden. We can say, "Lord, can you remove this trial? Is there another way my character can be developed without having to face this?" And we can receive encouragement in these inspired words:

> ¹³ No temptation has overtaken you that is not common to man. God is faithful, and he will not let you be tempted beyond your strength, but with the temptation will also provide the way of escape, that you may be able to endure it. (1 Corinthians 10:13)

This can be the personal word of encouragement for us. That can be the personal meaning of the Advent for us. Sweeping away the Santa Claus, cleaning up all the clutter caused by the free enterprise system that makes Christmas our greatest time of buying and selling and marketing and advertising, we can rejoice in the true meaning of Advent—the fulfilling of the promise that God would put enmity between us and evil. God gives us victory without removing the cup, just as he did Jesus. He does not remove it. He gives us the strength to endure. One of the results of Advent.

CHAPTER TWENTY-SIX

Watching unto Life

> "To live is so startling it leaves time for little else."
> —Emily Dickinson

MATTHEW 24:36-44

³⁶ "But of that day and hour no one knows, not even the angels of heaven, nor the Son, but the Father only. ³⁷ As were the days of Noah, so will be the coming of the Son of man. ³⁸ For as in those days before the flood they were eating and drinking, marrying and giving in marriage, until the day when Noah entered the ark, ³⁹ and they did not know until the flood came and swept them all away, so will be the coming of the Son of man. ⁴⁰ Then two men will be in the field; one is taken, and one is left. ⁴¹ Two women will be grinding at the mill; one is taken, and one is left. ⁴² Watch therefore, for you do not know on what day your Lord is coming. ⁴³ But know this, that if the householder had known in what part of the night the thief was coming, he would have watched and would not have let his house be broken into. ⁴⁴ Therefore you also must be ready; for the Son of man is coming at an hour you do not expect.

CHRISTMAS WASN'T MY BIRTHDAY

A little girl had just finished opening all her Christmas presents and a friend asked her, "Did you get all the presents for Christmas that you hoped for?" She thought for a moment and then replied, "No, but then, it really wasn't my birthday was it?"

Advent is that magical time of year when we are reminded again to watch. When we were children our parents listened carefully as we walked through the toy section of the department store pointing out all the things we hoped to get for Christmas. And when we pointed to those precious toys we were told, "Well, Christmas is coming!"

How many times did my parents utter that short sentence? And as a little boy it just seemed like Christmas would never arrive. But when it did I was watching. I was watching the presents pile up under the tree. I was watching to see if I could see any there for me. I was watching to see if I could guess what the presents were that had my name on them. It was a glorious experience in delayed gratification. And it was exciting if not frustrating—watching and waiting. I decided waiting was hard. Would Christmas ever come?

Jesus gave us direct counsel on that—not looking for our presents but looking for his presence. Advent is an experience in watching and waiting—being patient and knowing that in his own time God acts. Israel had been watching and waiting for Advent for hundreds of years and yet as we know, only a few were patient.

WATCHING IS A MESSAGE OF ADVENT

One night I came home from work and saw that Jennifer Lopez would be a guest on the Tonight Show with Jay Leno. I was interested in seeing an interview with a pretty and mysterious singer-actor who had been so successful in her career. I poured a bowl of cereal and ate it while Jay Leno went through his opening stand-up routine. Then I settled back to watch the interview. But something happened. As I relaxed I didn't see her, but rather there was a male guest and then a singing group. And I wondered, what happened? She was supposed to be Jay's first interview. Well, she was. I realized, to my disappointment, that I had dropped off for a few minutes in my tired state after having taught my college classes all day and I had seen the whole program except the one part I wanted to see.

Jesus told a story something like this in principle. There were ten young women who were waiting for a wedding. They were the bridesmaids. But the bride and the groom were late, and these young women were tired, and they fell asleep. They all had lamps instead of flowers and as they slept some of the lamps went out. Some had extra oil so when they woke up they were able to re-light their lamps. But some didn't and when they went to get more oil they returned to see that they had missed the wedding.

> [10] And while they went to buy, the bridegroom came, and those who were ready went in with him to the marriage feast; and the door was shut. [11] Afterward the other maidens came also, saying, "Lord, lord, open to us." [12] But he replied, "Truly, I say to you, I do not know you." [13] Watch therefore, for you know neither the day nor the hour. (Matthew 25:10-13)

We see from this that the coming of Christ required watching and waiting. But more importantly it required being ready. "Watching" was a much more inclusive idea than just being there looking around. It meant that they were prepared for a wait. So, while Israel may have been watching, many were not ready. They had become preoccupied with other things, thinking that when and if the Messiah would come they could quickly gather their things and follow him. But instead, many of them got so far off the track that they were never able to return. In this scriptural passage Jesus talks not only about the first Advent but also about his return. Again, he gives the instruction: Watch! Those who watch will be ready.

WHY ARE WE TO WATCH?

We are to watch because the coming of Christ is "our blessed hope." It is the culmination of the plan of salvation in which we are a major objective.

> [13] Awaiting our blessed hope, the appearing of the glory of our great God and Savior Jesus Christ. (Titus 2:13)

Have you ever had dreams about some event coming in your life and you were so worried that you would miss it that you dreamed you missed it? Some ministers testify that they dream about getting up in the pulpit and suddenly look down and realize they forgot to put on their pants. And there they are in shirt and tie and coat, but without pants. How embarrassing—how revealing such a dream is that this important event is anticipated but they are not ready.

I sat in O'Hare International Airport in Chicago one morning. I had flown in from Tennessee and was on my way to my graduate school in Michigan. I was tired and I had a two-hour layover in Chicago. I watched the planes as they landed and taxied in—waiting patiently for mine. I leaned back and relaxed and two and a half hours later I woke up with a start. I grabbed my carryon and rushed over to the gate just in time to see my plane taxiing down the runway bound for Michigan.

I had missed my plane. There I stood feeling and looking like a fool. The very reason I was in that airport was to catch that plane, and I had missed it. To live a whole life and miss the point of that life. To become so caught up in trivia that our lamps go out, or we sleep through the Advent like so many from Israel did. Advent, both first and second, represents the end of the rescue mission for sinners. So, Jesus says, "Watch!" We watch because we do not know when the Advent will occur. In the Hebrew scriptures there were signs given as to the general time or season of the Advent. The prophets told of the place and some phenomena that would occur, but they did not give the specific time.

Perhaps nothing is more frustrating than to invite someone over for dinner and then they are late. We gave a time, but they got stuck in traffic or someone had a last-minute emergency. There you stand, wringing your hands, frustrated by their insensitivity to your concern to have a hot meal to serve them. The gravy is beginning to separate. The potatoes are getting cold, the turkey is burning, the drink is getting warm as the ice cubes melt.

Jesus never gave us a specific time. Nowhere in prophecy was the date of either Advent explained. So how could we know? If I am to be at your house at 6:00 pm for dinner, I know what you are expecting. But if you just say drop in, what am I to do? Jesus couldn't give us a time.

> [36] "But of that day and hour no one knows, not even the angels of heaven, nor the Son, but the Father only." (Matthew 24:36)

He said that the Father hadn't revealed it to him. He said that the Father hadn't revealed it to the angels. He said that the Father gave him nothing to reveal to us. I think there was another reason: we might get stuck in traffic. We might have an emergency in the family. Here comes one of my students and he has a late paper. "I had an appendectomy, and I couldn't get this to you in time for the deadline." What am I to say?

"Sorry, the paper gets an F?" But he wasn't negligent, he had a genuine emergency!

Does Jesus wait for us to get our act together and when he finally comes we have the act together? He comes when we are ready? We watch because we only get one chance. When I missed my plane, I went and got an updated ticket and an hour later I was winging my way to Michigan. But that is not true with the Advent. If you missed it, you missed it. There are no second chances.

There is a set of books out in the bookstores right now which many have read. They are intensely interesting. They are downright exciting. But they represent a theology that doesn't coincide with this teaching in Matthew 24 for they suggest that if you miss the Advent you will get another chance. That is not the teaching of Jesus. In this passage Jesus makes it quite clear that only those who watch will be ready and those who watch get only one chance. However, we can find comfort in the fact that when the second Advent occurs all will be comfortable with their decision. There will be no need to keep things going anymore. Indeed, that is why he comes at that time.

We watch because this is our "blessed" hope.

> 37 As were the days of Noah, so will be the coming of the Son of man. 38 For as in those days before the flood they were eating and drinking, marrying and giving in marriage, until the day when Noah entered the ark, 39 and they did not know until the flood came and swept them all away, so will be the coming of the Son of man. (Matthew 24:37-39)

"As were the days of Noah," life was going on routinely and all seemed to be going well. The world was growing in civility. The families were happy. People were prosperous. God was the farthest from most people's minds. But they did not see themselves as God saw them. And the flood took them away. No second chance for those left behind.

> 28 Likewise as it was in the days of Lot—they ate, they drank, they bought, they sold, they planted, they built, 29 but on the day when Lot went out from Sodom fire and sulphur rained from heaven and destroyed them all— 30 so will it be on the day when the Son of man is revealed.
>
> 31 On that day, let him who is on the housetop, with his goods in the house, not come down to take them away; and likewise let him who is in the field not turn back. 32 Remember Lot's wife. 33 Whoever seeks to gain his life will lose it, but whoever

> loses his life will preserve it. ³⁴ I tell you, in that night there will be two in one bed; one will be taken and the other left. ³⁵ There will be two women grinding together; one will be taken and the other left." ³⁷ And they said to him, "Where, Lord?" He said to them, "Where the body is, there the eagles will be gathered together." (Luke 17:28-37)

"As it was in the days of Lot," life was going on routinely and all seemed to be going well. The city was enjoying its way of life. They did not see themselves as God saw them. And the fire took them away. No second chance for those left behind. Two men working in the field. One ready and watching, the other not ready and lost. The Advent takes the one and leaves the other—no second chance. Two women grinding at the mill. One ready and watching, the other not ready and lost. The Advent takes the one and leaves the other—no second chance. Both the first and the second Advents were the reward of the righteous—the vindication of those who watched. God saves those who have taken him at his word and are prepared to go home with him.

Both Advents represent eternal life for God's disciples on earth. They are our reprieve from slavery, from exile, from hopelessness. They represent our hope for eternity, that return to the world God created which was free of sin and despair.

I visited a lady in the hospital. I went to the hospital immediately upon hearing that she was there. But I was too late. She had died just minutes before I arrived, and I stood at her bedside remembering three weeks ago when she was in church. How much pain she was in, but how much happiness she exuded. I remembered how fond she was of my little three-year-old boy. I remembered how happy she was that she could be with us and how hard it was for her to climb the stairs. I remembered the moments we had spent together in my visits to her retirement center and the many times she put forth great physical effort to be in the company of other believers. And I prayed over her lifeless form. Here was a genuine saint who had lived a full life.

I couldn't help remembering my last visit with my mother, the same age as my church member. Her happiness was at having lived a full life on this earth and alive in the blessed hope that she would live again. Death was not a part of God's original plan. The scriptures call it the enemy of humanity. We were created to live and enjoy forever, not to go through the pains of death and discouragement. And again, I thought of the wonderful promise of Advent.

JESUS CAME TO GIVE US HOPE

Jesus came to give us hope. He did not come to satisfy our curiosity about the future or about magic. He came to say, "Those who believe in me shall live forever." Those who watch and are ready, those who believe in my name, shall eventually be rewarded. Those who watch will be watching unto life.

The Advent season on earth is a foretaste of the future eternal kingdom in which God will have his way in everything. The saints don't need a second chance. The second chance since Adam is the salvation in Christ. The lost have had all the chances they will get because they won't change. And yet our very task on this earth is to search out those who haven't made up their minds completely—they are to see in us a life eternal that has already begun. God gives us the grace to revisit that meaning of Advent.

CHAPTER TWENTY-SEVENTEEN

The Rapture

> "Toil, feel, think hope; you will be sure to dream enough before you die, without arranging for it."
>
> —John Sterling

REVELATION 1:4-8

⁴ Grace to you and peace from him who is and who was and who is to come, and from the seven spirits who are before his throne, ⁵ and from Jesus Christ the faithful witness, the first-born of the dead, and the ruler of kings on earth.

To him who loves us and has freed us from our sins by his blood ⁶ and made us a kingdom, priests to his God and Father, to him be glory and dominion for ever and ever. Amen. ⁷ Behold, he is coming with the clouds, and every eye will see him, every one who pierced him; and all tribes of the earth will wail on account of him. Even so. Amen.

⁸ "I am the Alpha and the Omega," says the Lord God, who is and who was and who is to come, the Almighty.

THE RAPTURE GUIDE

As I browsed through the religious bookstore, two sweet female voices interrupted my concentration on book titles. Although I could not see them, two women were chatting. I assumed they were clerks, for the sound came from around the corner.

"Have you heard the news?" inquired voice number one. "I heard a rumor yesterday that a building permit has been issued for the rebuilding of the temple in Jerusalem!"

"Praise God!" responded voice number two. "The rapture won't be far off now."

I slowly selected my books, secretly hoping for more information on this interesting bit of theology. But the ladies said nothing more. I stepped to the counter, and I met voice number one. I asked for my ministerial discount. It had been discontinued. I reached for my VISA card.

The sales slip was ready. I think I signed it, but my mind was preoccupied. "Thank you, sir," said the sweet, now familiar, number one voice. I turned to leave, but as though the victim of a plot, I was accosted by another rack. It contained literature with interesting, eye-catching titles. Voice number two found me this time. "Have you seen our 'Rapture Guide'?" I confessed I had not. I examined the pamphlet with a four-color painting on the cover showing cars being smashed by driverless automobiles, planes crashing for lack of pilots, buildings burning with no firemen to extinguish the flames.

The folder revealed that a seven-year tribulation would soon come on the earth. An "antichrist" would take over the world and rule for three and a half years (a time of "great" tribulation), during which life on earth would be almost intolerable. The guide told me that because of God's great love for his people, he would quickly take them to heaven (the rapture) just before this troublous time. And it would all start with the rebuilding of the temple in Jerusalem. I arrived at my van with two new books, my used VISA card, my "rapture guide," and something thrown in free—a determination to find out more about this "rapture." So, returning to my office on the college campus, I began my research.

THE *PRETRIBULATION* RAPTURE

I found that rapture is not as common a word today, outside of religious circles, as it once was. It means "caught up," but it has meant, and still means in theology, "a carrying away," or "being carried away in body and spirit." What the two feminine voices at the shop were discussing, the bumper sticker implying, the "rapture guide" asserting, was that Jesus Christ would soon return to carry away his church, so she would not suffer the wrath of God to be poured out in a soon-coming "tribulation" period. No one would see Christ do this; thus some have called this the "secret rapture."

Christians have always looked forward to the return of their Lord. But the pretribulation rapture concept splits that coming into two events: (1) a rapture (the translation of the saints) before the time of trouble, and (2) a revelation (the public, visible return of Christ with his saints) after the tribulation. At the rapture Jesus sneaks into history and catches up his saints. One modern rapture writer calls this "the great snatch."

But although the "snatch" is secret, the alleged effects are very public. Should you be so unfortunate as to miss being raptured, it is claimed, and you find yourself driving next to a saint on the freeway when this event occurs, you may discover his car forcing you off the four-tiered interchange, for, as the bumper sticker said, "This Car Will Be Driverless!"

A POPULAR DOCTRINE TODAY

Incredible as the implications of such a doctrine sounded to me, I discovered that literally scores of thousands of fundamentalist Christians believe it. Evangelical book houses have put forth great efforts to popularize the doctrine and to warn the non-expectant public. Paperback books in the millions expound this teaching in a simple and readable manner. Bumper stickers, paintings, charts, catchy sayings, include but a few of the methods being used in this campaign.

A basic theological guide which has found increasing popularity over the years is the *Scofield Reference Bible*, containing a set of notes that claims to make the Bible more intelligible to all who will rely on its comments. These notes teach a pretribulation rapture by following a system of interpretation which puts the bulk of last-day prophecies (especially the ones found in the book of Revelation) in our future.

As I studied the Scofield comments, I experienced a strange phenomenon. I found myself relying more and more on the notes and less and less on the biblical text. Then it dawned on me that I had better be careful not to put my confidence in commentators rather than the text.

I asked myself before moving on with the research, is it possible that a person's method of interpreting the Bible can become so detailed and exacting that scripture is subjected to charts and notes rather than having a chance to speak for itself?

As I studied, and as I interviewed people who believed in a pretribulation rapture, I found that chart study was extensive. I found a great number of charts for sale, most of them similar in nature. Some I found were free. One bookstore manager told me, "You can't understand the Bible without this chart." That was a claim I was skeptical about. I didn't have enough evidence to decide yet.

The popularity of a doctrine should never be confused with its biblical soundness. My search for truth revealed that, historically speaking, the pretribulation-rapture idea is new. Christians have believed Christ was returning ever since he left, but the idea that he would return secretly to translate his people has prevailed only a little over a hundred years.

THE BIBLICAL SECOND COMING

My study led me to compare the Bible words referring to the second coming. There are three. The first is parousia. *It means "coming," "arrival," or "presence." The New Testament uses it twenty-four times, and twenty-two of those times translate it "coming;" two times as "presence." Not one time is there even a hint that the* parousia *is unperceivable or secret.*

The favorite text of those who hold to pretribulation rapture is 1 Thessalonians 4:17, which is describing the *parousia* of Christ. The text reads,

> [17] Then we who are alive, who are left, shall be caught up together with them in the clouds to meet the Lord in the air; and so, we shall always be with the Lord. (1 Thessalonians 4:17. Emphasis supplied)

The context gives the surrounding events of this "catching up."
(1) God resurrects those who sleep in Jesus:

> [14] For since we believe that Jesus died and rose again, even so, through Jesus, God will bring with him those who have fallen asleep. (1 Thessalonians 4:14)

(2) All the resurrected saints and those who were already alive are caught up together.

> [15] For this we declare to you by the word of the Lord, that we who are alive, who are left until the coming of the Lord, shall not precede those who have fallen asleep. (1 Thessalonians 4:15)

(3) The Lord comes with a "shout," with the "voice" of the archangel, and with "the trumpet" of God.

> [16] For the Lord himself will descend from heaven with a cry of command, with the archangel's call, and with the sound of the trumpet of God. And the dead in Christ will rise first. (1 Thessalonians 4:16)

If there is one thing that this passage does not teach it is that the "rapture" will be in any way secret or even quiet! The noise is enough to "wake the dead." Any interpretation, therefore, which tones down the decibels of this event does not consider a natural understanding of the passage.

The second word that the Bible uses to describe the coming of Jesus is *epiphaneia*, used five times and translated "appearing" or "brightness." Paul wrote,

> [8] And then the lawless one will be revealed, and the Lord Jesus will slay him with the breath of his mouth and *destroy him by his appearing and his coming*. (2 Thessalonians 2:8. Emphasis supplied)

The Greek literally reads, "the *epiphaneia* of his *parousia*." If there is any inclination to make *parousia* secret and *epiphaneia* public, this text will not allow it.

The third word for his return is *apokalupsis*, which occurs eighteen times in the New Testament. The word means "revelation," and where it is used for the second coming of Christ, always denotes a public appearance.

These three words appear interchangeably in the New Testament scriptures to refer to Christ's second advent. No position has been successfully defended that tried to distinguish between them. If all the words used for the second coming indicate a public event, and none of them hint at a double event coming, how can there be a secret pretribulation rapture and a public post tribulation second coming?

FIVE BIBLICAL FACTS ABOUT THE SECOND COMING

I discovered at least five basic biblical facts about the manner of Christ's second advent. This event will occur suddenly, when least expected by the world in general. It is not sudden to God's saints, for they are watching.

Matthew 24 contains several references to this effect. For example, the world in Noah's day, said Jesus, was going on as usual when the flood occurred. The people had been warned; they had rejected the warning, and life had returned to normal. Then the flood came and "swept them all away."[1] This is how the days of the coming of Christ will be.

It will involve the *personal, physical return* of Christ himself. When Jesus ascended into heaven, he informed his disciples, through his attending angels, that he would return "in the same way" as he went. They saw him physically, literally ascend.

> [10] And while they were gazing into heaven as he went, behold, two men stood by them in white robes, [11] And said, "Men of Galilee, why do you stand looking into heaven? This Jesus, who was taken up from you into heaven, will come *in the same way as you saw him go into heaven.*" (Acts 1:10-11. Emphasis supplied)

The second coming will also be *visible*.

> [7] Behold, he is coming with the clouds, and *every eye will see him*, every one who pierced him; and all tribes of the earth will wail on account of him. Even so. Amen. (Revelation 1:7. Emphasis supplied)

The pretribulation-rapture view says that this text refers to Christ's coming at the end of the tribulation, but if the Bible points to only one return of Jesus, how can this be? We cannot make distinctions unless we establish that scripture will support them. Christ declared that the second coming would be so visible that it could best be described by comparing it to the flashing of lightning.

> [27] For as the lightning comes from the east and shines as far as the west, *so will be the coming of the Son of man.* (Matthew 24:27. Emphasis supplied)

It will also be *personal*. Christ will personally return for his people. The dead in Christ will be first to rise and together with the living saints will be caught up to meet him in the air.

1. Matthew 24:39.

> ¹⁶ For the Lord himself will descend from heaven with a cry of command, with the archangel's call, and with the sound of the trumpet of God. And the dead in Christ will rise first; ¹⁷ then we who are alive, who are left, shall be caught up together with them in the clouds to meet the Lord in the air; and so we shall always be with the Lord. (1 Thessalonians 4:16-17)

It will be a *glorious and triumphant* event. Christ comes for his saints. And he comes with his retinue of angels.

> ³¹ When the Son of man comes in his glory, and all the angels with him, then he will sit on his glorious throne. (Matthew 25:31)

SOME POINTED QUESTIONS

So, my trail of research came to an end with some pointed questions that had far-reaching implications. How about the bumper stickers—the signs telling me to cheer up because I would soon be dead, or the ones suggesting I honk if I wanted to be raptured? Do these exalt Jesus? Or do they provide just so much more grist for the ridicule of Christian faith? Do those who long for the life-giving power and the loving solace of an understanding heavenly Father receive comfort from the picture of a school bus full of little children crashing into the onrushing expressway traffic for want of a bus driver because theirs has been "raptured"?

How must that affect one's view of God's justice? Does not talk of Christ's Advent as "the ultimate trip" or "the great snatch" bring this sacred truth down to the level of the common—something to joke about, something to discuss "over a beer"? When truth is cheapened, it loses its power.

How about God's getting his saints out of the world before the tribulation? Has this ever been the case? Noah, Lot, and Rahab were saved from the wrath of God, but God did not take them out of the world. It was Christ himself who prayed,

> ¹⁵ I do not pray that thou shouldst take them out of the world, but that thou shouldst keep them from the evil one. (John 17:15)

God's people will never suffer God's wrath, of that we can be sure. But the Bible also makes it certain that God's people have not and will not always escape the wrath of God's enemies. For this reason, the word is full of God's promises to help his disciples prepare for times of trouble.

> ³ His divine power has granted to us all things that pertain to life and godliness, through the knowledge of him who called us to his own glory and excellence, ⁴ by which he has granted to us his precious and very great promises, that through these you may escape from the corruption that is in the world because of passion, and become partakers of the divine nature. (2 Peter 1:3-4)

Finally, what does the pretribulation-rapture concept do to the dignity and importance of Christ's victory day? Victors do not sneak around snatching their people, hoping no one will notice. The Lord has won the war! He does not need to hide his face. No Bible writer ever misses the chance to exalt Christ's victory day when writing about the second coming. Does not seeking Jesus as a celestial sleuth belittle the greatness of this event?

I still have my "rapture guide," but I now notice something is missing when I read it. It tells me all the events that will occur, it warns me about the great tribulation to come, and it promises me that Christ will "rapture" his saints. But it does not say anything about a story Jesus told in Matthew 25. In essence that story says there will be some waiting for the second coming of Jesus, but it will not occur precisely as they had expected, and as a result they will not be prepared for the event. As I look through my "rapture guide," I wonder where I will be if I put all my faith in being raptured and suddenly discover that the tribulation has started, and nobody is missing.

CHAPTER TWENTY-EIGHTEEN

AT PEACE WITH GOD

"Peace is not absence of war, it is a virtue, a state of mind, a disposition for benevolence, confidence, justice."

—BARUCH SPINOZA

ROMANS 5:1-11

¹ Therefore, since we are justified by faith, we have peace with God through our Lord Jesus Christ. ² Through him we have obtained access to this grace in which we stand, and we rejoice in our hope of sharing the glory of God. ³ More than that, we rejoice in our sufferings, knowing that suffering produces endurance, ⁴ and endurance produces character, and character produces hope, ⁵ and hope does not disappoint us, because God's love has been poured into our hearts through the Holy Spirit which has been given to us.

⁶ While we were still weak, at the right time Christ died for the ungodly. ⁷ Why, one will hardly die for a righteous man— though perhaps for a good man one will dare even to die. ⁸ But God shows his love for us in that while we were yet sinners Christ died for us. ⁹ Since, therefore, we are now justified by his blood, much more shall we be saved by him from the wrath of God. ¹⁰ For if while we were enemies we were reconciled to God by the death of his Son, much more, now that we are reconciled,

shall we be saved by his life. [11] Not only so, but we also rejoice in God through our Lord Jesus Christ, through whom we have now received our reconciliation.

THE TROUBLE WITH ADAM

One of the favorite motifs of the apostle Paul is to see this world in a battle mode against God. Paul has no trouble seeing the human race as an estranged crowd of people who fight God at every turn. The trouble began with Adam when he decided not to trust God but rather to try out the adventurous route of going it alone without God—that when God requested trust, to say, "No God, I think you are withholding something more beautiful than we have." That move turned the human race into a rebel force and set up the new work of God as working to reconcile a race of people and bring them back to full citizenship.

Recently a young man, born an American citizen, decided to turn away from all the benefits his citizenship offered in favor of a way of life that allowed for continuous rebellion against his homeland. He was discovered among the Taliban. His father defended him as a gentle, caring young man with convictions. But that is what fathers do. Meanwhile he was on trial, not for treason, which is a crime that is hard to prove, but for willfully planning to bring harm to other American citizens. You've read about him, heard about him on the news, and he went on trial. His loyalty was called into question since the Taliban had become a major enemy of this country.

It is this same kind of disloyalty that the apostle Paul accused the whole human race of participating in throughout his letter to the church in Rome. Paul spends three chapters in this epistle attempting to show that this rebellion, this disloyalty, has spread to all human beings who are caught in the confusion of the battle between right and wrong.

LEARNING TO HATE EVIL

When we read of what happens in our contemporary world what does it take to teach us to hate evil? A young mother takes her four little children and drowns them one by one in the family bathtub so that they will not be possessed by the devil. Is she crazy? Insane? Is she suffering from some disorder? Is she evil? Her motive was to "save her children." She seems incapable of accepting the fact that they will someday face the world, all its temptations and all its evils. So, she takes their lives away from them in order to avoid that.

A next-door neighbor sneaks into a house while the family is having a party and takes their seven-year-old daughter who is sleeping peacefully in her bed, brings her to the desert and kills her. Friends, relatives, and volunteers begin the search, hoping against hope that she has not been harmed, and three weeks later find her decomposing body rotting by the side of a trail. What possesses someone to do such a thing?

These are but two stories that flashed in the headlines recently, many more could be cited. And we still wonder about the evil hearts of people who have found no peace with God. How can we resist asking, where was God? And what can be done to bring our race into harmony with the wishes of God that are for our own good?

Here comes a man who wishes to be known as accepting and liberal. He asserts, "All religions are good and equal." And yet here is a religion that condones and encourages its members to hijack a plane and take not only the lives of those on board but the lives of people going to their routine jobs for the betterment of humankind and destroy them all in the name of God. Is this a picture of people who are at peace with God? The beat goes on. Next week these stories will simply be replaced with others just like them—like teaching sophomores in high school—the faces change but the behavior remains the same.

WANTING TO KNOW RIGHTEOUSNESS

The apostle Paul teaches clearly that no matter what we do we can't make things go right. We trust friends and they betray us. We place our trust in others and they deceive us. Rodney King uttered those words of immortal question: "Can't we all just get along?" And the answer comes from Paul, "No, we can't." No matter how hard we try, the old man of sin raises his ugly head and will do his best that we will fail.

We proclaim that we'd like to "get along." It is the accepted mentality of this age that to have peace we must have the most sophisticated weapons, the most brutal tactics, the most lethal approaches to intimidate the enemy. This mentality says that we can never have peace without preparing for the worst war in history. I don't doubt that mentality. I don't doubt that this is true. History testifies that when another nation thinks you are weak its leaders will try to take from you what they want.

But these are bandages on the wound; they are not cures for the problem. These are remedial measures; they are not preventive. Or they may be preventive, but they are not remedial. Either way we look at it there seems no way around the fact: "No, we can't all just get along!" Paul's words may be disputed but the evidence is clearly on his side.

> [9] What then? Are we Jews any better off? No, not at all; for I have already charged that all men, both Jews and Greeks, are under the power of sin, [10] as it is written:
>
> > "None is righteous, no, not one;
> > [11] no one understands, no one seeks for God.
> > [12] All have turned aside, together they have gone wrong;
> > > no one does good, not even one."
> > [13] "Their throat is an open grave,
> > > they use their tongues to deceive."
> > "The venom of asps is under their lips."
> > [14] "Their mouth is full of curses and bitterness."
> > [15] "Their feet are swift to shed blood,
> > > [16] in their paths are ruin and misery,
> > > > [17] and the way of peace they do not know."
> > [18] "There is no fear of God before their eyes."
>
> [19] Now we know that whatever the law says it speaks to those who are under the law, so that every mouth may be stopped, and the whole world may be held accountable to God. [20] For no human being will be justified in his sight by works of the law, since through the law comes knowledge of sin. (Romans 3:9-20)

So, do what you must do to keep peace but don't expect the threat ever to go away. Everyone will interpret a unique way to attaining it. Paul's solution is not to avoid evil, but to learn to love righteousness. It helps to hate evil, but that still doesn't solve anything. Here is a person who hates abortion, so he kills abortion doctors. Here is a person who hates injustice, so he kills judges. Here is a person who hates bad people, so he destroys them on his own. And the contradictions go on. Evil done in the name of God—bad things done allegedly to please God. Here is a man who hates homosexuals, so he drags the gay man behind a car by a rope until he is dead. And it all started with the simple thought of mistrusting God. God is withholding something from us—I guess we are learning what it was!

THE GOSPEL ANSWER

I only find one answer to the lack of peace in the world and that is what Paul writes here in our Lenten lectionary.

> [1] Therefore, since we are justified by faith, we have peace with God through our Lord Jesus Christ. [2] Through him we have obtained access to this grace in which we stand, and we rejoice in our hope of sharing the glory of God. (Romans 5:1-2)

Peace comes through reconciliation with God. Why? Because the initial war is between humanity and divinity. I find no evidence that this is anything but personal in its final application. The cross is significant in that it puts every member of the human family in a savable condition—it brings the race into a condition of where it can cash in on the legacy of Christ, but no one makes anyone else accept it.

Two young men tried to show me recently that creation has been proved. That science now has at its disposal proof that Genesis is correct,

In the beginning God created the heavens and the earth.[1] I confessed that I am a creationist and that I believe that text, but I did not agree that this had been or could be "proven." If it is proven, I suggested, then every scientist should acknowledge it. Why wouldn't they accept proof? It is my understanding that there is always room for doubt, questioning, skepticism, agnosticism. God does not act in the realm of scientific proof; he acts always in the realm of faith which means there will always be room to doubt if you chose to. And we all have a way of finding evidence for our doubts. Decisions involve *responsibility*.

We are at peace with God because of our faith that Jesus has reconciled us. He has justified us and put us first in a savable position and then when we respond, in a saved condition. Paul goes on to say that because of this new perspective brought about by the work of Christ on our behalf we are able to look at trials and troubles as opportunities for growth and rejoicing. But we don't have to. We can mope around and feel slighted because of them. We can feel betrayed and deceived by others and let that erode our faith. Hope and grace and perseverance need not reign in our lives if we choose not to let them. But God has still poured his love into our hearts. He has still moved to bring reconciliation, to create peace with his wayward family on earth.

---

1. Genesis 1:1.

PEACE *WITH* GOD NOT PEACE *OF* GOD

For those who choose to accept the benefits of the peace which God has already brought between him and us—they can have hope and perseverance and character. They can see in suffering, a result to which God wants that to lead.

We watched with awe as Sarah Hughes went through her skating routine several years ago. She shared that she didn't think she had a chance, so she relaxed and let it happen in her long program. In that relaxed mode she skated like she had never skated before. With the pressure off she did her thing, and it was awesome. Moving from fourth place to Olympic gold had never been accomplished before in the history of the games.

Here was a picture of being at peace—at peace with one's self. I thought of another skater whose team several years ago thought her only chance for the gold was to have the legs of her competition broken. We are not out of the ordinary when we naturally turn to the battle mode. Speaking in the battle mode, the apostle commented,

> [6] While we were still weak, at the right time Christ died for the ungodly. [7] Why, one will hardly die for a righteous man—though perhaps for a good man one will dare even to die. [8] But God shows his love for us in that while we were yet sinners Christ died for us. [9] Since, therefore, we are now justified by his blood, much more shall we be saved by him from the wrath of God. [10] For if while we were enemies we were reconciled to God by the death of his Son, much more, now that we are reconciled, shall we be saved by his life. (Romans 5:6-10)

Christ did not make us good in order to save us. He took us as ungodly people and accomplished peace with God. What we could never do, he did. Every attempt of humanity to make peace with God ends in destroying someone else in the process. Paul does not speak of the peace *of God* in this passage. He speaks of the peace *with God* which Christ accomplishes. When we enter that reconciliation with God we can then experience the peace of God. But that is not his argument here. Here he suggests that the center of our hope is found in Christ's work not ours.

> What is peace? To most people it means peace of mind; a psychological state in which they no longer fret, or a temperament which is always placid and unruffled, or the ability to look on the bright side. This is not what Paul means by peace with God.

> He was not saying that 'Now I'm justified, I have a peaceful kind of feeling about life'. He was not talking about a state of mind, but a restored relationship—peace *with* God not just peace. There is a difference. Many would give anything for peace, but not so many want peace with God. This is simply because, to be at peace with someone, you must meet and face them. . . . Peace with God means facing God—and the consequence of justification is that we *can* face Him and be at peace with Him.[2]

When we gather at the table of the Lord where we celebrate the meaning of Easter we all are there because the human race is at peace *with* God. We may be upset, we may be discouraged, we may be deficient in biblical knowledge. None of those things is an issue in the question of this Lenten message. The issue is that we have been justified, we have been reconciled, we are at peace with God.

---

2. Horn, *Go Free! The Meaning of Justification*, 54-55.

CHAPTER TWENTY-NINE

You Are the Light of God

> "A cynic is a man who knows the price of everything and the value of nothing."
>
> —OSCAR WILDE

EPHESIANS 5:8-14

> ⁸ For once you were darkness, but now you are light in the Lord; walk as children of light ⁹ (for the fruit of light is found in all that is good and right and true), ¹⁰ and try to learn what is pleasing to the Lord. ¹¹ Take no part in the unfruitful works of darkness, but instead expose them. ¹² For it is a shame even to speak of the things that they do in secret; ¹³ but when anything is exposed by the light it becomes visible, for anything that becomes visible is light. ¹⁴ Therefore it is said,
>
> "Awake, O sleeper, and arise from the dead,
> and Christ shall give you light."

THE BATTLE MOTIF

In the last chapter we looked at a common motif in the teachings of Jesus: the battle. Good and bad are in constant battle. This battle manifests itself in varying degrees of intensity. A quick trip around the cable channels will reveal the openness of this battle as we see all its aspects displayed. Today's generation of filmmakers have little reticence about displaying all the seven deadly sins that plague the human race. Immorality is presented as the "new morality." Unmarried couples living together without shame stand in the face of our own nation's definition of the term family: a man and a woman who are married and living under the same roof, rearing their 2.5 children.

Instead, we see many young people living together without the benefit of marriage, playing house, acting as though this is an acceptable and normal way to demonstrate their sexuality. This is followed even in the face of factual demonstration that young people who live together without marriage and later marry have a greater chance of divorce. Not only does the battle for good condemn such behavior, it appeals to us to look at the consequences of such behavior.

Murder, dishonesty, betrayal, sexual immorality, deviant activity, and uncontrolled infatuation have made Hollywood a land of riches because the fare appeals to the propensities of those battling for the bad in the guise of the "good life." In this chapter we will look at another motif. If battle doesn't grab you perhaps this one will: the motif of light and darkness. Those who push for the thrill of fighting for the bad are viewed in scripture as on the quest for darkness.

If the Christian strives for anything at all in his battle against the bad it is the quest for a qualitative, fulfilling life. This life is not just an attempt to keep the "old man of sin" in control, it is the attempt to live a life that is pure and guilt-free—a life which is described by Paul as the life of light.

THE LIFE OF LIGHT IS IN CONTRAST TO THE LIFE OF DARKNESS

The apostle Paul sometimes gives us catalogues of sins, a list of those things that will not be part of life of a disciple of Christ. Here in Ephesians he lists some things: fornication, impurity, and covetousness. These are unfitting, he says, to ever be found in the lives of those who are the saints of God.

> [5] Be sure of this, that no fornicator or impure man, or one who is covetous (that is, an idolater), has any inheritance in the kingdom of Christ and of God. (Ephesians 5:5)

Filthiness, silly talk, and levity. Deceptive "empty words." These are also "unfitting." Ours is a life of seriousness.

> ⁶ Let no one deceive you with *empty words*, for it is because of these things that the wrath of God comes upon the sons of disobedience. ⁷ Therefore do not associate with them, ⁸ for once you were darkness, but now you are light in the Lord; walk as children of light ⁹ (for the fruit of light is found in all that is good and right and true), ¹⁰ and try to learn what is pleasing to the Lord. (Ephesians 5:6-10. Emphasis supplied)

All these sins invite the wrath of God upon what he calls "the sons of disobedience." While these are overt and outward behaviors, they also have their internal counterpart. Here is a person who connives and conspires to live out his own narcissism. Life is his and everyone else be damned. We all have these propensities. We often rationalize them as products of our evolution, after all, only the fittest will survive, right? But scripture doesn't work from this evolutionistic thesis. It works from creationism; created in the image of God we fell, and Christ came to rescue us from that fall.

One of the favorite plot scenes in popular movies is the climb and the fall. From cartoons to heavy drama people are continually falling, from buildings, from platforms, from towers, from planes, from rocks, from mountains. These falls intensify the drama. Your knuckles turn pale as you dig your fingers into the arms of your chair. And the fall is into the unknown darkness. The more mysterious the fall, the more intense the drama, whether it be a fall down a rabbit hole into pitch blackness, or down a laundry chute with no idea of destination.

This fall into darkness is a common biblical theme as well, in which the writers try to visualize what it is like to fail to meet the original opportunities set for humankind. We were created in God's image and we fell through disobedience into the hopelessness of darkness.

THE DARKNESS MOTIF AND OUR FEAR OF BEING ALONE

As we examine once more the fall of humankind through disobedience we can't help but notice the thrill of disobedience. People who party often testify to the exhilaration of being out of control.

On the Splash Mountain ride at Disneyland, we ride along in the little cart, harmlessly, watching the interesting scenery go by, then into the mountain and then up the waterfall, instead of down, and then under the waterfall and finally to the top of the mountain only to notice a gaping hole up ahead. Then we realize that gaping hole is on our route and we are going to go down and there is no way off the tram. We hold on and the cart heads almost straight down into total blackness. It is the great rabbit hole, and we are going 50 mph into nothingness!

Such thrills are addicting. They certainly were for the descendants of Adam and Eve. Down, down, down the race went in its quest to fill the void that God had once filled. Groping around in the darkness became a macabre joy which substituted for the original, genuine article of peace with God.

The devil never comes to us promising *darkness*. This should be our first clue that darkness is really not a goal of a fulfilled life. The enemy promises enhanced *light*.

> ² And the woman said to the serpent, "We may eat of the fruit of the trees of the garden; ³ but God said, 'You shall not eat of the fruit of the tree which is in the midst of the garden, neither shall you touch it, lest you die.'" ⁴ But the serpent said to the woman, "You will not die. ⁵ *For God knows that when you eat of it your eyes will be opened, and you will be like God, knowing good and evil.*" ⁶ So when the woman saw that the tree was good for food, and that it was a delight to the eyes, and that the tree was to be desired to make one wise, she took of its fruit and ate; and she also gave some to her husband, and he ate. (Genesis 3:2-6. Emphasis supplied)

The enemy's promise, God is withholding something from you that you should experience. It is not darkness; it is a substitute light. In God's book anything that is not good, not honest, not filled with thanksgiving and purity and selflessness is darkness regardless of whatever anyone wants to call it.

An actress recently testified that when she parties she wants to party out of control. So, at a recent birthday party she decided to party. She got so drunk she was screaming at everyone. When the big birthday cake came out for the person of honor that evening, she decided to destroy the cake with her bare hands and start a food fight. This was her version of partying. It was a shifting of the focus from the birthday girl to herself. It was the disregard of all the guests so she could have fun. Such disregard for others is not unusual in this life of darkness. When she sobered up she regretted it and her publicist denied it happened.

WE LEARN OF THE LIFE OF LIGHT THROUGH CONTRASTS

One of the characteristics of darkness is that we do not find fulfillment in its constancy. The trip down the rabbit hole at the family park lasts possibly ten seconds at the most, probably less. Destroying a party of your friends cannot be sustained or you would have no friends. If everyone knew you would destroy their party you would never receive another invitation. Life is filled with people who destroy themselves and their influence through their behavior.

Occasionally you will find people who are admired for their "freedom." But society has trouble with these people. They are really societal freaks to most normal and sane people—these types may be admired but who would want their teenager to date them?

Yet this is viewed as light in a superficial way. Somewhere down inside us, regardless of what we may say outwardly, we know that such "freedom" is really slavery. Some entertainers have plots for new ways of keeping the public's attention. The amazing fleetingness of the dark side of life often leads the weaker people in our society to seek to sustain it. And so, we have the other outcroppings of drug abuse and alcoholism. But the newness wears off and eventually people sometimes end up on skid row or its class equivalent—the result of perceiving darkness to be light.

We see the contrasts, usually when it is too late. If I hold a stick of dynamite in my hand and light the fuse, I will know in the blink of an eye the results. I will spend the rest of my life without a hand if I survive the incident at all. But darkness comes in all degrees and the slightest deviance from God's instructions can start me down a road that ends in the same dire straits. The slippery slide of darkness is often much more gradual than the rabbit hole.

Paul contrasts the fornicator with the pure, the silly with the focused and the filthy with the clean. He paints the contrast of true light with deceptive darkness. Watch out for the fake "angel of light."

WE ALL COME FROM DARKNESS

In his conclusion the apostle drives the motif to the end. Darkness is where we all came from. Before Christ entered our lives we saw little contrast. We certainly didn't see Christ as the alternative. It may have taken the feeling of hopelessness that often accompanies real darkness to bring us to the possibility of Christ.

Paul not only tells us not to follow the life of darkness, he warns us against going after those who propose it.

> ⁶ Let no one deceive you with empty words, for it is because of these things that the wrath of God comes upon the sons of disobedience. (Ephesians 5:6)

Whether we wish to see this as the open and active wrath of God or simply as a cause-and-effect statement makes little difference here. Those on skid row are only the extremes, but none of them planned to go there. They did not grow up with the grand ambition of ending up on skid row. It was the result of various decisions and pursuits that brought them there. Cause and effect? Wrath of God? Take your choice, they both may mean about the same thing.

> ⁷ Therefore do not associate with them, ⁸ for once you were darkness, but now you are light in the Lord; walk as children of light ⁹ (for the fruit of light is found in all that is good and right and true), ¹⁰ and try to learn what is pleasing to the Lord. (Ephesians 5:7-10)

What a glorious metaphor! You don't just *have* the light of God; you *are* the light of God! Perhaps if we would dwell on that we could experience genuine humility. This truth should not make us proud; it should make us serious about our role on this planet. We have been reborn into a royal family and that carries certain responsibilities as well as privileges.

Some princesses are known for their wild and free life, but they are not revered for their meeting their responsibilities of royalty. A queen is often more respected for the way she handles the waywardness of her family and a lot of it has to do with the office the two hold. A queen would not act the way some princesses do. Those who are the light of God may find strength and direction that merely having the light of God cannot give.

¹⁴ Awake, O sleeper, and arise from the dead, and Christ shall give you light. (Ephesians 5:14)

Paul quotes from Isaiah, but he goes farther: *You* are the light of God!

CHAPTER THIRTY

Tuesdays with Morrie

"When fortune smiles, I smile to think, how quickly she will frown."
—Robert Southwell

LUKE 24:13-35

[13] That very day two of them were going to a village named Emmaus, about seven miles from Jerusalem, [14] and talking with each other about all these things that had happened. [15] While they were talking and discussing together, Jesus himself drew near and went with them. [16] But their eyes were kept from recognizing him. [17] And he said to them, "What is this conversation which you are holding with each other as you walk?" And they stood still, looking sad.

[18] Then one of them, named Cleopas, answered him, "Are you the only visitor to Jerusalem who does not know the things that have happened there in these days?" [19] And he said to them, "What things?" And they said to him, "Concerning Jesus of Nazareth, who was a prophet mighty in deed and word before God and all the people, [20] and how our chief priests and rulers delivered him up to be condemned to death and crucified him. [21] But we had hoped that he was the one to redeem Israel. Yes, and besides all this, it is now the third day since this happened.

²² Moreover, some women of our company amazed us. They were at the tomb early in the morning ²³ and did not find his body; and they came back saying that they had even seen a vision of angels, who said that he was alive. ²⁴ Some of those who were with us went to the tomb, and found it just as the women had said; but him they did not see." ²⁵ And he said to them, "O foolish men, and slow of heart to believe all that the prophets have spoken! ²⁶ Was it not necessary that the Christ should suffer these things and enter into his glory?" ²⁷ And beginning with Moses and all the prophets, he interpreted to them in all the scriptures the things concerning himself.

²⁸ So they drew near to the village to which they were going. He appeared to be going further, ²⁹ but they constrained him, saying, "Stay with us, for it is toward evening and the day is now far spent." So, he went in to stay with them. ³⁰ When he was at table with them, he took the bread and blessed, and broke it, and gave it to them. ³¹ And their eyes were opened, and they recognized him; and he vanished out of their sight.

³² They said to each other, "Did not our hearts burn within us while he talked to us on the road, while he opened to us the scriptures?" ³³ And they rose that same hour and returned to Jerusalem; and they found the eleven gathered together and those who were with them, ³⁴ who said, "The Lord has risen indeed, and has appeared to Simon!" ³⁵ Then they told what had happened on the road, and how he was known to them in the breaking of the bread.

A STORY ABOUT MORRIE

Some time ago a friend of mine back east sent me a book that had been especially inspiring to him. My wife and I read it together on one of our outings to a hilltop resort. The story is about Morrie, a professor of journalism at an eastern university. He was one of those exacting teachers whose students were guaranteed a measure of success if they succeeded in meeting his high standards. As time went by Morrie came down with Lou Gehrig's disease and word got back to one of his illustrious former students who was now a successful journalist. So touched by this news was his former student that he looked Morrie up—to thank him for all he had done for him.

It was not enough for Morrie just to accept the gratitude. He told about going to a funeral and hearing all the accolades and praises for the deceased. He said one thing was wrong—the one person who needed to hear these good words was the person lying in the casket. What is wrong with human beings that we get everything backwards? Why can't we have a funeral before the person dies? We know we will all die. On this basis Morrie's student began visiting with him every Tuesday afternoon and got the privilege of seeing how his acclaimed professor dealt not only with life, but with dying.[1]

EVERY CONGREGATION DEALS WITH DEATH

I often think about the two from Emmaus.

> [13] That very day two of them were going to a village named Emmaus, about seven miles from Jerusalem. (Luke 24:13)

As they walked along disappointed with the events of Passion Week, a third person joined them and reminisced over the happenings of that week. Here was the man upon whom they had placed their hopes and now he was in the grave, so far as they knew.

They chatted about good things and bad. They recalled their wonderful hopes for themselves and for the world. They thought cosmologically—in terms of the world, albeit the Jewish world. They thought and talked in terms of the kingdom that they all looked forward to. Here was the man who would change everything. The Jews would be freed from the iron hand of Rome and they would see the long-awaited and delayed fulfillments of all those promises God had made to these, his chosen people. Yet it hadn't happened that way at all. He had been executed by the very people he was to conquer, and these two were confused. Just talking helped them to feel a little better.

Sometimes it is profitable to devote a worship service to just sitting in a large circle in the worship center and talking about the future of your congregation. When we did that once one of our church members remarked that she had attended the funeral of a congregation and it was a horrible experience. For several weeks after that we heard of the church closing, moving, continuing, or shutting down. Back and forth the talk went and some became discouraged by it and left.

---

1. Albom, *Tuesdays with Morrie: An Old Man, A Young Man, and Life's Greatest Lessons.*

We invited a consultant to come and speak with us and talk about the many churches that close in America each day. We read the testimony of our denominational president who said, "if you want your church to die, try to keep it from dying." Perhaps those weren't the most encouraging words either, but Morrie knew he was dying. Morrie knew he had little time left, and he wanted to talk about the place of death in anyone's life.

THE CHURCH ON ITS DEATHBED

I had hoped that these members would be restored to full health and returned to us to worship and fellowship again. But many of these people were in their 80s and 90s and people in that phase of their life seldom come back for any significant amount of time.

Many churches come to the end of their life cycle every year in America. They apparently have served their purpose or have contracted terminal diseases that no matter what anyone tries to do ends in closing their doors. We can lament that, and well we ought, or we can praise God for what those congregations have meant to the people who have belonged to them over time. Congregations are often the fountain of friendship and the circle of spiritual fellowship. They are mountains of meaning in members' lives. Yet nothing some do has been enough to save them. In some congregations no one is to blame, it just happens.

As the two walked along it soon became apparent that they had misunderstood the purpose of Christ's mission to this earth. And when they became aware that the third person in their party was the resurrected Christ, they got a new look at that mission. It didn't change their previous hopes, but it renewed their hopes. It didn't mean that their sincerity was any less because they had been wrong, it just meant that they now had an opportunity to throw themselves into a new quest. And they were thrilled. They came to the disciples and testified that they had seen the Lord.

DEATH IS INEVITABLE

If Christ does not return soon all of us will die. So, what is our answer to death? Not just congregational death, but personal death? For many people death is a morbid topic. But I remember one of the first funerals I ever conducted as a new minister, fresh out of Seminary, a lady who was ninety-four years old.

She was delightful up until the last day. Then she just went to sleep. There standing by her casket were her two sisters. One was ninety-three and the other was ninety-two. And they weren't crying. They were smiling and rejoicing about two things: she had lived a long and influential life, and she had died in the blessed hope of Jesus Christ.

If indeed a congregation is to cease, it will cease. If a congregation is to discontinue services, then it will. If a congregation is at the last leg of its life cycle, then it will wrap things up in due time. It is not a question of who is to blame or who caused it. This is just what happens to congregations. But as early fathers of the church used to say, "the blood of the martyrs is the seed of the gospel." And what they meant was, every time a Christian was killed, ten more pagans were converted. It was frustrating to those who would see the Christian mission die on this earth.

Whatever church you may belong to, it is not alone responsible for bringing the world to the feet of Christ. It is only part of the body of Christ and the work of Christ will carry on without your congregation. In time a new church will rise up in your city to take the place of yours if it is in the purview of God's providence. You can be part of raising up the new congregation by leaving funds for that purpose or you can refuse to have anything more to do with this work through your denomination.

Some things will happen regardless of your votes or decisions. Your city needs your denomination to emphasize the importance of personal responsibility to God, to preserve the significance of free will and the integrity of the human mind. Whether you chose to be helpful in that by giving your money to that cause, is your choice.

No region, no central government, no voluntary missionary society, can force a congregation to cooperate or to live. When I stood by the bedside of a church elder for the last time, I had no power to raise him up, though I wished I had. By the same token, not one of you may have the power to raise your church back to what you remember it was or think it could be, though we have all flirted with the idea. Some walked away early in their suspicion. Those who are left must now make their decision.

WE ALL SERVE A PURPOSE

So, you look for another Tuesday, not knowing how many are left. Regardless of what happens to your congregation you can look back on your experiences together with a degree of happiness. You all served a purpose. You can lament that some left. But their staying would not have changed the inevitable. Ministry to the young today is a lot different than it was fifty years ago. Churches that do not reinvent themselves on a regular basis end up with chronic ecclesiastic diseases. How that happens is not always readily clear but those who wait too long eventually die.

I remember watching a church. It had a beautiful edifice. It had a seating capacity of eight hundred worshipers. But never since it was built were there that many people in it. It was a closed setting. It was hierarchical and a little clutch of people made the majority of the decisions. As the years went by this became a more critical problem. The attendance was down to around 125 when I studied it, mostly older people, but clearly the church was on its way to a lethal infection.

A new pastor came, the first female the church had ever hired. She sat down with the people and said, "Things will be different now. The only way you avoid change is to fire me." And she moved ahead. She sold the organ and the organist stormed out of the church never to return. She threw out the pulpit, and half the elders left the congregation at that point. She hired a band for music, and most of the trained musicians left at that point. Most of the people over fifty years of age left. That is those over fifty who did not have twenty-five-year-old minds. It was a great risk. People who should have stayed, left. But the changes paid off. The church was soon packed every weekend, with young people singing, praising, praying, yearning for the word of God. That church reinvented itself.

Morrie couldn't reinvent himself. He could hope for a cure that never came. But as congregations go, there is that rare time when someone steps up and has the courage to say, "Go if you must, but we are going to make this church the way it was when you were twenty-five years old and joined!"

CHAPTER THIRTY-ONE

THE CLASS OF '57 HAD ITS DREAMS

> "Keep your eyes on the stars, and your feet on the ground."
> —THEODORE ROOSEVELT

1 PETER 2:19-25

[19] For one is approved if, mindful of God, he endures pain while suffering unjustly. [20] For what credit is it, if when you do wrong and are beaten for it you take it patiently? But if when you do right and suffer for it you take it patiently, you have God's approval. [21] For to this you have been called, because Christ also suffered for you, leaving you an example, that you should follow in his steps. [22] He committed no sin; no guile was found on his lips.

[23] When he was reviled, he did not revile in return; when he suffered, he did not threaten; but he trusted to him who judges justly. [24] He himself bore our sins in his body on the tree, that we might die to sin and live to righteousness. By his wounds you have been healed. [25] For you were straying like sheep, but have now returned to the Shepherd and Guardian of your souls.

HIGH SCHOOL ANNUALS

I have always gotten a kick out of reading high school annuals. The "most likely to succeed." The "class clowns." The "most handsome." The "most likely to get married right after graduation."

And then the ambitions. John Jacob plans to be a *doctor*. Joe Schmooze plans to be a *bum*. Sally Jones plans to be a *mother of ten*. And so, they go. Some are jokes, others are serious. But not-so-hidden is that desire to bring change to the world. At last, here is a generation that is going to do something right. Like one senior said at a twenty-year class reunion, "I was always searching for Mr. Right. I just didn't realize his first name was 'Always.'"

But what senior classes chronically overlook is that they are not the first to spell out their dreams. A commercial ran on radio that interviewed the winner of a beauty contest where she was asked what her dreams were? And she answered, "I want to bring about world peace and see to it that all of us get along." And the announcer said, "Well, you're going to be a busy girl!"

It reminded me of the reality song of the Statler Brothers when they sang of their class wishes under the title I have taken for this chapter: "The Class of '57 Had Its Dreams."

In this song they sing of what actually happened to the Class of '57.

> Tommy's selling used cars, Nancy's fixing nails.
> Harvey runs a grocery store and Margaret doesn't care.
> Jerry drives a truck for Sears, Charlotte's on the make.
> And Paul sells life insurance and part time real estate.
>
> Helen is a hostess. Frank works at the mill.
> Janet teaches grade school and probably always will.
> Bob works for the city. And Jack's in lab research.
> And Peggy plays organ at the Presbyterian Church.
>
> And the class of '57 had its dreams.
> We all thought we'd change the world with our great work and deeds.
> Or maybe we just thought the world would change to fit our needs.
> The class of '57 had dreams.
>
> Betty runs a trailer park. Jan sells Tupperware.
> Randy's on an insane ward. Mary's on welfare.
> Charlie took a job at Ford. Joe took Freddie's wife.
> Charlotte took a millionaire. And Freddie took his life.

Johnny's big in cattle. Ray is deep in debt.
Where Mavis finally wound up is anybody's bet.
Linda married Sonny. Brenda married me.
And the class of all of us are just part of history.

And the class of '57 had its dreams.
But living life day to day is never like it seems.
Things get complicated when you get past eighteen.
But the class of '57 had its dreams.
Oh, the class of '57 had dreams![1]

NOT THE ONLY ONES WHO DREAM

Throughout the scriptures we see the dreams of God and his people. During his estrangement from his family Jacob had a dream in which he saw a great ladder that extended from heaven to earth and on that ladder were angels that walked up and down keeping this planet in connection with heaven. Jacob had his dreams that estrangement would be done away with and reconciliation between God and the human race was indeed the great goal of all people.

Nebuchadnezzar, the popular and capable king of Babylon, had a dream in which he saw a great image with a head of gold, arms and chest of silver, a belly of brass, legs of iron and feet of iron and clay. When the king asked his wisemen what this dream meant, the prophet Daniel, the spokesman for the wisemen, told him it represented kingdoms that would come on this earth during and after Babylon.

Daniel pinpointed Nebuchadnezzar as the head of gold. So enthralled was the king with this revelation he had his sculptors build a huge image but rather than make it of these various medals, Nebuchadnezzar had the image made all of pure gold. This defied the message of the dream that other kingdoms would follow him. But the king of Babylon had his dreams—his kingdom would rule the world for ever, he dreamed.

John the revelator had brilliant and terrifying dreams of the chaos on this earth. But in the end the dream of complete restoration of this earth from its sin would be realized in a clear and decisive way. Dreams keep us going. Dreams and visions are something that God often inspires to keep his people encouraged. The American pioneer Thomas Jefferson once said, "I like the dreams of the future better than the history of the

---

1. Reid and Reid, "The Class of '57."

past."[2] The poet Henry David Thoreau wrote: "I have learned this at least by my experiment: that if one advances confidently in the direction of his dreams, and endeavors to live the life which he has imagined, he will meet with a success unexpected in common hours."[3]

GOD ALSO DREAMED

Somewhere in time, in the quietness of his creative thoughtfulness, God dreamed that he would make a world that was so beautiful that all would want it. He would make the beauty of purple hills and white animated clouds. The sun would shine for warmth and trees would provide shade. And in this dream he saw charming flowers of all kinds, bees to pollinate the fields and guarantee perpetual beauty. Animals of all sorts would dot every conceivable habitation, and all would get along.

God dreamed a creature with free will to tend this world and offer a superior intellect to keep it forever harmonious. This creature he called "man" would build and be prosperous. He would create to his heart's content. He would clarify value according to the universe's standards and he would be only happy forever. It was a stunning dream. It was the "mother" of all dreams. It was the dream that could be shared, and it was the first vision given to human beings.

Life got complicated, not just when one became eighteen years of age, but by the entrance of an adversary. No one who has ever lived has been able to avoid something or someone interfering with his own dream. Either the dream was so expensive that it required donors who had their own ideas and required changes if they were going to be involved, or the dream was infiltrated by a hostile takeover of some who got jealous and decided to claim the dream for themselves.

The Bible story is narrative of one vast screw-up of God's dream. No matter what God tried, we screwed it up. No matter what language God used we misinterpreted it. No matter what illustrations he gave we rewrote the script.

---

2. Jefferson, *Letter to John Adams*.
3. Thoreau, *Walden; or, Life in the Woods*.

WHEN LIFE BECOMES COMPLICATED WE HAVE TO DREAM AGAIN

The principle of life getting complicated after we turn eighteen is intriguing. Think back about how easy it was to dream when your whole life was before you. People asked you what you planned to be? "A doctor" was the favorite response in the culture I grew up in.

A friend of mine was determined to be an engineer. He learned a trade to work his way through engineering school. He became a journeyman, the equivalent today to a desk top publisher who works in front of a computer screen all day. In the middle of his college education, he got married. The bills were mounting up. She wanted to be a teacher. So, he dropped out of school temporarily for her to finish her education.

Then she got pregnant. Now they had a child. He was still working at his job, with his dreams. But this was an era before the great government loans were available and she was still in school. He dreamed on—"when she finishes I will continue with my education and pursue that dream to be an engineer." Meanwhile, he had a good income at his trade.

Just before graduation she got pregnant again. Staying home with the two little children was a priority and so he continued to work at his trade. He made enough to keep the family afloat but not enough to pursue his dream, so he put it on hold again.

When the kids were ready for school he realized that church school was expensive but that was his wish and so they enrolled them, and his wife started to teach when she got pregnant again. By this time, he was 30, still working at his trade. Shortly after that they had another baby. By now they had two children in church school with its tuition, she was taking care of two more at home, and he was still at his trade. Would he ever follow his dream?

Life gets complicated after eighteen. Does that mean we quit dreaming? Maybe it means we alter our dream. Does that mean we let minor details become major obstacles to our dream? Or does it mean we dream again, a new dream? For him, the latter was his choice. He is retired today. His four children are educated, and his wife is retired. He never became an engineer, but I never heard him complain that his dream was void. He became an inspiration to me because of his ability to dream again, a new dream.

THE ART OF DREAMING

I pastored a church for a while that had been established back in the 1920s. The church bore great fruit. As time proceeded through decades they were reminded of Thomas Jefferson's remark: "I prefer the dreams of the future to the history of the past."

The members of the congregation began to realize that a church has its time in the world. The art of dreaming has to include that element of risk and revision. They had started out to change the world with all their "crazy schemes." Or maybe they expected the world to change to match their dreams. But life simply is not like that. Where would we be without the burger turners and the insurance personnel? Where would we be without the hairdressers and the desktop publishers? Isn't that what makes up life?

Becoming a doctor may not be all that it is cracked up to be. One of my friends worked most of his life to become a doctor and now he pastors a small church in the north. And when I asked him, is this enough to keep you busy, he smiled warmly and said, "As busy as I care to be." Being a doctor was fine, but it was serving people that attracted him to the medical profession and he found that fulfillment in the pastorate as well.

The ability to re-dream when life gets complicated is included in my idea of our creative God. When a congregation meets the end of its life cycle there is a chance to dream again. The entity may be gone but the body of Christ is not gone. Out there are many struggling congregations whose life cycle has not ended. They need our support. They need our offerings, our encouragement, our suggestions, and our presence. There are congregations that will inherit those who remain.

Regardless of how complicated life gets, dreams are carried on in the young people who came out of those homes, never in the same way, but in the same spirit. In that circumstance it is time to dream again, to refashion the chance to serve this world.

CHAPTER THIRTY-TWO

Praying in the Enemy's Land

> "Every act of rebelling expresses nostalgia for innocence."
> —Albert Camus

LUKE 11:1-13

¹ He was praying in a certain place, and when he ceased, one of his disciples said to him, "Lord, teach us to pray, as John taught his disciples." ² And he said to them, "When you pray, say:

"Father, hallowed be thy name. Thy kingdom come. ³ Give us each day our daily bread; ⁴ and forgive us our sins, for we ourselves forgive every one who is indebted to us; and lead us not into temptation." ⁵ And he said to them, "Which of you who has a friend will go to him at midnight and say to him, 'Friend, lend me three loaves; ⁶ for a friend of mine has arrived on a journey, and I have nothing to set before him'; ⁷ and he will answer from within, 'Do not bother me; the door is now shut, and my children are with me in bed; I cannot get up and give you anything'? ⁸ I tell you, though he will not get up and give him anything because he is his friend, yet because of his importunity he will rise and give him whatever he needs. ⁹ And I tell you, Ask, and it will be given you; seek, and you will find;

knock, and it will be opened to you. ¹⁰ For every one who asks receives, and he who seeks finds, and to him who knocks it will be opened. ¹¹ What father among you, if his son asks for a fish, will instead of a fish give him a serpent; ¹² or if he asks for an egg, will give him a scorpion? ¹³ If you then, who are evil, know how to give good gifts to your children, how much more will the heavenly Father give the Holy Spirit to those who ask him!"

MITCH WAS MY FRIEND

My friend Mitch died last Sunday. Heart attack. He went quickly. At the funeral, the preacher read a text that said something about "threescore and ten." Mitch did not qualify—he was too young. A lot of things make no sense in the enemy's land.

Mitch was a Christian. I met him for the first time when I was assigned to pastor a small church in the fruit belt of Southwestern Michigan back in the early 1960s. He was a thriving farmer and looked like he stepped out of a Normal Rockwell painting. He had it all—white forehead, bronzed skin, big hands, bowed legs. He was burly and tough, and his heart was pure fun.

As I viewed the bier and watched Mitch's family take their paces through the cruel procession, I questioned God. I thought of another farmer I once met who was strangely similar in appearance and disposition but quite different in conviction. Our conversation had lasted only a few minutes because he wanted nothing to do with preachers. He viewed me as an intrusion.

This second farmer was a World War II veteran—one who had not been converted in a foxhole. The gist of his theological contribution to our summer day's visit was simply, "I do not believe in God, and so I do not believe in prayer. I watched dozens of my buddies go into combat crying for their lives. Their God never heard them—they were cut down like cornstalks before a combine." I had dusted off my shoes that day and gone on my way, but his words have never left me. They returned to haunt me yesterday at Mitch's funeral.

THE ENEMY'S LAND

Too often we forget that we live in the enemy's land. If no evil existed on earth God could easily say yes to our every prayer request for our hearts would be pure and all our requests unselfish. With no enemy, all motivations would be perfect. But when God decided to allow sin to exist in an otherwise perfect universe, he did so with a full understanding that he would risk being misunderstood.

I have friends who say God is a myth because they see no evidence that God cares for them. They claim he never answered their prayers. Conversely, I have friends who say they know God is alive because they spoke with him this morning. Which group is right? Why the confusion? An enemy called Satan and the devil does exist, and when we discuss prayer we must never forget that important fact.

PRAYER IN THE POSTMODERN WORLD

The caricature of prayer in a postmodern world is not always pleasant for the onlooking believer. Notice the place prayer receives in routine American life as depicted on prime-time television. Perhaps it's a humorous or archaic grace at mealtime with the actor assuming a stained-glass voice. Prayer comes across as dated, set in the 1940s or the ancient past, but not something modern. The enemy would have it this way.

"O my God!" is a fervent biblical expression. But today people utter it as a flippant expletive, no longer said with the attitude or adoring sensitivity of the believing follower of God. Indeed, a week of perceptive TV viewing will convince you that if the television truly reflects modern society, then "intelligent" people must place no faith in God through prayer, or else they do not care about talking to him at all.

The church has been the traditional school of prayer, yet surprisingly no institution has received more criticism for formality and emptiness, frequently at the hands of its own theologians. Opposing definitions, theological nuances, disagreements over biblical interpretations, and even envy and jealousy, have contributed to the inability of the church to remove the confusion regarding dynamic prayer.

In both society and religion, the enemy is at work. He knows something about the results of a life that enters into "everything by prayer."[1] He saw in it the living of Jesus.[2]

"LORD, TEACH US TO PRAY"

Christ's closest followers approached him one day and overheard him praying to his father. Impressed with his seriousness and the reality of the moment, they implored, "Lord, teach us to pray."[3] They uttered these words from a perspective of human need, of respect and reverence for God, and from an uncanny recognition that only Jesus has perfect guidance on the subject. The request is vital to us for several reasons.

First, every person who would know God must eventually make this request. Many people say prayers, but only serious people pray. Parrots can be taught to say prayers, but those words are cheap. Meaningful words come from maturing, growing minds and carry proportional value. Sooner or later a person will either pray or quit saying prayers altogether.

Second, there are few people who will not honestly admit that they suffer some degree of confusion regarding prayer. Many are not clear on what to pray for. They often forget that the presence of the enemy created certain undesirable conditions that limit even God. Satan claims this world as his own and humanity has largely accepted his claim. Furthermore, he makes God out to be unfair and selfish. In view of this, God has chosen to let him prove it within certain boundaries: he cannot force us to remain his captives, but by the same token God appeals to our choice in the matter too.

The hostile environment of the kingdom of Satan creates an abnormal atmosphere. There would be no sick to pray for, no protection to claim, no disasters to avoid, if no enemy existed. And, although Satan has authored these conditions, we often blame God for them because he respects the "rights" of Satan for all to see whether his is a valid political economy.

Because prayer is confused and multi-defined, and because it is not always perceived in this larger perspective, many become careless

---

1. Philippians 4:6.
2. Matthew 4:1-11.
3. Luke 11:1.

in what they pray for. They become impossible and unintelligent beggars. The sick sometimes pray for healing when they ought to pray for the strength to reform their harmful habits or, sometimes, for the courage to die. Parents demand that God force his will on their wayward children, overlooking his respect for human choice. Students pray for good grades when they should ask for the maturity to study. Many pray for material wealth when they should instead agonize over their spiritual poverty. Because many requests stem from nonsensical ideas of prayer and of God, the answers are imperceptible or unacceptable and therefore confused. And the enemy rejoices.

FORMALISM IN PRAYER

A third reason that this request is crucial is the danger of formalism and presumption. A fellow minister asked me, following a funeral one time, why I had included certain accolades of the deceased in my graveside prayer. "You didn't believe those things," he chided. "You said them though you knew them to be false." It surprised me that I had employed churchly lingo and become a ploy of the enemy. According to him, I had not truly prayed.

Jesus warned against formality in prayer.

> [5] And when you pray, you must not be like the hypocrites; for they love to stand and pray in the synagogues and at the street corners, that they may be seen by men. Truly, I say to you, they have received their reward. [6] But when you pray, go into your room and shut the door and pray to your Father who is in secret; and your Father who sees in secret will reward you. (Matthew 6:5-6)

Praying for display or effect, using God to one's own advantage, spewing forth meaningless jargon that bypasses the mind and does not break forth from or seek to meet human needs—all violate the authenticity of a relationship with God.

> [7] And in praying do not heap up empty phrases as the Gentiles do; for they think that they will be heard for their many words. [8] Do not be like them, for your Father knows what you need before you ask him. (Matthew 6:7-8)

To treat God with a "don't-call-me-I'll-call-you" attitude is both irrational and insulting to a serious God. His work involves the greatest rescue mission in history. Presumption is close to formalism. To presume on God is to take him for granted. There are conditions to any relationship. In the case of sinful human beings, the tree of life was removed from our reach, so sin could not become an immortal institution.

> ²² Then the LORD God said, "Behold, the man has become like one of us, knowing good and evil; and now, *lest he put forth his hand and take also of the tree of life, and eat, and live for ever*"— ²³ therefore the LORD God sent him forth from the garden of Eden, to till the ground from which he was taken. ²⁴ He drove out the man; and at the east of the garden of Eden he placed the cherubim, and a flaming sword which turned every way, *to guard the way to the tree of life.* (Genesis 3:22-24. Emphasis supplied)

God plans to dispose of the enemy one of these days, and if we overlook the fact that he cannot bless those who pray simply to feed a sinful nature, we put ourselves in the path of the destroying angel.

Responding to God's wooing includes recognizing that he gives blessings as a trust to be used for unselfish purposes.

> ³ You ask and do not receive, because you ask wrongly, to spend it on your passions. (James 4:3)

> ²² And we receive from him whatever we ask, because we keep his commandments and do what pleases him. (1 John 3:22)

Prayer is for bringing us to God, it is not a coercive tool to transform God into our celestial genie.

Finally, this request to pray as Jesus prayed is important because too many people rely on too many other people for their instruction on how to pray and what prayer is. We are part of a humanistic age, and we thrive on self-help materials. But the solution to the sin problem does not lie with man. The disciples recognized that Jesus was the "wonderful counselor" who gave the truth about personal relationship with God. Good-intentioned Christians have passed on poorly thought-through ideas that have caused others to turn from God in confusing no assurance when the Bible might have cleared the matter up.

THE SAMPLE PRAYER

Jesus gave a sample prayer in answer to the request of the disciples. It was not to be another meaningless form, but it could illustrate the manner, spirit, form, and content of talking with God. He did not command them to repeat the prayer (neither did he forbid it), but he invited them to pray like this.

> [9] Our Father who art in heaven,
> Hallowed be thy name.
> [10] Thy kingdom come,
> > Thy will be done,
> > > On earth as it is in heaven.
> [11] Give us this day our daily bread;
> [12] And forgive us our debts,
> > As we also have forgiven our debtors;
> [13] And lead us not into temptation,
> But deliver us from evil. (Matthew 6:9-13)

Prayer is friendly communication with God in a child-parent relationship. It should never be confused by construing it as a friend-to-friend relationship of equals in which one's input is as good as another's and no submission or obedience is expected. God never relinquishes his position as our eternal parent. That would never work in the enemy's land.

God does not ask our advice. He is ever and always God—"hallowed be thy name." Part of being God is having the answers. Part of creaturehood is dependence—needing answers. It is God's omniscience (all-wise) that we rest on, and because we have none of our own, we may not always know where he is leading us. So, we walk by faith in his promises, not by sight, and he takes the responsibility to reveal his will to us. Because he is eternally secure in his government, he allows us to accept or reject that will.

In the enemy's land, rejecting God's will can be disastrous because then the enemy has a certain freedom to attack. But God, the faithful guide, continues to fight for us, through many approaches. He offers us enlightened eyes, and he limits the enemy so we can choose intelligently. He never coerces us. He is always the model parent.

PETITIONING GOD

Within this relationship we make our requests known to him, always recognizing that he is all-knowledgeable.

1. THY KINGDOM COME—that is, bring us under and keep us ever in your wise and loving rule, as we travel through enemy territory.
2. THY WILL BE DONE—bring us to acknowledge and voluntarily submit to your wise superintendence.
3. GIVE US THIS DAY OUR DAILY BREAD—sustain us through materials needs.
4. FORGIVE US OUR ... [SINS], AS WE ALSO HAVE FORGIVEN OTHERS—accept us and change our natural inclinations of self-centeredness. Take the enemy's land out of us.
5. LEAD US NOT INTO TEMPTATION—You have taught us that our ultimate need is deliverance from sin unto eternally walking in the ways of your kingdom.

Jesus' prayer includes praise, thanksgiving, adoration, dedication, and petition. But our confusion always rests with the last element—petition. In general, we learn from the Lord's Prayer that no one should feel guilty about asking God for blessings (there are five clear requests made here). And we learn that those requests can take on the nature of either material ("bread") or spiritual ("forgive us") needs.

Our confusion over petition resides in two problems. We are prone to forget about the enemy and his "rights" of claim on us and our world. And we often overlook the fact that prayer requests are of varying character.

KINDS OF REQUESTS

I can best illustrate this second point by using the same illustration that Jesus used—the Father-son relationship. When my son was eight years old there were things I loved for him to ask me for. But when he came to me with his annual list of toys from the Sears Christmas Wish Book, there was a limit.

Ideally speaking, my decisions to grant his requests in this area were based on my experience and position as his father, my projection for his best good, and my wisdom of his developmental needs for trial as well as the cultivation of desire. In short, his character was my constant concern, and to spoil him would make him stunted and selfish. I neither denied all his requests nor fulfilled them all. I attempted to calculate my decisions in a way I thought would stimulate truth in him and keep our relationship vibrant and growing.

A second category of my son's requests included his need for love and affection, for reassurance of self-worth. He occasionally asked me to forgive him, or he sought encouragement. These requests caved in my heart. The very purpose of my being his father was tapped—he hit the target. These were gifts I freely promised him, and all he had to do was claim them to realize them himself.

To stretch the illustration one more step, it was conceivable that my son would ask me for something that I must strictly forbid him to have. If he asked for a rattlesnake to sleep with or a strychnine soda to drink, my answer must be a flat refusal. If I granted him those things, I would be answerable not only to him but to onlooking society as well.

God's relationship with his sons and daughters is similar to this. We come to him with requests for three kinds of blessings:

1. Those that he has neither promised nor forbidden.
2. Those he has explicitly promised us as heirs of his kingdom.
3. Those which he has clearly forbidden in his word.

We may confuse ourselves by not bothering to notice which is which. If we would look more carefully at our requests, we would be less prone to blame God when things did not work out our way. God is not capricious, but we are often irresponsible.

SOME PRINCIPLES

Based on scriptural instruction concerning prayer, here are some principles that are helpful to a meaningful understanding of petitionary prayer.

That which is not specifically promised, or explicitly denied in name or in principle in God's word, may be responsibly requested only in the attitude expressed in the words, "thy will be done."

> [14] And this is the confidence which we have in him, that if we ask anything according to his will he hears us. (1 John 5:14)

> ¹⁰ Thy kingdom come,
> Thy will be done,
> On earth as it is in heaven. (Matthew 6:10)

We have desires that, if seen from a correct perspective, might be better termed luxuries than needs. God is too intelligent to spoil us or to make mistakes. He never guarantees to fulfill a desire of the human heart that is not in our best interest.

> ¹¹ What father among you, if his son asks for a fish, will instead of a fish give him a serpent? (Luke 11:11)

Whatever is specifically promised in God's word, we may *ask* for, believe that we receive it, and thank him that we have received it as a benefit of our personal acquaintance with God through Christ. God never withholds forgiveness from his confessing child.

> ⁹ If we confess our sins, he is faithful and just, and will forgive our sins and cleanse us from all unrighteousness. (1 John 1:9)

He freely grants his Holy Spirit to those desiring his strength and guidance.

> ¹³ If you then, who are evil, know how to give good gifts to your children, how much more will the heavenly Father give the Holy Spirit to those who ask him! (Luke 11:13)

He promises guidance to those who want it.

> ⁸ I will instruct you and teach you the way you should go; I will counsel you with my eye upon you. (Psalm 32:8)

There are many promises in scripture for peace of mind.

> ⁷ And the peace of God, which passes all understanding, will keep your hearts and your minds in Christ Jesus. (Philippians 4:7)

And promises for help in spiritual growth.

> ¹⁴ Wait for the LORD; be strong, and let your heart take courage; yea, wait for the LORD! (PSALM 27:14)

> ¹⁵ Rather, speaking the truth in love, we are to grow up in every way into him who is the head, into Christ. (Ephesians 4:15)

The promises include rest from trying to make ourselves perfect.

> ²⁸ Come to me, all who labor and are heavy laden, and I will give you rest. ²⁹ Take my yoke upon you, and learn from me; for I am gentle and lowly in heart, and you will find rest for your souls. ³⁰ For my yoke is easy, and my burden is light. (Matthew 11:28-30)

And victory under temptation.

> ¹³ No temptation has overtaken you that is not common to man. God is faithful, and he will not let you be tempted beyond your strength, but with the temptation will also provide the way of escape, that you may be able to endure it. (1 Corinthians 10:13)

And joy under stress.

> ² Count it all joy, my brethren, when you meet various trials, ³ for you know that the testing of your faith produces steadfastness. ⁴ And let steadfastness have its full effect, that you may be perfect and complete, lacking in nothing. (James 1:2-4)

Whatever is specifically denied or forbidden in God's word is not granted by God. To insist on one's own way in any relationship is the prelude to dissolution. It may be that the enemy, in his effort to confuse, takes advantage of selfish, ignorant requests by answering them himself and passing them off as being from God. He is the great deceiver. We may be sure that God will not give those things which he has specifically forbidden in his word. We need to study the Bible carefully to understand this. We can be sure that anything denied or forbidden by God is not for the good of people of faith or society in general.

NOT BLIND FAITH

God is not our pawn to move. If he were, we would soon grow tired of him, for no god is big enough to challenge us who is not superior in wisdom, strength, intelligence, and sovereignty. But though he is not maneuverable, he is nevertheless understanding and patient. Those who go to destruction will do it on their own, with God still calling them back to the abundant life.

When one walks with God, it is not a blind faith. God has given us his promises so we can know his will. They are found in his word for all to see. We have a lot of evidence of a living God even in the enemy's land.

We can have surety of his leading, won for us at Calvary and demonstrated in the daily evidence of a living relationship.

Praying specifically will yield specific answers. Studying the scriptures will reveal his will. God guarantees what he promises, he grants many requests that he decides are for our good, but he denies us those things that would destroy us. When we understand this, it will help us in realizing that even in the enemy's land we can experience the kingdom of God.

Bibliography

Albom, Mitch. *Tuesdays with Morris: An Old Man, A Young Man, and Life's Greatest Lessons.* New York: Broadway, 1997.
Aquinas, Thomas. *Summa Theologiae.* Garden City: Image Books, 1969.
Babcock, Maltbie D. "This is My Father's World" *United Methodist Hymnal.* Number 144. 1901.
Barclay, William. *Gospel of John.* 2 vols. Philadelphia: Westminster, 1956,
———. *Letters to the Galatians and Ephesians.* Philadelphia: Westminster, 1958.
———. *Gospel of Matthew.* 2 vols. Philadelphia: Westminster, 1975.
Bonhoeffer, Dietrich. *Life Together.* San Francisco: Harper & Row, 1954.
Earles, Alice Morse. *Sabbath in Puritan New England.* Williamstown, MA: Corner House, 1969.
Edwards, Jonathan. "Sinners in the Hands of an Angry God." Enfield, CT, 1741.
Farrar, F. W. *Message of the Books Being Discourses and Notes on the Books of the New Testament.* London: Macmillan, 1884.
Geld, Gary, and Peter Udell. *Shenandoah.* Milwaukee: Hal Leonard, 1982.
Goodman, Ted, ed. *Forbes Book of Business Quotations.* New York: Black Dog and Leventhal, 1997.
Horn, M. Robert. *Go Free! The Meaning of Justification.* Downers Grove: InterVarsity, 1976.
Jefferson, Thomas. "Letter to John Adams." In *Papers of Thomas Jefferson*, 10:285. 1816.
Kipfer, Barbara Ann. *14,000 Things To Be Happy About.* New York: Workman, 1990.
Maslow, Abraham. *Motivation and Personality.* New York: Harper Bros., 1959.
Reid, Don, and Harold Reid. "The Class of '57." BMG Rights, 1972.
Thoreau, Henry David. *Walden: or, Life in the Woods.* Boston: Ticknor and Fields, 1954.

www.ingramcontent.com/pod-product-compliance
Lightning Source LLC
Chambersburg PA
CBHW060602230426
43670CB00011B/1931